GRAIN TRADE

GRAIN TRADE

The Key to World Power and Human Survival

JOHN FREIVALDS

STEIN AND DAY/Publishers/New York

First published in 1976
Copyright © 1976 by John Freivalds
All rights reserved
Designed by Ed Kaplin
Printed in the United States of America
Stein and Day/*Publishers*/Scarborough House,
Briarcliff Manor, N.Y. 10510

Library of Congress Cataloging in Publication Data

Freivalds, John.
Grain trade

The key to world power and human survival
Bibliography: p. 221
Includes index.
1. Grain trade—United States.   I.   Title.
HD9035.6.F74   380.1'41'310973   76-10134
ISBN 0-8128-2075-1

To Tetis, Pidge, and Jilly

CONTENTS

FOREWORD

But for my grandfather's disaffection with mules, I probably never would have written this book. According to family legend, my father and grandfather were out plowing our grain farm in Latvia when my grandfather abruptly stopped the mules—the main source of power in those days—looked at my sweating father, and informed him, "I want you to go to the university so you don't have to spend the rest of your life looking at a mule's ass." That was quite a break in tradition, for my father, grandfather, and I were born in the same house and room, and slept in the same crib, in Skujene, a rural Latvian town of thirty inhabitants that most people have trouble pronouncing and I still have difficulty locating on a map.

My father did go to the university and became a journalist, but the love, if not a fascination, for the land stayed with him and was passed on to me. Perhaps this has made my path predictable—from rural development work with the Peace Corps, to agricultural consulting, to international commodities trading. Thus, this book is as much a professional autobiography as it is an explanation of how the grain trade works.

Since food prices are such an emotional issue and it is fashionable to find a villain, many of the previous works on the grain trade have taken a dismal view of its activities. I have tried to be even-handed to both consumer and producer, which usually results in getting the enmity of both.

No single volume can definitely embrace the grain trade from farmer to table, but I decided to provide some brief sketches that hopefully will bring everyone's food costs into better perspective as to how they are made up and how we as consumers affect them.

Traveling through the grain trade, I was provided many insights and much guidance. Chief among those who deserve special recognition are William Warne, Harald Frederiksen, and Burton Joseph. Chuck and Judy Reynolds's enthusiastic listening and comments did wonders for me when I didn't feel like going on.

Writing a book on the grain business brings the temptation of bombarding the reader with statistics; I have tried to minimize them and make them as useful to the eating reader as possible. Professionals should therefore recognize some of the liberties I have taken to explain the grain trade. And the statistics that I did include were humanized by some interesting people I met in writing this book. My thanks therefore go to four farmers: Dale Yahnke, Gordon MacClean, Lester Wolverton, and Harvey Hovland. Equally helpful were Allenby White of Northrup King and my longtime Tar Heel friend, Hervey Evans of the McNair Seed Company. Atherton Bean and his colleagues at International Multifoods, Monte Beeson, Andy Gillette, and Dave Mona, who arranged it all, get special thanks. The hassles of food retailing were amply brought out by Red Owl Stores' Catherine Searight. Sam Kuhl gets special thanks for giving me an enthusiastic tour of his North Dakota mill. Thanks also go to many officials at the U.S. Department of Agriculture, Cook Industries, and Continental Grain, who took time to provide information and comments.

Patricia Day's editing was more than helpful in giving the book a better perspective. Marsha Walsh was a lifesaver with her typing, as was my friend Susan with proofreading, editing, listening, and all-around soothing.

Minneapolis, May 1976

GRAIN TRADE

1

PUTTING IT ALL TOGETHER

In the same way every person has his or her favorite food, everyone seems to have a favorite villain to blame for high food prices. During the past three years, the Russians have come in for a piece of the blame. Others discount supply-and-demand altogether and blame the big food oligopolies that are found in the marketing chain. Advertising, Henry Kissinger, George Meany, Earl Butz, Pope Paul—the list is endless. The truth is that they all have an effect on food prices.

On any given day, decisions are being made that affect our food supply and the price we and the rest of the world pay for it. It's a long day and begins on the farm. Before it's over, presidents and peasants both will have made important decisions that we literally have to pay for. If you had the opportunity to be a witness to the decisions, they would go something like this:

Even on a beautiful spring morning, windswept Gilbey, North Dakota, does not conjure up visions of great wealth, but on closer inspection it rivals California's Central Valley in value of farm production. Gordon MacClean's blue eyes gleam as he tells you this and the fact that his family has farmed here since 1883. Gordon now farms 3,500 acres but feels he can do more. Now forty-three, young by comparison with other farmers, Gordon has his eyes set on picking up some more land that is up for sale. "Why?" I ask him. "Because it's there," comes the response.

In August and September 1975, longshoremen refused to load grain on vessels bound for the Soviet Union. President Gerald Ford remembered that when Earl Butz became Secretary of Agriculture he had promised he would fight like a "wounded steer" for higher farm prices. Farmers wanted the exports, for they meant higher farm prices; George Meany, president of the AFL-CIO, wanted them stopped because domestic food prices might go up. Ford looked up as one aide read some figures: "In 1974 there were 2.8 million farmers, while during the same year the AFL-CIO had a membership of 14 million." A moratorium would be placed on exports.

Barry Gordon had had a rough day at the office, as his proposal for office consolidation had been thrown out. His wife Laila hadn't fared much better in her work at J. C. Penney's as a salesclerk. She was tired of being blamed by customers for this or that item's not being in stock; she just worked there. They had planned to have dinner at home, but Barry did not want to wait for dinner even if Laila wanted to make it. "They deserved a break today" and headed off to McDonald's for hamburgers. They liked to go out to eat, and the manager recognized them as they hungrily walked in.

Hong Kong's atmosphere is unlike the strict austerity of the People's Republic of China, which surrounds it. Bright neon lights, bars, and banks—lots of banks. These banks, in particular, have made the PRC tolerate the presence of this capitalist enclave, for foreign exchange flows into mainland China from this crowded colony. Lin En-lai worked for a large PRC bureaucracy with a large name: the China National Cereals, Oils, and Foodstuffs Import and Export Agency. This agency negotiates the purchase of foodstuffs from overseas, and Lin knew that the PRC needed 200,000 tons of wheat. He wanted to buy soon, but after he had called a friend at one of the Hong Kong banks, he decided to wait. The United States was going to devalue their currency in two weeks, his friend "assured" him. And when they did, the dollars the PRC now had would buy much more American grain. As Lin told his buying strategy to his colleagues in Peking, a Pan Am jet landed at Hong Kong's airport. One tired businessman from San Francisco turned to a passenger next to him and asked, "How come the Reds allow Hong Kong to stay capitalist?"

The noise shook him, but Lou Thomas just snuggled up closer to his warm wife. The phone rang again, and now he finally had to answer. As he reached for the loud monster, Lou noticed it was 4:00 A.M., and before he heard the voice at the other end, he knew it was a

European trader. In Italy it was 10:00 A.M., and the European traders had already been at it for a couple of hours. Lou is a Minneapolis grain trader for a firm active in the international "resellers" market. The Italian trader at the other end of the line had bought American wheat three months earlier, and, with shipment to a U.S. port on the Gulf of Mexico a month away, wanted to sell it before the market fell (a friend who "knew" had told him it would). This same grain had already been bought and sold thirteen times and would probably "change phones" a couple of times more before the wheat actually left the numerous country elevators it was stored in. Lou felt the market for wheat was strong, and he bought it. He muttered something unkind about Italians as he hung up the phone, watched the digital clock flip to 4:19, dug his nose into his wife's hair, and fell asleep.

The atmosphere at Moby Dick's bar, whose motto is "A Whale of a Drink," is always smoky and most certainly funky. Apart from air hockey, football, and the most active pool game in Sacramento, lots of interesting and strange people can be seen; one frizzy-haired guy came in last year with a steering wheel tied around his neck—Halston had better watch out. As the night wears on, Joe (it seems all bartenders are named Joe) is really busy pouring beer and handing out popcorn. His job is tougher now, for he gets complaints about the 25-cent increase in the price of a draft, and because the popcorn, which was free six months ago, now has to be paid for.

All you see out the front window is the eight rows of corn being taken into Steve Yahnke's $40,000 combine. The stalks are cut, taken into a screw conveyor, and then devoured by a shredder that separates the energy-rich corn kernel from the cob. The smashed cobs and bits of stalk are spewed out the back until they fall to the earth, while the kernels end up in a bin that Steve will unload at the end of this row. The air conditioning keeps the dust out, while Hank Snow's rendition of "I'm Moving On" coming in on the AM-FM radio makes the work easier. While this John Deere is no racehorse, it can harvest six acres of corn an hour; this is enough corn to keep a Mexican family of six going for ten years.

Saturday mornings are particularly enjoyable for four-year-old Christopher Camp. Bugs Bunny, Shazam, and Fat Albert can all be seen in the same day. Chris likes the commercials, especially for the sugar-coated cereal in the neat box with the free racing emblem. Mommy is taking Chris shopping in the afternoon, and she has promised him he can pick out what he likes.

The workmen have just installed Mustafa Bahktiari's long-awaited telex machine. Mustafa presses the "local" and "here is" buttons and beams as the machine prints out: "T-R-A-D-E-C-O-M Tehran." Bahktiari likes the sound and is confident that the new machine will help him put commodity deals together. The *farangi* ("foreigners") know nothing about trading with petro-dollar countries, and Bahktiari feels that with his contacts in Tehran, Riyadh, and Baghdad, American firms will engage his services. He turns the machine off, closes the door, and heads toward his Mercedes parked in the sun. As he drives past a bakery making flat Arab bread, he remembers that a wheat tender for Iran is only two weeks away and that an American company will pay him a good fee to get that business. *"Enshallah,"* he mutters to himself.

After looking at all the figures he could gather on production, inventory, and usage of wheat, Charley McInerny, chief market analyst for a Minneapolis grain firm, figures it's time to "short" wheat. Charley started out as a geographer, but ever since he wrote a paper on peanuts in India, everyone has respected his view on commodities. He has been wrong before, but unless the Russians botch up his calculations, he could make a tidy bundle. A bonus would help things out for his seven-member family.

In Grodno, Belorussia, P. M. Masherov addresses party and collective workers, urging that grain production be increased, for "the next year will determine the level of the development of agricultural production in the next five-year period . . . the jumping-off point toward the new and even higher and more strenuous tasks which the Belorussian Communist Party and all the republic's working people will have to solve." But even as he speaks, Exportkhleb, the Soviet grain agency, is trying to figure out how much grain they should buy from the Americans.

Dave Auslam looks up at the TelePrompTer and notices corn has passed through its "resistance" level. He anxiously calls one of his Minneapolis clients and tells him his wheat position is going against him. "Let's leave it, Dave." The position stays as Dave returns to the charts on his desks. A quick glance reveals terms such as "moving averages," "head-and-shoulders," and "inverted fulcrums." Dave eats wheat but otherwise knows very little about it. He does know about charting commodity prices, though, and interpreting price movements tells Dave what he needs to tell his customers, many of whom took their dollars out of the stock market and put them into commodities. Dave wants a bonus also, but he feels that you should "go long" on wheat—that is, buy it now and hope the price goes up.

A Minneapolis mother of four sighs as she stirs yet another macaroni-and-hamburger casserole. With a food bill approaching $400 a month, Sally Kraska now relies on the cheaper cuts of meat and "juicy blend," a blend of hamburger and soya protein sold in some parts of the United States, as the mainstay of the family diet. Bacon is only a fond memory, and steak is brought out for special occasions. She finds she buys more spices to jazz up the casseroles, and her husband Paul has begun making their own bread. Their food purchases are now made at a wholesale warehouse.

A cool mist blows past Miguel Garavito's furrowed cheeks as he sets out to plant corn on a weathered mountainside in the Colombian Andes. The elevation is 8,500 feet and not suited to corn, but Miguel's father, and his father before him, planted it. There has always been a crop, although in recent years his yields have been low and have led him to buy extra grain in Gacheta, a small town at the end of a serpentine gravel road sixty miles from Bogotà. Constantly in debt, Miguel is also illiterate. He doesn't know that the grain he buys in town is marked in red-white-and-blue letters: "Not to be sold. A gift of the American people."

Pines and lots of sandy soil abound as you drive into Laurinburg, North Carolina. It's good farm country and the home of McNair Seed Company. There's lots of tradition here, but talent as well. Hervey Evans, president of McNair, would be at ease anywhere and brings home what the new agribusiness executive is like. His walls show a diploma from Princeton and a Harvard MBA. Noticing you're looking around, Hervey interjects, "I spent a year at North Carolina State, studying agriculture, as well." Hearing this background, you don't question the ability of farm suppliers to meet farmers' needs, as Hervey leans back in his chair, puts his feet on the desk (revealing a hole in his shoe), and recounts the corn blight of 1970. "One day we thought we had a good seed crop, and the next day we had to abandon it all. Following that, we went to Central America, planted seed hurriedly with farmers we had never met before, supervised the production, built a processing plant, shipped the seed back both by ship and by air, and managed to get it planted in the spring of 1971. We worked night and day when the seed was being delivered, and many of our people never went to bed for a week or more, simply sleeping on the floor of the warehouse or catching a nap whenever they had a chance."

Michele Yvon shudders as the North Dakota winter wind whips through the threads of his stylish French coat. He has just made another purchase of foundation wheat seed and hopes it will arrive in time to plant. This is not his first trip to North Dakota, so he should not be surprised at the size of the farms. He is, though, as he recalls that someone has just told him that farms of 1,000 acres are not unusual in these parts; the seed he has bought will go to French farms of 50 acres, and even those are above average size. The new seed will help yields somewhat, but farm production costs in France will remain higher than those in the United States, assuring that the long tasty French bread he likes so much and misses on these extended trips will continue to be made from cheaper American wheat.

Fifi is just like any other member of Dallas's Johnson family, except she is a mite smaller, has more hair, and barks—except when she "sings" to accompany Paul Johnson when he plays the harmonica. She has been with the family ten years and, like some of the older members of the Johnson family, has developed a slight paunch. Since the Johnsons eat a variety of foods during the week, Fifi gets a variety as well. Everyone thought it was a neat idea when Paul Johnson spotted a dog cookie jar in Nieman-Marcus's Christmas catalog and suggested this as Fifi's Christmas present. As the catalog said, "How the world got along without our dog cookie jar is anybody's guess."

"It tastes *guud*," Dr. Mattil of Texas A&M University drawls as he bites into a cookie made of "tamunuts." Tamunuts (named after *Texas A&M*) are a new type of cottonseed which researchers at A&M hope will find commercial outlets in baking. It's high in protein, and researchers feel that this new, edible cottonseed will give Texas farmers a greater portion of the marketing dollar and create a new source of protein.

Hanging over Monte Beeson's shoulder is a picture of a man praying over a meal of bread and soup. Monte is equally reflective as he pores over weather reports he gets from five separate weather services. International Multifoods, where Monte works as the head of grain operations, is ready to make wheat-purchase decisions to supply flour for its retail business and expanding Mister Donut franchises. Weather is crucial, but Monte sort of shrugs when he looks up from the reports and tells one of his colleagues, "I don't know what position to take. Three said we're going to get plenty of growing rain, while two indicate we're in for a hell of a drought."

Louis Boudreaux loves to tell people near his Iowa, Louisiana, rice farm that he "speaks Cajun and talks turkey." He can't see too much wrong with the government's getting into agriculture. "Sure, they control my acreage, but they've opened some markets." Boudreaux explains that a lot of PL 480 programs shipped rice, particularly to Cambodia and Vietnam. "I made some good money." But, peering out from under the brim of his ten-gallon hat, Boudreaux can't understand why he can't sell his rice to Cuba. "Look, *mon ami*, them Cubans will pay cash money for my rice. I want to sell it, the mill wants to process it, but politics say you better not try it. What harm is a plate of rice going to do? I ain't fought with anyone at the dinner table."

Even though towns in southern Brazil have such German-sounding names as Blumennau and Novo Friburgo, some of the most progressive farmers in that area are Japanese. Takashi Kamini came to Brazil twenty-five years ago with very little and now is one of the largest soybean growers in the state of Paraná. Speaking in his accented Portuguese, Kamini is proud to recall Brazil's ascendence in ten years from nowhere to become the world's second-leading producer and exporter of soybeans. Kamini has read that American farmers are upset that his beans have taken away markets and lowered prices. "Listen, my friend, the world's a hungry place, and everyone has to produce. Apart from the gringo and the Brazilian, no one else can produce enough beans. Let me tell you something, we both need oil, but we always can leave the car in the garage. Can the rest of the world leave their stomachs in the refrigerator when there is no food? Brazil and the United States could form a protein alliance. My tractor is the most powerful weapon Brazil has. Why should you Americans worry? I have seen pictures—your tractors are much larger."

Bloomington is the fastest-growing suburb of Minneapolis. Lots of new, shiny buildings dot the area, including the much-admired headquarters of the Minnesota Vikings football team. One of the newest buildings is the Country Plaza supermarket. It's got it all: air doors that keep winter and summer out through a wall of forced air; carpets to muffle the sounds of shopping carts as piped-in music soothes the nerves; a home nutritionist always on duty with free recipes. Everyone seems to smile, except Louise Mugre when she gets the bill from the check-out clerk. She grudgingly writes out a check and asks, "Why do your prices always seem higher than other places?"

These scenes and some of the decisions made in them may have shed some light on food prices, or they may have confused the issue. In any event, you are probably still reluctant to pay $2 for a pound of bacon. The following chapters provide the background for this typical day in the world of grain.

In trying to piece together the many aspects of the grain trade, I talked to farmers, exporters, food processors, union and government officials, health-food advocates, and consumers. Everyone was unanimous in one aspect—they were not responsible for high food prices. I went into this with some grocery shoppers I talked to, one of whom best summed up the situation by telling me, "That's fine, but when I leave the supermarket, I'm left holding the bag." She had a point.

2

GETTING THE CROP IN

Nature had taken out her paintbrush as I headed south along the Minnesota River valley. Although the eye was attracted to the brilliant foliage, the real wealth of the area was in the dry and dust-colored cornstalks and soybean plants dotting the valley floor on that October day. As I climbed out of the valley, which, incidentally, is where the Jolly Green Giant lives (or at least a billboard tells you so), the land became more rolling as it stretched south out into the Corn Belt. The northern tier of this belt is firmly anchored by Minnesota's aptly named Blue Earth County.

Harvest was under way, and, everywhere I looked, tractors and combines weaved dusty, hypnotic, back-and-forth patterns. As I turned up the gravel road to Dale Yahnke's farm, an old dog slowly got up, his tail wagging rhythmically. I got out of the car and headed for the tidy white farmhouse.

The only noise you could hear was the breeze; no chickens or cows provided any barnyard noise. A dull buzz came from Yahnke's grain dryer; Dale met me with your basic down-home smile on his pleasant, angular face. A slight man, Dale was wearing work clothes and a cap bearing the insignia of a fertilizer company. Harvest was in progress, and he was rushing to get everything organized.

Dale took over this 400-acre farm nineteen years ago because the owner didn't have the ambition to make a go of it. His farm is not the best in Blue Earth County because of the sandy soil, but the years—and lots of fertilizer—have enabled him to make a go of it. "A lot of folks said we would starve to death." His rosy cheeks convinced me that this had not yet happened.

When Dale began farming on this piece of land, he had cows,

chickens, pigs, and an assortment of crops. Today, he has nothing but corn and soybeans and has no qualms about it. He gave up livestock two years ago because of poor prices and the work involved, leaving his barn and silo as empty reminders. Apart from a large vegetable garden, the Yahnkes are as dependent on the supermarket as any Park Avenue banker. Dale's wife is "too busy" to bake bread.

Like the banker, Yahnke knows where his money goes. Dale never went to college, but this doesn't prevent him from having a "sharp pencil." He needs it, for, with his land and equipment, the value of his farm exceeds $300,000 and brings in gross sales of around $200,000.

All the finances are conducted on a businesslike basis, including those involving his two sons. Steve, an exuberant thirty-two-year-old, can't wait to go skiing, farms 600 acres, and shares equipment with his father. Dale has a huge tractor for plowing, as well as three trucks for hauling grain, a grain dryer, and an 80,000-bushel storage complex (about what two World War II Liberty Ships would hold). He uses his storage as a marketing tool; his 1975 crop of corn wasn't to be sold until June 1976. "Them Russians are going to wait—and pay for this crop." This equipment is charged to Steve at cost; he, in turn, charges his father for the use of his $40,000 harvester and smaller tractors. Steve is quick to point out, "We actually pass checks back and forth."

Blood is thicker than water, for both farmer and son have undertaken large investments, knowing they can spread the costs on their combined acreage. Waiting in the wings to join this group is seventeen-year-old Marvin, who is farming forty acres he rents from Dale. Marvin plans to go to the University of Minnesota Agricultural School and then return to farming because "I figure I can make some money at it and be my own boss."

Dale explains the positive attitude his sons have toward farming by his never having complained about farming. He reasons, "If you complain, how do you expect to have kids stay around?"

How Dale does in a given year is less a matter of consumers and the government conspiring against him than of how efficiently he manages his operation. Fiercely independent, Dale puts the responsibility for the success or failure of his efforts on himself.

He does, however, get information wherever he can and is particularly proud of the Corn Economics Group to which he belongs. The group consists of some Blue Earth farmers who occasionally meet to discuss their farming operations. Invited speakers include county agricultural agents, university professors, and representatives of seed, machinery, and chemical companies—"as long as they don't hawk their wares."

Dale, however, needs the farm inputs these companies provide. Inorganic fertilizer, for example, has enabled him to plant corn on the same field for seventeen consecutive years. As to environmentalist claims that we are polluting our earth with too many farm chemicals, Dale responds, "Well, that's fine—if you want everyone to starve."

"We've talked too much, let's go out and harvest some corn." Dale and I climb into one of his red trucks and head out to the fields where Steve is harvesting. Few farms today are in one parcel, but have fields strewn in the area. Dale's is no different, and he probably will add additional pieces as time goes on. As we rumble down the road, Dale points out which farmers will no longer be around in five years. It makes him angry that these poor farmers will last that long, as they mistreat their soil. Equally certain of the farm failures, Dale also knows he will be picking up more land; he figures he and Steve can handle another 500 acres with the equipment they already have. For the time being, however, he will have to wait, as no one is selling, and renting land is done on an auction basis.

The asphalt ends and we come upon a rutted farm road. The truck leaves long, dusty, vapor trails as we near the field where Steve is harvesting.

Dale and Steve have worked out a unique harvest system. While Steve runs the harvester through the eight-foot corn, Dale shuttles one of the three trucks back and forth between the field and the dryer. The two other trucks remain at either end of the field to be filled. Then, when Dale gets back from emptying one truck, he takes back another, and the cycle starts over again. During this time of year, Dale's wife and Steve's fiancée also help with the truck driving.

Watching an eight-row corn harvester is akin to seeing a science-fiction movie. A big green machine with drawn-out prongs gobbles up a sixteen-foot swath of corn, separates the grain from the cob, and spews the stalks and mulched-up cobs out the back. Dale sees my fascination with the green monster and adds, "I still don't know how they do it." I hurry to climb aboard as Steve approaches.

For Steve inside the cab, harvesting is merely a hydraulic routine. Helping him pass the time are some country-music sounds coming in on his FM radio, making the time he spends in his air-conditioned, soundproof cab more enjoyable. There is a feeling of power moving that machine through the fields, for the stalks yield quickly. "I wonder where the corn off that stalk will end up—Moscow or Cincinnati?" Steve interjects as he turns the harvester to unload.

Steve respects Dale not only as a father but as a farmer. "He's the best source of information around. I do get mad at him, though, for he won't let me make my own mistakes." Although the harvester is large and unwieldy, Steve guides it smoothly through the fields until he senses something wrong in the steering. "It's the damn oil line again."

Anticipating what he needs to do, Steve turns the machine around, steps down, and begins fiddling with the oil line. The wind blows the now flowing, if not boiling, oil away from us as Steve tries to find the source of the problem. Dale drives up, and then all three of us are trying to get at the root of the problem, but only succeed in getting hot oil all over ourselves. "Yessir. You let all those New York people you write for know how much fun us farmers have." I grin back at Dale's comment.

Steve finds and fixes the problem, but vows to have a new harvester in a couple of years. He wants to farm more land and won't be able to afford too much maintenance time. I believe him when he says he'll get it, even though it will cost $50,000.

The harvester goes on gobbling up corn at the rate of six acres an hour as I get back into the truck shuttle with Dale. Dale is like many farmers—conservative politically and a staunch anti-Communist churchgoer, but don't you dare stop sales to the Russians. He wants the government to stay out of farming altogether and is proud that he never took any part in the set-aside programs that once paid farmers not to farm.

In spite of this independence and pride, Dale has gotten out in the world. He went on trips organized by the state of Minnesota to visit farms in Poland and Mexico and could not decide which country's agriculture was worse off. Dale's favorite picture hangs in the dining room and depicts a Polish farmer harvesting by hand. "I felt sorry for those people."

After his family and fields, the thing that probably gives Dale the most pride is the Crystal Cooperative where Dale markets his grain. Begun in 1926 to sell petroleum products to area farmers, by 1959 the co-op had an elevator and a grain dryer.

Dale eagerly showed me through the place. "Look there, everyone around here likes farming"—pointing out a pretty teenager (who was a cheerleader for the high school), driving in a twenty-ton truckload of soybeans. Although the co-op office was dusty and dark, it was cheered up by a steaming pot of coffee and lots of fattening doughnuts laid out for co-op members. On the co-op board for sixteen years, Dale recently helped push through the construction of a unit-train siding. Unit trains are groupings of at least twenty-five rail cars which enjoy a preferential rate from the railroads, meaning the co-op can ship farther for less. Most farmers have a lot of trust in this co-op, for it hasn't paid a dividend since 1964; all surplus has gone into building up the facilities.

The co-op is indispensable for Dale's farming operation now. Co-op representatives come out and do a soil test to determine the rate of fertilizer application, sell him the fertilizer, seed, and herbicides, and buy his grain when he's all done. Dale figures all this has made him more efficient, and gets upset when consumers blame him for high food prices. "They're just ignorant of the truth."

Whither the Farmer?

Dale Yahnke is not unlike the remaining 2.8 million farmers in the United States who provide us, and most of the world, with food. The opinion of farmers I met coincides with what Abraham Lincoln said about them and their labor in 1859: "No other human occupation opens so wide a field for the profitable and agreeable combination of labor with cultivated thought as agriculture." The farmer is still the salt of the earth, but he has changed drastically over the years. Conventional wisdom would dictate that farmers farm by the seat of their pants and read the nostalgic *Farmers' Almanac*. Few do, however; most, like Dale, take part in seminars and read scientific agricultural journals. As a result of this change, each U.S. farmer now feeds 55 Americans, compared to 7 in 1900. By way of comparison, the Russian farmer of today feeds the same number of people as did the American farmer in 1900, while the Chinese farmer feeds only 1.2 people!

Most of today's farmers are willing to concede that there is still some "romance" in being a farmer, but insist that they have to get a fair return and recognition. During Emperor Hirohito's 1975 trip to the United States, which included a visit to Donald Baltz's Illinois farm, one farm journal remarked, "The real emperor is a farmer like Donald Baltz, and it's about time we realized it."

Catering to this heightened image of the farmer, an organization calling itself the Professional Farmers of America got under way in Cedar Falls, Iowa, in 1974. In addition to providing market information, the organization offered farmers "attractive two-color letterheads . . . show others you're a businessman . . . your Pro farmer membership certificate tells office visitors that you're a proud member of a proud profession."

John Kenneth Galbraith feels that our farm system produces so much because of the self-exploitation in agriculture. "The market system, as we have seen, allows self-exploitation and encourages it as a convenient social virtue." Farmers do work hard when they have to, but Dale Yahnke insists that I do more physical work than he does.

Statistics bear Dale out. Although U.S. farm output from 1940 to 1972 increased 90 per cent on essentially the same acreage, farm labor input fell by two-thirds. At the same time, fertilizer use on U.S. farms grew almost ninefold and mechanical power and machinery increased two and a half times. These factors have also enabled average farm size to increase by 16 percent in the last ten years, to 385 acres. More significant, perhaps, is the fact that the average farm operation is now worth $150,000, sells $23,000 worth of farm products a year, and is run by a farmer in his early fifties. With this amount of capital required to get into farming, a farmer's children are among the few who can afford the luxury of feeling the earth. And with rigid Federal inheritance laws, even the farmer's children are having a hard time taking over the operation.

Present Federal inheritance laws require a substantial tax to be paid—in cash—once a farm is passed down; a farm worth $300,000 might cause the survivor to pay $50,000 in taxes. Many farm groups are now working to change this situation by increasing the tax exemption allowed on inherited property and by valuing land for its agricultural rather than development potential, thereby lowering the tax rate.

These changes have called for a redefinition of the word *farm*. Time was when a farm was any place over ten acres with annual sales of $250 or more, or any place of ten acres selling $50 or more. Now the Bureau of the Census will define a farm only as an establishment having sales of $1,000 or more.

Farm specialization is increasing, due to the high cost of farm machinery and equipment. The range of services produced on a farm has declined. Fertilizer is purchased rather than manure spread, since many farmers like Dale have gotten rid of their animals altogether. Furthermore, seeds are bought rather than saved from the farm crop, and feed is bought rather than raised. There are a few exceptions to the rule. Gordon MacClean in Gilbey, North Dakota, farms mostly grain, but he adds, "I wouldn't feel like a farmer unless I had some cows to look at."

There has been a substantial decline in the value of farm-raised food consumed by the farm family. Grandpa's farm used to have milk, cream, vegetables, eggs, smoked meats, and apples, but no longer. In 1951, the total value of its production consumed on the farm reached $2.3 billion; it has now declined to less than a third of that.

In 1967, the Harvard Business School coined the word *agribusiness* to describe modern farm operations, and in view of the economic changes on the farm, it is an appropriate term. For a farmer to be successful nowadays, merely growing a crop is not enough. Considerable attention has to be given to knowing what to produce, how much and which farm supplies to use, when and how to market—not just sell—and when and how to borrow. But Gordon MacClean told me that he still feels like a farmer, even though his banker lists him as an agribusinessman on his loan application. Regardless of his title, Gordon likes to point out to his banker that a farmer is a unique member of society who "spends seven dollars when he only earns five, and owed six already."

The large investments required in farming are worrying many farmers who see better-financed farming corporations waiting to gobble them up. Although nonfamily corporations own and operate 10 million acres in the United States, or 1 percent of the total, these farms produce 3 percent of agricultural sales. Nevertheless, 66 percent of the farm output still comes from family farms, which occupy 58 percent of the land. While corporation farming has not yet made inroads in grain production, it is found in vegetable production, livestock raising, and citrus, sugar, and pineapple plantations. To keep the family farm going, Minnesota and North Dakota prohibit corporate farming.

But possibly of more concern to many farmers is the growth and concentration of the food-processing corporations, which lead to contract farming. Critics of this type of arrangement feel that it ultimately turns the farmer into little more than a sharecropper. Quite common in broiler production and the raising of sugar beets and vegetables for processing, contract farming has not yet entered the grain business. Dale Yahnke gave it a try one year by growing sweet corn for Green Giant, but could not stand someone telling him when he should harvest. "I'm just too independent."

Although the threat of corporate farming is greater than the reality, corporations supplying the family farm are becoming increasingly important, so much so that observers like Galbraith state that they have made the farmer technologically obsolete. "No innovation of importance originates with the individual farmer. Were it not for the government and the farm equipment and chemical firms, agriculture would be technologically stagnant." Whoever is responsible, technology has revolutionized agriculture, enabling crop production per acre to double in the past twenty years, beef and veal output to increase by 50 percent, and net farm income to rise to $32 billion in 1974, three times the 1960 level. The trend is not expected to stop, as farm output per man-hour is expected to be about 75 percent higher in 1985 than in 1970.

The benefits to our economy are clear: Food costs in relation to income are the lowest in the world—17 percent of disposable income—and the increased efficiency on the farm has released workers to other sectors of the economy. And in view of our increased imports of oils, it doesn't hurt to have those $22 billion in foreign exchange. The United States is the granary for the world, as we export two-thirds of our wheat production, half our rice and soybean production, and 25 percent of our corn production, making the United States the largest world exporter of these commodities.

Technology

It all starts with the seed, and if you wanted to meet the neatest seed grower in the world, Harvey Hovland of Northwood, North Dakota, would come close. The fields Harvey prepares to grow registered and certified seed have a sculptured look, and his newly painted white home set among the brown fields offers a pleasing accent to the eye. Harvey belongs to a small but active group of farmers who grow seed for other farmers. Although he sells some of the seed himself, most of it is grown for the major seed companies.

One of Harvey's 40-acre wheatfields will provide enough seed for 2,500 acres.

Harvey started farming like most other people, growing crops and raising livestock, but turned to specializing in one aspect. Harvey is the neat and careful type of man that Northrup King, the world's largest seed company, and others like it, want to produce seeds they have developed.

Allenby White, a vice-president, explains that Northrup King's research budget is $5 million a year, enabling 250 researchers to get into all aspects of plant breeding. Although tremendous yield advances have been recorded in recent years, White sees further progress and credits good legislation as one reason. In 1971 the Plant Variety Act was passed, which gives companies a "copyright" to seeds they develop. Prior to that time, a variety could be copied by anyone; now, with this protection, White estimates more money will go into research.

Along with more sophisticated research, seed companies are changing their selling techniques as well. Previously, the town merchant would get the seeds and then resell them to farmers. Now, with fewer and larger farms, the companies use a more direct route: farmer-dealers.

One interesting concept employed by Northrup King is to recommend one main variety to a farmer, along with several minor ones suited for his area. Using this system, a farmer can spread his risk. There are over two hundred varieties of wheat being used in the United States today. The risks of seed production are also spread out, as Northrup King has winter seed-multiplication farms in Arizona, Florida, Hawaii, and Mexico. All seed companies employ this practice.

But where White feels that seed research has really excelled in the United States is in understanding genetics—that is, mixing one good characteristic of a plant with another. Henry A. Wallace, the founder of another leading seed company, Pioneer, recognized this in 1955 in his statement: "We hear a great deal these days about atomic energy. Yet I am convinced historians will rank the harnessing of hybrid power as equally significant." From some of Henry Kissinger's food-policy actions, you get the feeling he does not want to wait for historians.

One reason our agriculture is so far superior to the Soviet Union's, according to Allenby White, is our emphasis on plant genetics. The Soviets, according to White, have neglected this area of research due to the influence of their political philosophy on plant breeding. A Soviet theoretician by the name of T. D. Lysenko decreed that everything is caused by environment; this, and not genetic background, is the important area of research. Accordingly, the Soviets have built huge multistory buildings, called phytotrons, to simulate different environments and their impact on production. In his prime, Lysenko called anyone who attempted a different approach an enemy of the state, a title no one wanted to face Stalin with. U.S. seed companies have concentrated on genetic rather than environmental research. White, however, reports that Soviet plant breeders are now openly studying genetics, but reasons that they have a lot of catching up to do.

Many farmers are no longer waiting for rain to fall to sprout their seeds, and are introducing irrigation. Irrigated acreage now totals 5 percent of all cultivated cropland in the United States. Using irrigation, some Nebraska farmers now get 150 bushels an acre, or about three times the yield of unirrigated land. The cost is greater, as some center-pivot systems—those with a sprinkler shooting water out in a circle—come to a total fixed cost of $265 an acre. But the extra yields make up for the cost and make successful farming more a science than an act of God.

Hybrid seeds and irrigation are just part of the technology the American grain farmer has available to him. American farmers now apply 19 million tons of primary plant nutrients (nitrogen, phosphate, and potash) every year, as well as 466 million pounds of active pesticide ingredients. These numbers are overwhelming and might better be understood by thinking in terms of a corn farmer applying 100 pounds of nitrogen per acre. A good farm manager gets even more precise and minute than that. Dale Yahnke found a boron deficiency in one field and added one-half pound of boron per acre.

But the modern technology of farm chemicals has not been able to eliminate some farm slang expressions. For even though the modern herbicides bear such modern-sounding labels as Treflan and Kerb 50-W, their purpose is to eliminate such nostalgic pests as cheat grass, chickweed, quack grass, wild oats, smartweed, foxtail, and shepherd's purse.

By far the greatest application of these farm chemicals has been in the Corn Belt. Are all these chemicals necessary? Secretary of Agriculture Earl Butz thinks so. "Without the modern input of chemicals, of pesticides, of antibiotics, of herbicides, we simply couldn't do the job. Before we go back to an organic agriculture in this country, somebody must decide which 50 million Americans we are going to let starve or go hungry." As one fertilizer spokesman pointed out, the Midwest soil has now been used for an average of sixty-five years, and high yields remove nutrients from the soil three times faster. "Something is needed to fill the gap."

In spite of Butz's statement, several organizations have questioned the economic and environmental effects of the heavy use of chemicals. The Center for the Biology of Natural Systems, which includes among its members Barry Commoner, recently came out with a paper stating that the heavy application of chemicals is not necessary for successful farming. The center, located at Washington University, St. Louis, Missouri, studied thirty-two mixed crop-livestock farms in the Corn Belt, sixteen organic and sixteen inorganic, and concluded: "There was no difference between the two groups' crop production trends." In some farm circles, this was tantamount to heresy, to the point that a fertilizer company telephoned the National Science Foundation, which supports the Center's work, to suggest it cut off the Center's funding.

One important impetus for the study was the impact of the energy crisis on agriculture. For example, from April 1973 to April 1975 the price of anhydrous ammonia tripled. Since this petroleum-related fertilizer represents an appreciable part of the Corn Belt farmer's production costs, the trend toward higher chemical costs threatens farm income. The center put the study together in the hope that farmers would remember there is an alternative available. Whatever the result of this work, the American farmer uses more chemicals than any other farmer in the world. One critic of this system feels the farmer now depends more on the fertilizer companies than on his land.

One farm organization, the Farmers' Union, feels the educational system has helped to dupe the farmer into heavy chemical use. Tony Dechant, the president of the union, points out that the farmer "has relied on the advice of the land-grant college system that has sometimes been less than devoted to the genuine long-term interest of farm families. So the farmer has adopted practices that sometimes damage the environment. These include the use of chemicals, cropping land that should not be cropped and over-use of some fertilizers."

Dechant's lament echoes that of other critics of the land-grant colleges, who say that they have looked for and recommended the most "cost-efficient" means of improving production through chemical fertilizers and expensive equipment, thus forgetting the environment and the family farm. But Secretary Butz, when asked what he felt about people who criticize modern agriculture and want to go back to a simpler way, stated: "It means they're blowing smoke out their ears, that's what it means."

Maybe we could go back to organic farming, but it would be a heck of a fight. I like to think back to the agriculture that America had at its beginning. When the Pilgrims planted corn, they always had to put five seeds together, throw in a fish, and chant the following refrain:

> One for the blackbird,
> One for the crow,
> One for the cutworm,
> And two to let it grow.

One final criticism of the energy intensiveness of our agriculture comes from Rural America, Inc., which suggests we put more energy into growing, harvesting, and processing our food than we get out of it. As one critic pointed out, "While the average American consumes 3,300 calories per person per day, it takes an additional 10,000 calories to produce that amount of food. The Indian who consumes 1,990 calories, expends only 763 additional calories to generate his food. Per capita daily calorie consumption in the United States is, therefore, over 9,000 calories more than in India."

After the farmer has collected his seeds, fertilizers, and other chemicals, he has to get them into the ground for crops to grow, and out of the ground to make some money. With the decline in animal and human labor on farms, the machine has taken an ever-increasing role. Combines that used to be pulled are now self-propelled, and four-wheel-drive tractors have replaced the familiar two-wheel-drive. One giant tractor offered by International Harvester enables a farmer to plow 160 acres a day "at trotting speeds of 4 to 6 mph." The cost: a cool $45,000.

In spite of the rising cost, American farmers are now spending $7.5 billion a year on farm equipment and machinery, with an upward trend indicated. One indication of this was the 75,000 people who attended the Twenty-third Annual Farm Progress Show in

DeKalb County, Illinois, in October 1975. Billed as the "largest, most sophisticated farm exhibition in North America," the show had on display such items as a giant 620-horsepower tractor, valued at $100,000, which can pull a 14-bottom plow over 200 acres a day. By comparison, in 1924 it took 30 horses to pull a 9-bottom plow over 24 acres. Now it's faster, as well as soundproofed, air-conditioned, and with stereo music. And it avoids a problem an ad for a farm tractor in 1925 indicated: "No fear of dead horses in hottest weather." The modern tractor suits Harvey Hovland fine. He says, "I have an office in the house, but now do most of my thinking on the tractor."

The comment you hear most often about the new equipment is that the farmer, having enjoyed three good years, wants to show off to his neighbors. There may be some of that, but the fact is that the extra days the larger machines give a farmer are worth the cost. For the top 10 percent of U.S. farms, which have sales of $40,000 or more and produce 61 percent of the nation's food, these machines are a must.

New technology in farm machinery is eliminating some old sights of farming. I remember my tall, sinewy brother Karl's spending a summer on the Little Big Horn ranch in Montana baling hay. According to Karl, one day he lifted 1,000 of those rectangular 50-pound bales we are used to seeing. That may have been the traditional bale's last stand, for new balers have since been developed to cut labor costs. The new equipment that a farmer can handle makes a 6-foot-diameter superbale weighing 1,200 pounds.

Joining the bale in obsolescence is the bushel. There was a time when crops were picked by hand and thrown into bushel baskets. But bulk harvesting by huge machines has eliminated the bushel everywhere except as a unit of measure.

The new machines also have their inefficiencies. For even though Steve Yahnke's combine can reap enough corn in an hour to keep a Mexican family of six in tortillas for ten years, one Illinois group found that machines are leaving a lot of grain behind.

This group, in Eureka, Illinois, called the Gleaners, goes over fields that have been picked mechanically; they then sell the grain and donate the money to charities. According to the Gleaners, one-fifth of the country's corn crop is missed because farmers can't afford to handpick what is left behind. The Gleaners solve the labor issue by doing the work at no charge.

In spite of the inefficiencies and the criticisms leveled at present-day crop farming, farmers using the new methods not only provide the consumer with ample amounts of bread, but also contribute to a thriving livestock industry.

Livestock technology has also made rapid advances through genetic improvement and better nutrition. Few farmers today can afford scratching chickens and feed that was not good enough to make it as food. Dale Yahnke remembers trying to mix feeds himself for the sixty head of cattle he had, until he realized that the already prepared formula feeds were better than anything he could produce. Demand for livestock products has made better feeds essential, and even though feeds with names like Leo's Wholesome Feeds have a good, down-home sound, they cannot compete in quality with the better mixed feeds, such as the more modern-sounding Nutrena and Formax.

Just as in crops, specialization is occurring in livestock production, but in many midwest states you can still find the farmer-feeder. In fact, about half the corn produced in the United States is fed to animals on the same farm where it is grown. Iowa is the main farmer-feeder state, growing corn and raising cattle and hogs. But here the beef-and-hog operation is still often seen as another way to market corn, rather than as a separate industry.

Other areas of the country show a marked trend away from farmer-feeder operations. The Texas Panhandle has scores of feedlots, which are basically spas for cattle. Cattle are brought in, fed, cared for, and sold. The largest feedlots can accommodate 200,000 head of cattle. Cowboys with all their romance have been replaced by cowmen-businessmen. The feeding efficiency of these feedlots has enabled cattle to put on a pound of meat for every six pounds of feed they consume. Cattle go from cute calves to market-ready steers in eighteen months.

Dairy farming is still mostly a labor of family love, and more and more dairy farmers are giving it up. Milking cows twice a day has worn many farmers out. The best indicator of this is that the number of milk cows has dropped 35 percent since 1958, yet milk production per cow has increased by approximately the same amount. Those who have remained in dairy farming have become more efficient and have cows that can produce seven tons of milk a year!

The cattle industry now commonly uses artificial insemination and a variety of growth hormones. One such hormone is DES, which, while it enables a steer to gain 10 to 15 percent more weight in a

230-day period, is feared to be cancer-inducing. Grain farmers would not mind its banishment, for it would enable them to sell more grain.

Poultry production in the United States has gone even farther into specialization. Now fully 85 percent of the poultry produced come from fully integrated raising-and-processing operations centered in the Southeast. Efficiency in these feeding operations has now reached the point where two pounds of feed produces one pound of chicken. But Chicken Little can no longer tell us if the sky is falling, for no modern chicken gets to see the sky from the enclosed coops.

Although the jokes about the farmer's daughter and the traveling salesman will continue, the salesman who sells all this technology has of necessity become more of a technician. Gordon MacClean summed it up when he grinningly told me, "Farmers aren't near as gullible as they once were." Gordon, like other farmers, now brings a healthy skepticism to bear on new promotions, for "many highly promoted items are designed only to separate you from your money."

The influx of technology has given a lot of farmers problems in knowing just how to use it all. And looking at tide tables and solar charts in the *Farmers' Almanac* won't really provide the answer.

How Gordon MacClean manages his farm is probably how many farmers do it today. From gleaning through the twenty or so farm publications Gordon gets, plus the thoughts he picks up from seminars "where you can rub shoulders with the elite," and the inevitable sessions at the local elevator, an idea forms as to what to plant. The price trends for certain crops give only one side of the picture. Consideration must also be given to the type and size of equipment you have, your storage, labor availability, credit, and soil conditions. After doing this, Gordon then puts his muscular fingers around one of his ball-points (which read: "North Dakota Livestock Association") and etches out a cropping pattern for each of his numbered fields. He then estimates how many inputs he will need to reach his harvest objectives, although sometimes he doesn't go exactly by the numbers, for he "gets a feeling for things."

With his numbers and feelings, Gordon gets the necessary seeds, chemicals, and machinery ready. From this point on, everything done to a field is recorded. For example, "Whiskey Quarter: cultivating two hours." Although most of his fields have numbers, Gordon clings to the old names of some fields he has. The Whiskey Quarter (140 acres) got its name from a local sort who said that the piece of land wouldn't produce enough to buy a quart of whiskey.

Gordon tried a computerized management service once, but they made too many mistakes for his liking. For the time being, Gordon plans to rely on his colored maps, cost sheets, and feelings to make a profit.

Due to the complexities of being both planner and operator, many farmers who can afford it have turned to professional farm-management firms to help them decide the who, where, what, when, and how of farming. According to the American Society of Farm Managers and Appraisers, since 1968 the amount of land under the control of outside farm managers has risen from 11 million to 20 million acres. By comparison, total cropland in the United States comes to around 472 million acres. Those numbers give me a headache, since I have a difficult time figuring out what to plant in the huge expanse of my quarter-acre garden.

Doane Agricultural Services is probably the largest farm-management company today, managing over 1,300 farms ranging from 2.5 to 6,000 acres. Many of the farms belong to absentee landlords, so it is not surprising to see Doane advertising its services in the *Wall Street Journal.* Some of the improvements it brings to a farming operation are quite easy to observe and recommend, such as digging a drainage ditch. The real fun comes in analyzing whether a farm has the right product "mix."

With hundreds of variables to analyze, Doane and other farm-management services have turned to the computer. There are hundreds of computerized programs available to farmers, many through the land-grant colleges. Most of the programs work in essentially the same way. You first fill out the necessary forms, which in some programs have up to 650 questions. There are no magical solutions provided by the computer, which merely analyzes the farm information you give it and makes a recommendation. Considering the $30 to $90 cost for running a farm problem through a computer and the costliness of farming operations today, it is not surprising to see more and more farmers turning to them.

Recently, International Harvester began offering computer services to farmers by having computer terminals put in many of its Midwest farm-machinery dealerships. Called Pro-Ag, this computer network reached about 4,000 farmers in the fall of 1975. One of the technicians who helped design the program feels its real value is in having farmers examine the value and cost of tradition. As he explained, "Many farmers have strong parent messages about how to farm, and they don't consider changes. I tell these guys to remember that our fathers thought the greatest revolution in farming was the switch from the two-horse to the five-horse plow."

These technological changes may have sounded the death knell of the old down-on-the-farm life as we have known it. One Ralston Purina executive put it this way: "Farming isn't a way of life anymore, it's a way of making a living. . . . That's a fact, whether or not you like the sound of it."

3

HOME COOKING

The most distinguishing feature of the landscape in Pretty Prairie, Kansas, is that there is none. Not much goes on in this flat, low-keyed farming community except a terrific amount of wheat growing, something that Lester Wolverton and other area farmers can get emotional talking about. The faded picture of Lester's grandfather that hangs in the "sitting room" conjures up the past when the farmer had fewer restrictions to deal with. It was an era when the farmer pitted himself against nature, whereas today he has to contend with government regulation and increasing consumer scrutiny.

Lester is unique in his farm community in that he really likes to eat out. By his definition, this means driving the ten flat miles to the Otley Diner. Why does he like it? "The trouble with home cooking is that you get too many people in the kitchen." Lester feels the same way about farm policy—that too many folks and interests are involved, many of whom ruin the resources that we have. But with food such an emotional issue, it does not appear that the efforts of the farmer organizations, the consumers, or the politicians that represent both groups will diminish in their efforts to influence domestic food policy.

Working Together (Sometimes)

It is true that the American farmer is an independent sort, but he nonetheless bands together with fellow farmers now and then. The economic power is there, as only four U.S. corporations have greater sales than the total sales of U.S. farmers. But how to get 2.8 million farmers to speak with one voice?

Attempts to give farming more economic power are not a new thing. In the 1920s, the Kansas State Board of Agriculture asked Bernard Baruch to examine the poor state of the farmer's existence and find a solution. Baruch's report, entitled *Putting Farming on a Modern Basis,* made one significant point: that "agriculture's troubles were compounded by its organization, or rather the lack of organization." The individual farmer competed with other farmers for a small group of buyers. As long as this situation continued, Baruch contended, every sale the farmer made was a forced sale. So farmers have tried to organize to bring some power to their efforts.

Most farmers belong to some sort of crop producers' organization, such as the American Soybean Association, the American National Cattlemen's Association, or even the American Dairy Goat Association. These groups, which often take the form of cooperatives, can exert considerable force; witness the change in the milk-support price which the Associated Milk Producers, a dairy farmers' cooperative, helped push through in 1972. Of course, this was through political power bought by campaign contributions—"the milk fund"—but it does illustrate that farmers can feel their oats as well as grow them when they have to.

Many of the special farm organizations find their voices fading as their membership gets smaller. Accordingly, many are consolidating their forces. For example, the American National Cattlemen's Association and the National Livestock Feeders' Association, which to any consumer and most congressmen sound the same, are working to make one organization.

Apart from the specific producers' organizations and cooperatives, there are four main farmer-advocate organizations at work in the United States: the American Farm Bureau, the National Farmers' Union, the National Grange, and the National Farmers' Organization. All share the basic premise that the family farm is a way of life, not a way of making a living; but more than that, they believe that the family farm is an essential part of the American heritage.

Several of the farm groups are getting more vocal in trying to prevent the paradoxical situation that the individual farmer now feeds more people than ever before, yet finds himself with a smaller voice in national affairs. "The Farm Bureau fights for legislation to provide a favorable climate in which farmers can earn and get high per-family net incomes. It also fights legislation which would jeopardize this objective." So reads the largest farm organization's statement of its goal.

With 2.4 million members, the Farm Bureau projects a conservative yet forceful voice in national affairs. It was not coincidental that President Ford chose to address this group's 1976 convention. Apart from the stands it takes on individual issues, it has also set out its overall policies on the world at large in a lengthy sixty-two-item treatise in which it takes a position on items ranging from river-channel dredging to welfare, voting, and pay television: Farmers are against them.

William J. Kuhfuss, president of the Farm Bureau, has recently been quite visible—and audible—concerning government influence in negotiating grain sales to the Soviet Union and Poland. Calling the entrance of the government into negotiations "a step in the wrong direction," Kuhfuss expressed the farmer's apprehension that "the more we go to political management, the more we lose." Kuhfuss takes the position that since the grain is the farmer's, the farmer should be able to do with it as he pleases. The Farm Bureau wants a totally free market for agricultural commodities, where supply and demand alone govern price. However, on the production side, the Farm Bureau is not totally opposed to an administered farm program, including price supports. The Farm Bureau is the "establishment" farm organization, as one South Dakota farmer told me.

Just as committed to the family-farm concept is the National Farmers' Union (NFU), which has 250,000 family memberships and includes 750,000 people. Founded in 1902, the Farmers' Union makes no bones about its stand on the family farm. "The small business structure of the family farm is the nation's strongest bulwark against communism and fascism. It is essential to the democratic way of life."

This Denver-based organization distinguishes itself by the emphasis it places on forming farmers' cooperatives, both for buying farm supplies and for selling farm products. The co-op–development effort brought charges in the 1950s that it was a Communist front, and due to the growth of some of the cooperatives, the union is now charged with being just another big business. Two of the co-ops that the Farmers' Union helped develop have turned into the country's largest grain-marketing co-op and one of its largest supply cooperatives.

Since the 1930s the Farmers' Union has held that agricultural stability can be achieved only through effective supply management and price supports. In other words, it believes in some sort of governmental tinkering with agriculture. Tony Dechant, president of the NFU, takes issue with Secretary Butz's gambling each season with his free-market policy. Dechant feels Butz's policy can get by as long as there is a bad crop in Russia or somewhere else. He reasons that on given occasions when supply and demand get out of whack, the government should step in and help the farmer. In a brochure sent out to its members, the NFU states that the Ford administration's policy is "the same as that of the opponents of the legislation that brought agriculture out of the Great Depression of the 1930s."

It is fitting that Norman Rockwell is a member of the National Grange, America's oldest and most traditional farm organization. When it began in 1876 as the Patrons of Husbandry, the purpose of the Grange was to heal the wounds of the Civil War and to give the farmer a voice. At that time, 47 percent of the public was engaged in farming, yet only 7 percent of the Senate and House members were farmers.

The tradition of the Grange is as thick as the paint on Rockwell's American easel. All Grange activities contain a "fraternal ritual based upon the most exalted laws of God and nature." No mundane titles such as executive director and district manager appear in the Grange hierarchy, but rather "Grand Master, Faith, Hope, Charity, Fidelity," and it seems each position runs from the "First to Seventh Degree." The Grange contends such ritual instills pride and discipline, while one farmer in Iowa—where the Grange has few members—said, "Who needs all that?"

The Grange was quite active and influential in the late 1800s, fighting the railroads and monopolies. Partly due to the Grange's efforts, the Interstate Commerce Commission and Sherman Anti-Trust Act were enacted in 1887 and 1890, respectively. Proud of their efforts, a Grange historian wrote: "Except for the Grange laws regulating monopolies and the Grange's sponsorship, America might well have gone the road to communism." The Grange members probably come as close to the "American Gothic" image of farming as any other farm group. A family organization, the 1974 Grange convention passed resolutions not only on corporate conglomerates and tax-shelter farming but on multiflora rose bushes as well.

Conservative in its politics, the Grange expresses its history in

Herbert Hoover quotes. Grange patriotism and belief in God are unfailing, requiring "the American flag ... on display at every meeting. The open Bible is on the altar in full view of members."

Today, the Grange's 500,000-member strength in forty-one states is based mainly in the West, although it was founded in Fredonia, New York. It has been losing members in recent years and sometimes finds itself out of step with the other farm organizations. The Grange was the only major farm organization that supported the administration on the November 1975 United States–Soviet grain accord. Of the four main farm organizations, the Grange is the only one to have its national office in Washington.

By far the most militant of the four major farmers' organizations is the National Farmers' Organization (NFO), with headquarters located in the Corn Belt community of Corning, Iowa. The NFO makes a big point of stating that its headquarters is without carpeting. The NFO is familiar to most people as the group that shoots animals and spills milk to protest farm prices. No words are minced by the NFO, which laments the cancer of low farm prices and refers to its start in 1955 as the Biggest Farm Story of the Decade. The NFO is not universally loved by farmers. In Gilbey, North Dakota, and other farm communities in the Midwest, some farmers regard the NFO as a "dirty word." So did Richard Nixon, so the NFO had the distinction of being the only farmers' organization on the "enemies list." They are proud of the listing, and a blowup of it is to be found in the Corning headquarters.

Oren Lee Staley is the first, and so far only, president of the NFO, and has made it his goal to take full advantage of the Capper-Volstead Act of 1922. This act allows farmers and ranchers to join together to set prices when they market their products. If industry did this, it would be called price fixing, but the NFO and other farm groups refer to it as collective bargaining.

With an almost missionary zeal, Staley has set out to put 30 percent of the nation's farm products under NFO control. As an NFO bulletin states, "If 30% of farmers—just 3 out of 10—put their products together, the block would be large enough to gain fair prices for farmers."

Although the NFO has not yet reached the 30 percent mark—estimates of its farm members are put at 40,000—it has staged a number of holding actions in its short but tumultuous history. The holding action in August 1964 on swine, cattle, and sheep sales was referred to as "the greatest show of bargaining power that American farmers had ever made."

This might be somewhat of an exaggeration, as a number of holding actions or strikes had occurred previously. In 1932, the Farmers' Union in North Dakota, angered by wheat prices that were below $1 a bushel, and by Herbert Hoover's lack of leadership, pushed for a farmers' strike and formed the interestingly named "North Dakota Holiday Association." When the strike began in September 1932, a manure spreader was pulled through several towns with a banner proclaiming "Hoover's Platform."

This strike in 1932 and the NFO strike thirty-two years later did not change prices, but they did draw attention to farmers' problems, and perhaps in this light were not in vain.

In 1974, the NFO held a public shooting of calves to protest low farm prices. Arnell Beckman, a Coon Rapids, Minnesota, man, shot off an angry letter to Orville Voeltz, an NFO spokesman in Wisconsin whose calves were some of the 600 shot in October 1974.

Beckman wrote Voeltz that if he were raising calves he wouldn't complain and that he could take one of Voeltz's calves and raise it for a profit. Voeltz called his bluff and showed up one day at Beckman's house to ask when he wanted his calf.

The bet was on, and Beckman's calf soon grew to slaughter weight, earning the name "Big Mouth" because of his voracious appetite. When Big Mouth was slaughtered in December 1975, Beckman found that he, like Voeltz, had also lost money—around $200.

Using any number of techniques, the NFO plans to continue its fight, since farmers need a "counteracting force to meet existing economic forces that have been established, i.e., processors and retailers." If it does not reach its goals, the NFO feels, Armageddon may be at hand, for "If NFO, in the end, fails, then the millions in rural America will have to seek their destiny elsewhere, and NFO will still have the biggest story of the century if only because it furnished the last hurrah as private enterprise and democracy went down the drain."

In trying to reach its objectives, the NFO has run afoul of many government agencies, including the Securities and Exchange Commission (SEC), which claimed the NFO acted illegally in 1974 in receiving $8 million in loans from members. To pay farmers for the grain they had sold to the NFO, the NFO gave as collateral "dues in arrears." The SEC, however, felt these back dues were bad debts that would never be repaid, and thus farmers who accepted these dues as collateral were being misled. The SEC thought the NFO should be placed in receivership to clean up the "hopelessly insolvent" organization, but a Federal judge stayed the SEC order, and the NFO continues to fight to be heard.

Another farm organization, the Associated Milk Producers Inc. (AMPI), which controls most of America's bulk milk sales, declared in 1975 that there is a "dangerous probability" that the NFO will reach its goal of controlling 30 percent of all farm production. AMPI is upset, since milk it controls would pass over to the NFO, thus weakening its bargaining position with farmers and buyers.

The NFO does, however, find itself in agreement with the other organizations from time to time. The NFO was against the United States–Soviet grain pact, too, but used far harsher terms in denouncing it than the other farm groups. Stating that the Ford administration exercised "dictatorship with a vengeance," Staley resented Ford's use of farmers as political pawns in making the agreement.

Courting City Cousins

While the various farm organizations have taken different approaches in helping their members to earn more money, all agree that the consumer needs to understand farming better than he does, since the 95 percent of the population who are not farmers have a lot to say about how much and what is going to be planted and to whom it will be sold. Gordon MacClean expressed his views on the matter by stating that to consumers "milk comes out of a paper carton, and the cow be damned." Turning his already red cheeks redder in talking about city folks, Gordon added that the "only livestock that guys in Brooklyn ever saw were rats running in the streets."

The worst feelings toward consumers in general, and labor unions in particular, came when George Meany, the cantankerous AFL-CIO boss, told longshoremen not to load ships with grain bound for Russia. Farm prices for wheat went down, for with no grain moving to Russia, this unloaded wheat added to domestic supplies. Claiming his action was not antifarmer, Meany stated on September 3, 1975: "The current grain sale to the Soviet Union, undertaken in the name of this thing called détente, is another billion dollar ripoff of the American consumer that will bring little benefit to the average family farmer." In any event, when Meany took his action, a county extension agent in Minot, North Dakota, told me if Meany showed up in town "he could be hanged."

Even the Farmers' Union, which is more sympathetic to labor unions than the other farm organizations, turned against Meany. The president of the Kansas Farmers' Union urged President Ford to call out the National Guard, if necessary, to see that the ships were loaded. An Iowa farmer added, "I don't have anything to say about their labor contracts, but they want to price my grain."

Particularly incensed was John Maynard, of Wilmot, Arkansas. With his Ozark drawl picking up in volume, Maynard pointed out that soybeans were selling at $6.20 a bushel before the administration imposed a moratorium on export sales in August 1975. When President Ford extended the moratorium to October, bean prices fell to $5.20 at the end of September. "How'd you like to have your income cut twenty percent by a politician?" asked Maynard.

Equally traumatic to farmers and the prices they receive were the various beef boycotts of 1973 and 1974. Consumers were protesting high beef prices and put most of the onus on farmers.

Partly to blame for that "meat mess" was the fact that beef prices and production had become distorted by tax-shelter cattle feeding. Seeking to shelter income, city investors began driving up the price of feeder cattle in 1974, which worried the administration.

The Federal government lifted the price freeze on many products but kept the beef freeze another sixty days. Farmers held up selling until the freeze was over, and when it was, the market, instead of going up, collapsed. Ken Monfort summed up the feeling of many cattle feeders by stating: "The presence of the tax-gimmick people cost the industry dearly." The mechanics of these tax shelters are further explained in Chapter 8.

With boycotts and freezes to contend with, it has become apparent to farmers that, although they are responsible for sending the grain to market, they have less and less say about the prices they receive.

With the realization that hanging George Meany would not narrow the communication gap between farmer and consumer, an experiment of sorts was set up in the latter part of 1973. With the theme "Let's keep in touch, together we'll grow," the Agriculture

Council of America (ACA) began a program to bring farmers and consumers together. The ACA was founded with the help of farm and agribusiness groups to get their story across. One of the first activities of the ACA was to set up a toll-free number that anyone with questions about farming and agricultural economics could call to get the story "straight from the horse's mouth." One farmer said he was manning the phones so he could "separate the wheat from the shaft."

Other approaches used by the ACA center around getting city folks to visit farms, and a mayor's-acre program. The mayor's-acre program would involve an acre of land being planted with crops bearing an urban leader's name. Proceeds from the acre, if there are any, the ACA warily points out, will go to the urban group each participating leader believes is doing the most in its area to promote better rural-urban understanding.

Strangely enough, the ACA is probably the best way to approach the farmer-consumer communication problem, for the U.S. Department of Agriculture—despite Earl Butz's declaration: "I'll fight like a wounded steer for higher meat prices"—is geared more toward the consumer's than the farmer's interests. Superficially, this is readily apparent by going through the 1974 *Yearbook of Agriculture*, which covers such timely farm topics as "Picking the Right Types of Pipe," "Your Own Pool to Get in the Swim," and "Don't Rush Out for a Ski Outfit: Make Sure It's Your Snowflake."

This erosion of purely agricultural emphasis has been noted by USDA staffers for a number of years. Thomas Hughes, administrative assistant to Orville Freeman, Secretary of Agriculture under Presidents John F. Kennedy and Lyndon Johnson, stated that one of the reasons they fought to keep food stamps at the USDA was to maintain a farm voice and leverage with consumer interests. A typical trade-off in that era between a USDA official and an urban congressman might go something like: "Okay, Senator, we'll continue to expand food stamps in your state, but we need your help in getting more funds for agricultural research."

Dan Paarlberg, director of agricultural economics at the USDA, publicly stated in September 1975 what had been suspected for a long time: "The agricultural establishment has, in large measure, lost control of the farm policy agenda." Paarlberg defined the "establishment" as "the farm organizations, agricultural committees of the Congress, land-grant colleges and the Department of Agriculture."

What was the old agenda of agricultural policy? According to

Paarlberg, it was concerned primarily with commodities and specif-
ically with influencing supplies and prices in the farmer's interest.
The new agenda, Paarlberg noted, deals with food prices and how to
hold them down, food stamps and school lunch programs, ecology,
rural development, land use, civil rights, and collective bargaining. A
blunter statement on this shift came in 1973 by Gary L. Seevers, then
a member of the President's Council of Economic Advisors, who
stated: "Agriculture has become far too important to be left to the
agriculturalists." So it came to pass that officials who could not tell
sow from soil came to run the agricultural show, as one farm organization official dejectedly explained to me.

Faced with this shift, farmers, Paarlberg says, can pursue one
of three paths: confrontation, capitulation, or cooperation. When
George Meany raised his voice to stop grain sales to Russia, many
farmers' groups passed resolutions to stop using American machinery
to present Meany with a tit-for-tat. This raised voices further.

On the capitulation issue, Paarlberg says, "If there are more
people in favor of coyotes than of lambs, side with the coyotes." But
few farmers are willing to capitulate. Evidence of this is a bumper
sticker I saw moving south near Bakersfield, California: "Eat
American Lamb: Lots of Coyotes Do!" The coyote issue, of course, is
tied into the overall attacks on the use of farm chemicals—in this
instance to poison coyotes who enjoy mutton.

The programs of the Agriculture Council of America demonstrate that farmers are willing to cooperate in understanding some of
the issues. Paarlberg says that since the USDA has reoriented some of
its farm policies, such as giving up subsidies to large farming
operations, farmers should also bend a little. But it will be hard to
bend on some of the new agenda items, such as collective bargaining
for farm workers. Many farmers find it difficult to accept unionized
help on the farm. To many farmers, a union connotes less work and
more pay for the workers. In addition, many farmers feel collective
bargaining would take away from their authority. But whatever the
case, the farmer knows a communications problem exists and is
seeking to solve it.

The City Cousins Themselves

The real issue in the consumer-farmer relationship is basically
that the bill for bread and other foodstuffs is, in large part, marketing

charges rather than raw-material costs. In fact, the nation's marketing bill is twice the value of the farm products themselves. Yet, since most of the onus of high prices is put on the price of grain, the Russians, the middlemen, or whomever, few consumers think that their preferences have anything to do with the increasing cost of the food they get out of Gordon MacClean's wheatfields and barnyard or Dale Yahnke's corn and soybean harvest.

Ed Cook, president of Cook Industries, one of America's largest grain exporters, points out, in defending grain exports: "The price of wheat is an insignificant part of only 12–14% of the final consumer price of bread . . . if bread prices were as sensitive to wheat prices as many would lead you to believe, one must wonder why bread prices did not decline when wheat prices dropped 50% from February 1974 to June 1975 . . . retail bread prices actually rose approximately 10% during this period." What did Safeway say about this? Speaking before the Joint Economic Committee of Congress in December 1974, William S. Mitchell, president of Safeway Stores, said that "strong, effective, anti-inflationary competition is the name of the game in food retailing." And so it goes.

No one part of today's marketing chain will admit it is responsible for the increase in food costs. One way of analyzing who gets what part of the grain dollar is to look at marketing spreads—not a new type of margarine, but rather the cost components of retail foods.

During 1974, the American consumer spent $147 billion on foods; yet, of that total, only 37 percent went to the farmer. The rest was the marketing bill, which is: 51 percent labor costs—the meat cutters, truck drivers, checkout boy; 12 percent packaging—those four-color packages of food; 3 percent advertising—the television commercial that Christopher Camp looks at on Saturday morning; 6 percent corporate profits and other miscellaneous charges. Indicative of the significance of costs other than grain in food is a comment by an official of a major brewery who told me, "People don't know this industry. We don't sell beer, we sell packaging." It is disheartening to know that the wrapper on a loaf of bread costs more than the wheat needed to make the loaf.

Within the individual food categories, the farmer can fare better or worse in his share of the marketing dollar. For example, of the $43 billion spent on meat products in 1974, the farm value of this expenditure was $20 billion. Less transformation and processing occur in getting meat to the retail marketplace than with bakery goods. In the latter case, only 23 percent of consumer expenditures for bakery items went to the farmer. A loaf of bread, for example, may cost 35 cents but contain only 5 cents' worth of wheat.

Separating retail food prices from farm prices even further is the increasing amount of dining out by consumers. In 1974, $44 billion was spent for food in restaurants. According to the USDA, the actual value of the food eaten in restaurants was only $9 billion, or 20 percent of the total bill. You have to pay not only for the bread and beef but for the Golden Arches as well. The allure of eating out is increasing; in 1964 one meal in five was eaten away from home, compared to one out of three now.

Today's consumer is buying convenience as much as he is buying calories. Our free-enterprise economy pits all the sellers of convenience food against each other to capture the food dollar. Due to the nature of food manufacturing, you can make more profit in selling individually wrapped cupcakes than on plain old flour. Some product differences enable a company to advertise its product over someone else's. Some observers go further to state that collusion—not just competition and advertising for the consumer's food dollar—is the real culprit in the farm-retail marketing spread. A report of the Agribusiness Accountability Project, a Washington-based watchdog of the food dollar, says that the only "competition that exists is on merchandising techniques, animated television commercials, radio jingles, package designs, contests and other promotional gimmicks."

Another factor that food buyers don't take into account in shopping is how much they waste. University of Arizona archaeology professor William Rathje began a project in 1971 to examine people's garbage. He believed that we can use today's garbage to see what's going on in our society.

And what's going on, according to Rathje, is a lot of waste. After four years of going through a selected Tucson area's garbage cans, it was found that the average Tucson family wastes about 10 percent of the food it purchases. Rathje's students, in spite of the jeers directed at the program, are scientific about their project as they go through garbage bags, record the weights listed on packages, and weigh the food thrown away. The program has now gained some credibility, as it receives financial support from the National Science Foundation and several companies.

Another factor in the farm-retail spread that has grown to

noticeable proportions has been cases of union and supermarket bribery and corruption, particularly in the beef industry. As a result, the term "New York cut" has taken on a different meaning. Americans eat 116 pounds of beef a year, and no one enjoys beef more than New Yorkers. And since the beef industry is so large, it becomes very easy to add on a few cents for special considerations to get your beef to move better.

This was the problem facing Iowa Beef Processors, the world's largest meat processor, when it introduced the boxed-beef concept in 1970. Instead of shipping carcasses to wholesale and retail outlets after slaughtering, the carcasses would be cut up and packed in boxes. This breakdown would get rid of waste, cut transportation costs, and, according to Iowa Beef, save consumers 9 cents a pound. Super idea, except that butchers around the country felt threatened; with no carcasses to cut up, they would lose their jobs. Thus, boxed beef can't be sold in Chicago, Kansas City, and Minneapolis. These markets Iowa Beef could work around, but it had to sell to New York to make a profit.

Union leaders in New York rejected the boxed beef until Iowa Beef's chairman began paying "commissions" to one beef broker named Moe Steinman. Eventually, Steinman and Iowa Beef's chairman, Currier Holman, were convicted of conspiring to bribe butchers' union officials and supermarket chain executives to get Iowa Beef's boxed-beef products into New York's market. The State's attorneys claimed the $1.5 million Currier paid Steinman from 1970 to 1973 constituted bribes, not commissions. The arrangement "guaranteed" the sale of 16,000 carcasses of boxed beef in the Big Apple each week, with 25 cents per 100 pounds going for "commissions."

What did this and similar arrangements do to meat prices? In hearings held by the Joint Economic Committee of Congress in December 1974, Senator William Proxmire (D-Wis.) stated the arrangement cost consumers "¼ of 1¢ to 4–5¢ per pound, and in some cases as much as 15¢ per pound."

In trying to place the blame for this situation, the judge who passed sentence on Iowa Beef said, "In a certain sense, this court will always consider you a victim of the extortion practices of union officials and supermarket executives in New York." But the whole affair cast some doubt on the wholesomeness, if you will, of meat marketing elsewhere. Speaking about bribes, Nicolas Scoppeta, commissioner of investigation for the City of New York, stated: "I think there is every reason to believe they are not unique to New York."

Recognizing the costs of labor on food the USDA now gives wage costs and raw-material prices equal billing in predicting food prices. At its annual outlook conference for the upcoming year, held in late 1975, a USDA economist ran through crop conditions, storage, foreign demand, and all other fundamentals that affect food prices, and then went on to state that between January and June 1976, 250,000 food-processing worker union contracts would expire, which represented a "major element" in food costs.

The New Agenda

The essence of the tug-of-war going on in Washington and state capitals is between farmers who want more money to grow and consumers who want to spend less to cook. Unfortunately for farmers, the Secretary of the Treasury, the Chairman of the Federal Reserve Bank, and the Secretary of State have more power over agriculture than the Secretary of Agriculture. And even the vocal, folksy Earl Butz finds himself running an organization in which two-thirds of the budget goes for consumer-oriented food-support programs, for example, food stamps and school lunch programs.

The images most of us maintain of the old farm policies include that ignominious term "the farm problem." The way this problem manifested itself is in set-aside programs which paid farmers not to grow, and the vision of that Iowa farmer who drove his set-aside-payment Cadillac to Washington to protest the situation. With presidential elections nearing in 1972, the Nixon administration paid farmers almost $3 billion to withhold 60 million acres of grain land from production. Even the reduced acreage produced surpluses, which then went into government-paid-for storage. In 1970, storage of farm surpluses was costing taxpayers $1 million per day.

The myriad government legislation in regard to agriculture created lucrative, if not illegal, opportunities for those who could figure out the maze. Before being caught, Billie Sol Estes and Tino DiAngelis accumulated millions by defrauding the government's agricultural programs. When storage facilities overflowed, the government disposed of the surpluses through the Food for Peace food-export programs. For commercial exports, the government provided export subsidies. Farm prices stayed low, and during the surpluses of 1970–71, farmers used a barter system to buy consumer goods. One Bismarck, North Dakota, appliance store offered a "Color 25-inch console TV now only 440 bushels of wheat"! Consumers were happy, as food was cheap; the subsidies showed up in the Federal budget, which was accepted to be permanently in deficit and going up. Besides, taxpayers have little empathy with figures in the millions, but try raising bread from 35 to 40 cents, and a potential battle, or at least a boycott, is on your hands.

But the inexorable laws of supply and demand changed all this. Poor crops in Africa, the disappearance of Peruvian anchovies, and the huge Soviet purchases of grain in 1972 put the emphasis on keeping up with demand rather than managing supplies. In the transition, some things got caught in the wash—and the public eye: Export subsidies and set-aside-acreage payments continued beyond their usefulness and purpose. The official burial of the old farm policy came on August 22, 1975, when the USDA announced the sale at auction of nine Quonset-type buildings, the last government-owned structures used to store farm surpluses.

In both the old and new farm policy, the farmer was primarily concerned with parity—that is, maintaining farm income in line with income in other sectors of the economy. Farm parity levels were established in 1914 and had legal sanction for many years. Now, however, when farmers ask for parity, it is an economic rather than legal concept.

The new farm policy orientation could be traced from the election of the Ninety-fourth Congress in November 1974. *Feedstuffs*, a prominent agricultural publication, stated that this Congress "will provide a more favorable legislative climate for organized labor, consumer groups and environmentalists." Where Shirley Chisholm once resigned from the House Agriculture Committee, stating her membership had no relevance to her constituents, Margaret Heckler (R-Mass.) joined in order to push urban consumer programs. Another member of the House Agriculture Committee was of a similar ilk. Peter Peyser, a New York Republican who represents Westchester County—where the cash crop is money itself—had his open letter to freshman congressmen published on the Op Ed page of *The New York Times*. This letter stated that if new members wanted to make a difference, if they wanted to face international and domestic problems, they should join the Agriculture Committee.

Sensing the increasing complexity and changes in agriculture, the new—and liberal—chairman of the House Agriculture Committee, Thomas S. Foley (D-Wash.), asked for a quintupled budget to hire more researchers to study the myriad issues. (W. R. Poage, the longtime conservative Democrat who headed the committee for more years than I can remember, often returned committee budget monies unspent.)

One of the first challenges facing Foley, as well as the new Congress, was a new farm bill. Similar to the one passed in 1973, which bore the interesting title Agriculture and Consumer Protection Act of 1973, the 1975 bill, HR 4296, called for "target" prices to be set for corn, wheat, soybeans, and cotton and to raise the dairy-support price. If market prices fell below these levels, the government would step in to support the prices. The 1973 bill also had target prices, but at levels that were only a third of prevailing market levels. The 1975 bill, however, upped the target level and, while still below market levels, was getting close to where "target prices will be increased to a point where they become incentive prices," as Secretary Butz admonished.

Debate was lively during hearings on old 4296. Representative Keith Sebelius (R-Kan.), whose stationery bears the notation "Be Fair to the Farmer—He is the Backbone of the Nation," argued that the "support levels are realistic from the standpoint of giving farmers some protection and will encourage farmers to produce at optimum levels in line with our food and fiber needs here in this nation and throughout the world."

The *Washington Star* and other big urban papers called it bad farm legislation, since "It also is likely to mean increased costs to consumers just when the price of food in grocery stores finally seems to be coming down a bit." What irked proponents of 4296 was that the *Star* and other opponents used cost figures of the bill supplied by the USDA that had been proved wrong yet continued to be used. For example, the incorrect USDA figures stated milk prices would rise by 6 cents a gallon, against the correct figure of 1 cent.

But most of the lobbying against the bill was directed at King Cotton. HR 4296 would have raised the target price 20 percent at a time when, Representative John M. Ashbrook (R-Ohio) stated, "This ... means farmers would be encouraged to produce an unneeded, nonfood crop rather than food crops. . . ." Ashbrook made big use of the fact that the American Farm Bureau was against the farm bill.

Meanwhile, in windswept Gilbey, North Dakota, Gordon Mac-Clean shook his head at most of the debate news, stating, "Doesn't matter one way or another." Farther to the south, at the National Farmers' Organization's expanded store-front headquarters in Corning, Iowa, lobbying continued in support of the bill.

What did bakers say? Remember them? They were the group that claimed bread would reach $1 a loaf if wheat sales to Russia were allowed. The bakers, through their trade association, the American Bakers' Association, saw some value in raising the target price to adjust for the impact of inflation. At the same time, the ABA said that any change in the floor price, as represented by the target, requires, as a matter of equity, establishment of a ceiling price for wheat.

All the action wasn't centered in the House alone, as 4296 echoed through the Senate Chamber. Hubert Humphrey lent support, if not eloquence, to the bill, questioning, "What is the cost of doing nothing? How many more bankruptcies on the part of our farmers do we need to convince the Department that a roller coaster agricultural situation is not in the interests of our farmers or our consumers?" The Senate chose to agree with Humphrey and other agricultural big guns, like Robert Dole of Kansas, John Stennis of Mississippi, and Herman Talmadge of Georgia.

Finally, the House of Representatives approved the bill in April, after earlier Senate approval, with the National Consumers Congress and Common Cause arguing against the measure. President Ford, heavily influenced by Butz and his economists, who reminded him of a mounting Federal budget deficit, vetoed it on May 1. Ford held that the bill would add another $1.8 billion to the Federal deficit and be a "detriment to consumers and farmers."

Immediately following the veto, pro-4296 forces sought to get a two-thirds' vote to override the veto. Although the National Farmers' Organization, National Farmers' Union, AFL–CIO, Consumers' Federation, and National Milk Producers lobbied hard, the vote fell 40 votes short, 245 to 182. The Consumers' Federation fought for the farm bill not so much for the family farmer, but to protect consumers from what might happen if he were not around. Carol Foreman, executive director of the federation, said that the government wanted to get out of agriculture so that large corporations could make the marketing decisions and consumers would have even less to say about food prices.

While this bill provoked some consumers' ire, other USDA food legislation has also come under criticism, particularly by farm groups. The Farm Bureau is concerned over the misuse of food stamps, and suggests that the whole program be turned over to the Department of Health, Education and Welfare. Chairman Foley of the House Agriculture Committee disagrees with that proposal by adding, "I wouldn't be comfortable with a situation in which the Agriculture Committee was concerned only with farmers."

Beef, a widely read farm publication, considers food stamps a consumer subsidy and wonders if the cattle industry isn't being too helpful by seeming to subsidize everyone with "low prices for those who can well afford to pay more for beef and give-away to those who don't want to work."

Ironically, the food stamp program grew to its present size under a Republican administration. In 1969, when Richard M. Nixon took office, the program cost about $500 million. Although food stamps are now a $5-billion program with a host of critics, President Ford's veto of another food program—subsidized school lunches—in October 1975 left him without too many friends. Citing the program as inflationary, Ford vetoed the $2.7-billion program, only to find himself without any Senate or House allies. The Farm Bureau couldn't see his thinking. Nor could the NFO, as farmers see the lunch program as another market for their products.

Inflation fighting pervaded the Ford administration's farm policy decisions. Probably the biggest uproar over any administration veto came with the moratorium on export sales in September 1975. First the administration refused the target-price system, preferring free-market agriculture. Yet when farmers started to export, that market was closed by government fiat. Wilbur Lewis, an Iowa corn farmer, was mad. "Darn Feds got you coming and going. I figure the moratorium already cost me $5,000. What are they going to do next?"

The brief moratorium on exports of grain to the Soviets was imposed in 1975 because many people conjured up visions of the 1972 sale and the price increases that came in its aftermath. That fear probably indicated that few people had paid attention to the world agricultural picture in the intervening three years, for the situations were entirely different. U.S. stocks had been built up, and record harvests had been brought in, and, most importantly, everyone knew the Russians were coming. Even so, the mere thought of another Russian sale led to the Secretary of Agriculture's burning in effigy in corn oil covered with wheat, flour, and corn in front of the Milwaukee hotel where President Ford spoke in September 1975.

Even though the American farmer produces more than the American consumer can possibly eat, consumer groups felt that if this sale were allowed, food prices would rise unconscionably. No less a believer was the International Longshoremen's Association, which in July 1975 refused to load Soviet-bound grain carriers.

President Ford did not know what to do, since Secretary Butz was for the export sales. But with elections on the way, and the workingman already dissatisfied with the state of the economy, George Meany's personal intervention in the foray led Ford to place an embargo on export sales.

Particularly angered at Meany's export-embargo stance was Warren Lebeck, president of the Chicago Board of Trade, the world's largest commodity futures exchange. Pointing out that in the case of a 35-cent loaf of bread, the value of the wheat is only 4 to 5 cents, Lebeck added, "The major cost component—in case Mr. Meany may want to make note of it—is labor. At roughly 11% a loaf, it accounts for over 30% of the retail price of bread."

Farm groups sent their predictable telegrams to the White House. "We have great production this year: the largest forecast ever on the corn crop; the best wheat crop on record has been harvested; rice production is another record, and soybeans are close to it. Why then," asked the American Farm Bureau, "can't we export?" Senator Hubert Humphrey lashed out at the embargo, calling it another example of the bankrupt leadership of the Department of Agriculture in pursuing a sort of ad hoc agricultural policy.

Supporters of the grain embargo felt not only were consumers getting a break, but also farmers were being saved from the "unscrupulous throes of communism and the big grain export companies."

To bypass the big grain companies and other middlemen, many farm groups supported legislation to enable farmers to deal more directly with consumers. Opposed by the Ford administration was a small, but significant, bill introduced by Joseph P. Vigorito (D-Pa.), the Farmer to Consumer Direct Marketing Act. Geared mainly toward bringing farmers and consumers closer together in the fresh fruit and vegetable trade, the bill, passed by the House in November 1975, calls for the Department of Agriculture to "initiate, encourage, develop or coordinate methods of direct marketing from farmers to consumers in those cases where it is feasible."

A three-year budget of $1.5 million was provided for this effort, which should help direct the marketing efforts of such groups as the National Farmers' Organization, which has been direct-selling cheese and beef from the back of its trailer trucks for several years. Oren Lee Staley, president of the NFO, makes no bones about the value of this direct-marketing effort. "Weeds have taken over the marketing system. They are sucking all the nutrient out of it to feed the coffers of the huge overgrown corporations and conglomerates which have sprung up between farmers and consumers, draining them both."

Back to Nature

Attempts to make marketing a more uncomplicated, if not more natural, affair have also been made in the beef industry, which is undergoing some controversial changes resulting from the banning of growth hormones and the revision of meat-grading standards.

Diethystilbestrol (DES) is the first farm drug that the U.S. Senate ever voted to ban. This growth-promoting hormone enables cattle to consume 10 to 15 percent less feed, yet maintain the same growth rate as without the drug. DES is suspected by some health authorities of being carcinogenic in humans, but many cattlemen claim this fear is unfounded. Up to 75 percent of the 40 million cattle slaughtered annually in the United States receive DES. Banning DES (which the Federal Drug Administration is considering) will help grain farmers, but hurt cattlemen, who will have to buy more feed grains.

Most of the farm legislation that attracts public attention deals with the price and quality of food. Of less visibility yet of equal importance are the various environmental bills that are being proposed, and passed—many times to what the farmer considers his disadvantage.

One indignant Illinois soybean farmer stated that he would like to follow up Rachel Carson's book *Silent Spring* with one of his own, *Silent Harvest*, for that is what he claims we would have if we gave up farm chemicals, as Carson proposed. The issue is a heated one, with environmental groups like Ralph Nader's Center for the Study of Responsive Law on Food, Safety and the Chemical Harvest urging controls, while farm interests are wondering what the furor is about. Secretary Butz is open in his disdain of Nader's efforts. "Nader is a screwball. He doesn't know the difference between a hayfork and a manure fork."

Many environmental groups want greater control of pesticide use by farmers. Writing in the Nader Center–sponsored book *Sowing the Wind,* Harrison Wellford, one of the original Nader's Raiders, feels farmers are incapable of judging the use or misuse of farm chemicals. "For over twenty years, the agribusiness establishment has conditioned the farmer, through economic incentives and propaganda directed by the chemical companies, with little thought for their ecological impact." As a result of this "indoctrination," the farmer forgets or abandons all the cultural controls at his disposal to stop pests.

What Nader's group wants is for the Environmental Protection Agency (EPA) to exert greater control of farm pesticides. The issue is far from resolved, for most farm organizations, not to mention the chemical companies themselves, are against such action. To add to the turmoil, prominent agricultural scientist and Nobel Prize winner Norman Borlaug calls attacks against farm pesticides "hysterical propaganda." Nevertheless, public pressure has succeeded in giving the EPA authority to regulate pesticides and related chemicals. The extent of support for this authority is shown by the 89-to-0 Senate vote in November 1975, extending the EPA's regulatory powers in this area.

Adding further controversy to the whole farm-chemical situation is the claim of a Harvard University scientist that the earth's ozone shield may be imperiled by fertilizer use. Michael McElroy, professor of atmospheric sciences, predicted that the projected increase in the use of nitrogen fertilizers in the next twenty-five years could reduce the ozone layer 20 to 25 percent. Putting the ozone situation in a wider perspective, McElroy states that the depleted-ozone-layer problem is mainly of concern to sun-sensitive, light-skinned persons, who probably won't get much sympathy from the dark-skinned inhabitants of developing countries that need fertilizers for increased food production.

4

GAMBLING IN GRAIN

Most of America's grain is grown by conservative, God-fearing folk; the Corn Belt and the Bible Belt are often synonymous. Yet, these stable, hardworking farmers—and most everyone else in the marketing chain handling grain—take risks with it. Granted, risk taking in Las Vegas is a lot flashier than in Gilbey, North Dakota, but then you have to remember that H. L. Mencken discovered that the word *crapshooter* was first used to describe a manure spreader.

There are, of course, substantial differences between Gilbey and Las Vegas. Gilbey is a place where wealth is created, while Las Vegas arose basically as a place to take wealth away. Where the similarity lies is that the people in both places are always weighing the odds and playing hunches to try to come out ahead of the game. And some tobacco-chewing farmers I know, decked out in their faded overalls, have made a hell of a lot more on their hunches than the razor-cut, white-shoed slicks that you find hustling Las Vegas.

Agricultural commodity markets are unique in an age of increasingly administered prices. The prices of Dale Yahnke's bushels of corn and soybeans and Gordon MacClean's wheat are determined by the tug and pull of an open marketplace.

Measuring Markets

The first thing I learned about agricultural markets was that they are feminine and acrobatic. "She's up today, but I expect her to be sidewise by afternoon. Tomorrow morning she should rebound and be up by noon." That's the way one knowledgeable commodity trader at the Minneapolis Grain Exchange explained the wheat market for me one day.

Actually, there are two commodity markets; the cash, or spot, market and the futures market. Without a doubt, the futures market attracts the most press, but the cash is equally important. Although cash and futures markets can be found in numerous locations (for example, the elevator at Pretty Prairie, Kansas, is a cash market for Lester Wolverton's winter wheat), most of the activity is centered in a few locations. The Minneapolis Grain Exchange is the largest cash grain market in the world, while the Chicago Board of Trade is the largest commodity futures market in the world.

The cash market at any time is the price you can get for a given commodity physically delivered. The cash market is made up of individual sales, like Dale Yahnke's selling his soybeans to the Crystal Cooperative. The futures market is, of course, the price you can get for a promise to deliver at some future date. The futures market is best characterized by the determination of price through trading in a public auction, and where the physical commodity need not change hands. Contrary to popular belief, 95 percent of futures contracts, which are obligations to buy or sell a given quantity of a commodity during a certain time span, are closed out before actual delivery of the commodity takes place. But the fact that, if held to maturity, a futures contract requires delivery of the commodity, makes commodity futures purchases more than a game. The two markets work hand in hand.

Futures markets developed as a response to the wild swings of the cash market: Either too much grain was around at harvest, or not nearly enough right before it. People in the grain industry came up with the idea of contracts for future delivery to smooth out the peaks and valleys.

One authority on futures markets has stated that the first futures trading occurred in Japan in the 1600s, while the first U.S. futures contract was made in 1851. Today, New York, Chicago, Minneapolis, and Kansas City are the main futures centers.

Two types of traders can be found at futures markets: hedgers and speculators. Hedgers are people like farmers, farm-elevator operators, flour millers, food processors, livestock raisers, exporters, and officials in foreign grain-marketing agencies who assume a position in the futures market equal and opposite to an already existing or expected cash position.

An elevator in Pretty Prairie, Kansas, for example, might purchase 10,000 bushels of Lester Wolverton's wheat. When it does, it acquires a "long" position in this amount of wheat and is exposed to the risks of price changes. To avoid the damages of the potential losses, this amount of wheat either has to be sold immediately or be hedged. It is hedged by selling 10,000 bushels on a futures contract that will mature at a specified later date.

The elevator is then afforded protection because prices in the cash and the futures markets move together. Both markets tend to respond to the same factors of supply and demand, so if cash prices go up, futures should rise also. And since the hedger's position in each market is equal and opposite—a purchase in the one and a sale in the other—a loss in one market is approximately equaled by a gain in the other, no matter which way prices move.

But for the hedger to be able to operate, someone needs to be on the other side of the transaction. Enter the speculator. The speculator "plays a vital role in the U.S. economy, assuming risks which are an integral part of the free market," according to the Chicago Board of Trade. Simply put, he's the buyer who takes the position opposite a hedger.

The speculator hopes that the market will go up if he has taken a "long" position (bought futures), or down if he is "short" (sold futures). In the case of the long position, a speculator who buys corn at $2.50 a bushel hopes the market goes up to $3 before the contract period expires—say, in six months. He can then "close out" (sell) his position and make 50 cents a bushel. Conversely, the speculator who goes short has accepted an obligation to sell a given quantity at some future time. He, therefore, hopes the price will fall; if he sold short at $2.50 and the market falls to $2, he can cover his obligation by "buying in" at the lower market price, and make 50 cents a bushel.

The escalating prices of commodities, publicity about the Russian wheat deals, and a faltering stock market have combined to send speculators into the commodity futures markets in droves. It sometimes seems like the gold rush all over again, with all the talk about a "killing in pork bellies." Actually, 85 percent of the speculators who trade in commodity futures markets lose money, but that does not seem to stop them. Just a few years ago, there were only 50,000 speculators, whereas today we have 1 million, and may reach 5 million by 1980! How come?

Commodity futures speculation offers a tremendous amount of

leverage, more than most other investments. For a small margin—down payment, if you will—you can own a lot of commodities. To be sure, this increases your chances for gains, not to mention losses.

The other attraction commodities futures have is that they are a promissory note for something "real." With the disastrous economic declines, stocks have fallen to all-time lows. And with New York City in a shaky condition, municipal bonds are losing their attractiveness. All types of investors have turned to commodity markets. In a study done by the Chicago Board of Trade (CBOT) on the nature of people trading on a given day, the CBOT found that in one day's wheat contracts only 39 percent of the traders were actually employed in the grain trade. Among the other 6,000 traders were 273 housewives, 127 bankers, 458 chemists, and 92 stenographers. You can still hear the famous story of the Kansas City housewife who had to take delivery of two railroad cars of wheat because she had forgotten to dispose of the "buy" contract she held.

Even more nongrain speculators are entering the market through commodity mutual funds. The first of these funds appeared in 1974 and gave the speculator the opportunity to invest in a number of commodities. By the end of 1975, some $30 million had been attracted to these funds.

While the greatly increased numbers of investors have added liquidity to the market, they have also brought volatility. For the most part, this group of speculators is unwilling to hold their positions for any length of time. They are all looking for the quickies and will bolt should the market turn. New volume records are being set every year: During 1974, 19.3 million contracts to buy and sell were traded, with a value of $388 billion! Since contracts are bought and sold several times, the volume of grain they represent on paper is many times the actual grain production.

The increased volatility has caused the trading ranges—that is, allowable price fluctuations or "limits" of the various commodities—to be changed, particularly in the soybean complex (soybeans, soybean meal, and soybean oil) and wheat. For example, to prevent too big a swing in commodity markets, market rules allow wheat to go up or down 20 cents per bushel on a given trading day. If it does this, then wheat is "up or down the limit."

There is considerable resentment about this speculation, even though it is regulated. Most of the resentment is of the sort expressed by Senator William Drew Washburn (R-Minnesota), speaking on the

Senate floor in 1892. "Wheat and cotton have become as much gambling tools as chips on the faro-bank table. . . . The producer of wheat is compelled to see the stocks in his barn dealt with like the peas of a thimblerigger, or the cards of a three-card monte man. Between the grain producer and loaf eater, there has stepped in a 'parasite' between them, robbing them both."

However, there is a limit to what a speculator can do. The Commodity Futures Trading Commission (CFTC) has regulations to stop someone from artificially cornering the market or spreading false rumors. On several occasions, the chairman of the CFTC, William Bagley, has come on strong in bringing regulation to commodity futures markets. Many grain traders were bothered when, in July 1975, Bagley asked that "major grain firms report cash grain sales to foreign governments on the date agreement is reached regardless of whether a contract has been formally signed."

In itself, the extra disclosure was no big change; what was, was Bagley's added comments that "the request is designed to enhance the CFTC's market surveillance system and help prevent insider manipulation of the futures exchanges, thus protecting the consumers against the prospect of higher prices."

Along with the two types of people you find in the commodity marketplace—hedgers and speculators—you also find two ways of analyzing markets: the fundamental and the technical approaches.

The fundamental approach, as practiced by Dale Yahnke, Gordon MacClean, and every farmer and insider I know, emphasizes that the fundamentals of grain supply and demand will determine the market price. In the farmer's case, knowing what supply and demand are requires knowledge of crop conditions, weather outlook, and domestic and overseas demand.

Technical analysis, first used in the stock market, refers to that school of thought characterized by the "chartists," who are convinced that the market's future can be inferred from a study of past price and volume patterns. No matter that the Russians are in the market this Friday, analysis of the last sixty Fridays' market prices shows a downward trend, so you sell rather than buy. A lot of technical traders don't know, or even care, what corn or soybeans look like. They feel it is impossible to analyze all the fundamental factors and give each one its proper weight. It is easier to be a technician—all you have to look at are price, volume, and open interest (outstanding contracts). Most of the new speculators belong to this group, as it is easier to understand averages that rely on numbers than to anticipate crop conditions, changes in consumer preference, and so on.

Give Me That Old-time Religion

Charley McInerny has been in the grain business thirty years and serves as the chief market guru for the I. S. Joseph Company, a Minneapolis-based international commodities firm. Charley, with a wisp of Irish in his voice, daily thumbs through thirty publications on crop conditions, exports, and imports, the most useful of which end up dog-eared from constant use. In addition to the mass of papers on his old-fashioned glass-top desk, you can always find an ear or two of corn as well as a dish of soybeans. No, they are not hors d'oeuvre for the visiting traders, but samples from the most recent crop.

Charley is your basic fundamentalist, and a successful one. Among traders, Charley's claim to fame came when he pulled off an item from the Reuters news ticker that buzzes incessantly near his desk. The item dealt with rainfall in Lima, Peru. "But it never rains in Lima," Charley thought to himself. A geographer by education, Charley was fully aware of the peculiarities of the cold Humboldt Current, which skirts the coast of Peru and causes a constant and enervating mist—but never rain—to fall on Lima. Lima, the story goes, was situated in its present location on the malevolent advice of the conquered Incas. When Francisco Pizarro, the Spanish conqueror, asked an Incan chieftain where he should found the capital city, the Inca, who knew the mist would be constant and depressing, pointed to where Lima now stands.

But if rain was falling on Lima, the current wasn't doing its job. Further investigation with the oceanography departments of several universities revealed that the Humboldt Current had shifted. This meant that the millions of anchovies that thrive on the plankton in the current might have gone as well. The anchovy is the raw material for Peru's fish-meal industry, a major source of protein for animal feed. Prior to their disappearance in December 1972, anchovies were used so much in animal feeds in California that some people complained about the fishy flavor of their pork.

With the coming of *el Niño* (a Spanish name for the shift in the current, which means "the Christ Child," since it takes place about every seven years near Christmas), a world shortage of protein was around the corner. Fortunately, Charley was able to use this fundamental research into weather patterns, fish movements, and the demand for fish meal for some modern profits. The old-time religion paid off.

Farmers, millers, processors, and bakers all follow this basic type of information closely, paying attention to USDA estimates on production, stocks (inventory), disappearance (use), and exports. Almost every day of the month, some type of report comes out, ranging in subject matter from meat in cold storage, to USDA purchases of milk, to peanuts in India, to the all-important crop production reports.

Required by law to issue a report on the grain and feedgrain crop sizes during the production and harvesting season, the USDA uses a number of unique measures to make sure no leaks occur before the 3:00 P.M. Washington time release; most commodity markets are closed by then.

This report is all-important, for the estimates it contains will determine U.S. grain exports to Russia and elsewhere, grain supplies and loans to developing countries, farmers' income, and the cost of meat, bread, and other items we buy in supermarkets. In turn, this information sets the marketing strategy for farmers, processors, exporters, and food retailers. Even though it is done, it is hard to raise the price of flour in the face of a record crop.

In addition to the effects of nature on commodity prices, a close watch is kept on economic and political developments. For example, if the Morgan Guarantee Trust announces that it will raise interest rates one-quarter percent, flour millers anticipating higher interest charges for stored grain will cut back purchases, and so lower grain prices. Similarly, currency devaluations have been quite important, particularly the ones the United States has undertaken, since overseas buyers find it easier to buy U.S. grain now that their currency is worth more in terms of dollars and thus they can buy more grain for less.

A strange phenomenon occurs with major political developments. Nixon's Watergate throes made American industry unsure of itself, and thus stock prices fell, yet the uncertainty boosted up commodity prices. The same would happen in the event of a major strike: Stock prices in industry would wane while nervous speculators holding short positions in commodities ran to close out their contracts, fearing that the strike would cut the commodity pipeline and bring about higher prices.

Some commodity traders feel everything is, or has to be, either bullish or bearish regarding commodity prices. Accordingly, when Saudi Arabia's King Faisal was assassinated, a Reuters analyst found it necessary to ticker: "Faisal Death Has Minimal Impact on Grain Exports."

The USDA crop estimates are based on questionnaires sent out to about 80,000 farmers throughout the United States, who record what they think their crop is going to do. Some are very conscientious about the effort, while others have a tendency to underestimate, hoping, thereby, to raise prices. In addition, the Statistical Reporting Service (SRS), which is the USDA's division in charge of putting out this report, sends its own enumerators out into the country. And they really get down on their knees and count plants.

The questionnaires and enumerator forms are then sent to Washington, where a dozen or so commodity experts gather in a windowless room at 5:00 A.M. Security is tight and elaborate, since an advance leak of the crop estimates could earn someone a small fortune in the commodity futures market. Accordingly, all telephones in the room are disconnected, no one who enters at 5:00 A.M. is allowed to leave until the 3:00 P.M. release, and the wall clock is locked in glass to ensure that the hands aren't moved. All this security has prevented leaks, except once in 1905. In that case, a USDA statistician, using a window shade, signaled the information to a confederate. The statistician lost his job but made a bundle.

When the report is released, scores of reporters grab the white sheets of estimates and quickly contact their papers or companies to relate what "Unkie" predicts. Are the reports accurate? You could say so, as a University of Wisconsin study revealed that from 1959 to 1968 the government's first production estimates were just 4.5 percent off from the final figures. Overall, the Wisconsin study showed, reports are getting better, as the 1930s estimates were sometimes off by 10 percent.

The reports have been improving even since 1968, since farms are larger and easier to contact and new techniques like aerial photography are being used. The reports have a tendency to stabilize the market, for in a monthly report there are fewer surprises than there are in the two reports, one at planting and one at harvest, that the Soviets issue each year.

It was the lack of information about the Soviets' crop size, if not their intentions, that, combined with the disappearance of the anchovies, helped propel grain prices out of sight. A USDA expert, it was later reported, had predicted that the Soviets would have a bad crop, but his report did not surface.

The Soviets made a good deal, for they had knowledge of the fundamentals of supply and demand and the value of hedging their purchases, while the American farmers, exporters, and government did not. As a result, considerably more attention is currently being given to what goes on in Russia.

It is not that Russia has had three bad crops in a row, but rather that Russia is always a lousy place to grow grain: 90 percent of Russia is north of Minneapolis, and as a result has a short and tenuous growing season. So the assumption you start out with is that Russian crops will be poor, but until the Russian-American grain accord, the Soviets were unwilling to say how bad. Why should they, since it would mean they would have to pay higher prices?

With the Soviet reluctance to discuss their crops, the grain trade has searched for other ways to find out what's going on. Those weather reports that Monte Beeson and his colleagues pore over at Multifoods represent one such attempt. One weather-service firm is Agromet, which for $650 a month will supply maps and a daily data sheet on the Soviet Union. But they have the same problem as the man on the evening news: how to make a good forecast. Agromet admits it's hard and therefore limits forecasts to short (three-day) and mid-range (six-day) outlooks "to guarantee a near-perfect service." Particular emphasis is placed on snow cover, for if it is lacking, the cold Soviet winter will kill grain planted in the fall.

The CIA has also entered the Soviet grain picture and has begun to make Soviet crop information available to the grain trade. During the 1975 Soviet grain purchases, grain traders were faced with the following Reuters ticker information: "USDA down—CIA up on Soviet estimates." The CIA appearance in these public types of announcements or in private sessions that are held in the halls of the Minneapolis Grain Exchange has supplied more solid facts on Soviet buying intentions.

Traders also pay attention to Soviet gold sales, which are used to buy U.S. dollars to pay for wheat purchases, and to Soviet chartering of ships to transport the wheat. To an international grain "house," word that the Russians are coming should provoke the following steps: Buy wheat (buy wheat now, since Soviet purchases will drive prices up), sell gold (Russian sales of gold to buy dollars will lower gold prices), and buy dollars (the value of dollars will go up, since the Soviets will want them to pay for wheat).

But if trying to get hard marketing information on the USSR is difficult, consider the situation with the People's Republic of China. In recent years it, too, has come into the world market and has had a sizable impact on prices. Part of the problem is Chinese secrecy, which comes across in the following fashion, according to the Commercial/Economic Section of the U.S. Liaison Office in Peking. "Their system of releasing information now consists of partial and not very precise reports like cotton production is 2.6 times the largest production" (for which there are no statistics), or "36% greater than in 1963" (for which no figures were published), or sometimes simply "comparatively good" (which means not very good), or a "bumper crop" (which means a good crop).

By carefully watching all this information, you will (should) eventually know which way things are going. However, the market may not react to this information as fast as you thought, so, although you are right, your timing may still be wrong. A true example:

You see a government figure that rye production is going to be up, yet you go out to the fields and see that the crop is drought-ridden and awful. Yet everyone believes the government figure, and the market goes down just after you have bought a bunch of rye, anticipating the shortage. The market keeps going down; no one wants the rye you bought at the high price; and since you need your storage you eventually are forced to sell at a loss. Three months later, the government revises its figure downward. You were right, but you lost money, leading one grain trader to remark, "You have to be flexible or the market will force humility on you."

Commodity markets therefore bear a close resemblance to politics, in that what is believed to be true is often more important than the truth itself.

Chartist's Corner

Not necessarily scoffing at the seemingly endless supply of fundamental information, the technician examines his charts and sees what they tell him. One technical trader I know made a concession to all that supply-demand jazz by wanting to know only if the fundamentals were bullish or bearish on a given day.

It's a lot easier to learn technical trading than it is to make yourself an agricultural expert. But I personally have a hard time believing that the price of Dale Yahnke's corn is determined by such phrases as "a price pattern rarely seen in commodity charts, the diamond formation is a hakitui of high volume tops." Some of the patterns have more unusual, if not sensuous, names, like the "selling climax." Others are more anatomical, like "inverted fulcrum," "head-and-shoulder," and "rounded bottoms."

Whatever the case, some traders make money using this "technical" technique and, according to long-timers in the grain business, have affected commodity markets.

Interest is growing in using computers for technical analysis. For example, if a technical trader were to see that corn had set a three-week high at the end of the trading day, consulting a computer, he could immediately determine what happened to the price of corn each time it reached a three-week high during past periods. The object of this effort is, of course, to help the trader decide whether to hold, buy, or sell corn.

First used by specialty commodity houses, these computer programs picked up steam when Merrill Lynch began using them in conjunction with a commodity mutual fund it offered. The computer programs do have their failings, for they did not predict a sharp rise in the price of wheat during the 1972 Soviet wheat purchases. In that case, it took a human decision to get out of the wheat market. Nevertheless, a Merrill Lynch spokesman feels the computers are here to stay in the commodity markets. "They're so fast and accurate and they remove human emotion. They can be impersonal and look at the market objectively."

Just as computer science has entered commodity marketing, so have some offbeat things such as astrology. How so? One Panamanian firm believes that stars move us all. Their May 1975 prediction for grains rambled on as follows: "Venus is in Cancer, a very bullish sign. However, it is square to Pluto on Thursday. This is a very bearish indication for grains. On the other hand, the wheat crop is being severely destroyed by the weather," and so on. Anyway, after a few more paragraphs of this, you get told to sell. Crazy as it seems, some traders follow the stars, and one leading commodity publication put in a "Futures Gazing" column. Why not try astrology, it might give you an edge.

Despite all of these techniques for analyzing commodity markets, one billion-dollar grain-and-flour firm felt they were not enough. Accordingly, they gave their traders ESP tests to see if they could provide the key to why one trader has better hunches than another.

Any new theory or approach gets consideration these days, for the old rules don't seem to apply anymore. I remember leaving the Minneapolis Grain Exchange and hearing a trader I knew mumbling, "Thirty years, thirty years I've been in this business, and I don't know what's going on."

Once a trader chooses the theory he will use, the action begins. In the "pits" of commodity futures exchanges, anxious, perspiring men wave finger signals back and forth, trying to get their price. The men in the pits represent brokerage houses and grain companies, each trying to outdo the other. A visitor from Spain was amazed when one trader collapsed with a heart attack and was removed with hardly a glance from anyone else. It had happened before.

Cash grain business saves you from the pit, but makes your constant daily companion the telephone. Someone is always on "hold." Dialing is cumbersome and time-consuming, so you add an automatic dialer. Trading millfeeds—the by-product of flour milling used for animal feed—is perhaps the most hectic. "Bid me, damn it. You won't? Well, the hell with you." That's how the fraternity talks sometimes, trying to "scalp" one another. Trading is a rugged game, and scalping is getting between buyer and seller and adding on a dollar or two a ton for your efforts.

The cash grain business is unusual in that it is one of the few trades in which oral contracts are admissible in a court of law. Once a trader says he will buy or sell, that settles it.

Some have questioned the relevance of this type of trading to the consumer. A trader buys grain, sells grain, earns his margin, but the stuff hasn't moved an inch if he has merely sold it to another trader. Somewhere along the line, a final buyer enters the picture and the action stops. Farmers are interested in cooperatives so as to avoid a lot of this trading, which they feel doesn't benefit them or the consumer.

5

FOLLOWING THE
HARVEST MOON

Down on the Farm

Even before Dale Yahnke gets his corn and soybeans in the ground, someone is guessing—if not betting—not only what he will harvest but also what price he will get.

When one of Dale's groaning red trucks is filled with corn, it heads back to the farm, where the corn is dried by a natural gas burner and then put into storage. High farm prices in the past couple of years have enabled Dale to put up new storage in the form of gleaming steel bins.

This arrangement provides Dale with a lot of flexibility. His dryer enables him to pick his corn while it still has a high moisture content, which cuts down on field losses. His storage, meanwhile, enables him to avoid those long, dusty lines at the Crystal Cooperative and lets him wait out the market. It was his intention that the corn he harvested in October 1975 should remain in his storage until May of the following year.

In holding onto his crop for some length of time, Dale is not unlike many other Corn Belt farmers. Current estimates show that on-farm storage has increased 70 percent in the past six years, from 3.5 billion bushels to 6 billion bushels, or, in other words, enough to store the nation's entire corn crop. Most of the increased storage facilities are going up in the Midwest, where farming returns more than in the East, where farms are smaller.

As a market alternative, apart from storage, some farmers are looking at forward selling. Using this method, a farmer would sell his future crop or a portion thereof to an elevator, processor, or livestock operation at what they agreed was an equitable price, taking into account the cost of production of that crop and providing a return to management and capital. One Missouri farmer explained: "It makes sense to start negotiating price before beginning production. That's how industry does it. The farmer's game is production. Let the speculators play the markets."

To be sure, a forward-pricing contract makes you forego any increase in price, but at the same time it will protect you from any declines. Advocates of this approach feel that it would help stabilize food prices all around.

Forward selling is really another type of hedge like that already available on commodity futures markets. Farmers are also using the futures markets themselves, for as farms grow in size, they produce commodities in quantities that better fit contract sizes. Twenty percent of a group called the Top Farmers of America have indicated that they intend to hedge their crops from now on. If the price of a commodity looks good in the futures market, they will hedge their upcoming production at that price. Then, regardless of what happens to markets, they will have assured themselves of a certain price, presumably enough to cover their costs of production. Lester Wolverton smiled as we discussed this, and said, "Can you imagine a Merrill Lynch office in Pretty Prairie?"

The logic of farmer hedging becomes obvious when you examine the fluctuation in the price of soybeans during 1975: from $4 to $8 a bushel. Most farmers know there's nothing they can do to cut their production costs, so they're trying to do a better job as sellers.

The interest of farmers in futures seems universal. On a European trip in 1974, the publisher of a leading grain-trade publication noted that sales of the *International Herald Tribune* in rural France had doubled in the past year. These sales were attributed to the fact that the *Herald Tribune* is the only European newspaper printing the full price closes of the Chicago Board of Trade.

During the winter months, Dale Yahnke gets kind of fed up with sitting around home and heads to the office of the Crystal Cooperative, where he knows hot coffee and fresh doughnuts are always waiting and the noise of the market ticker casts a hypnotic spell. Dozens of other farmers have the same idea, and so the place is packed and alive with talk about markets. It is probably at sessions like these, held in cooperatives or cafés, that the decision of when to sell their crop forms. Farmers work hard at this. A little to the south, in the rich soybean and corn country around Eagle Grove, Iowa, farmers spend the winter mornings at one café in town, then hop over to the other one in the afternoon, not wanting to miss a word or a rumor anywhere in town.

Waiting out the markets is not easy and gets expensive if you guess wrong. Consider the atmosphere at Kingsley, Kansas, on July 8, 1972, when Elmer Frick sold his entire wheat crop of 4,000 bushels for $1.27 a bushel. But then, right after he did it, President Nixon announced the Russian wheat sale. The smoke-filled cafés and frenetic commodity exchanges really began to buzz, and two weeks later, Frick's bushels of hard red winter wheat would have brought $2.14 each.

Critics of the wheat deal claim the farmers were robbed at the expense of the grain companies and the Russians because they sold before learning of the impending sales. Secretary Butz didn't see it that way. "Farmers didn't lose money because of early sales; they just didn't make the additional money they might have made." In any event, farmers are a lot more wary now of what the market can do for—and against—them, and spend a lot more time thinking about marketing rather than production only.

The buzz in these sessions goes something like: "It'll take $2.80 to get me interested. I've sold one-third for January delivery and have a fair average on that corn; $3 would buy the bulk of what's left." When the day to sell does come, they call the local elevator, get a price, and if it is good, tell the elevator operator to send his heavy trucks over. The grain farmer has completed his job.

These calculations occur at the beginning of the year as well, when grain farmers consider which grain will bring the most. Gordon MacClean can choose to grow barley or wheat, while Dale Yahnke can decide between corn or oats.

The grain-livestock farmer has to do a little more thinking before he begins growing grain for sale or for raising and feeding animals. Most of the corn produced in the United States goes to this type of farmer, as statistics reveal that 50 percent of corn production is fed to animals on the spot. Dale Yahnke made his decision two years ago when he realized that feeding grain to cattle was not returning enough money, so he turned strictly to grain. He could make more money selling the grain direct than he could by feeding the grain to livestock and then selling the livestock for meat. Dairy, hog, and poultry farmers have to make the same decision in their operations. Feed is the important cost—up to 75 percent in the case of hogs—in raising livestock. As one poultry farmer told me, "A chicken is nothing but walking corn and soybean meal that clucks." The figures, for those of you who are interested in such stuff, are that, of the corn used for feed, 17 percent goes to chickens, 34 percent to porkers, and 39 percent to cattle of one ilk or another.

The year 1974 was probably the worst ever for cattle feeders, when it cost 55 cents to add a pound of meat to a steer, yet cattle sold for only 40 cents a pound because of depressed demand and consumer resistance to higher meat prices. Cattle feeders thereby lost $100, $200, and sometimes $300 a head. Total losses that year were somewhere around $3 billion.

Grain farmers who have livestock also try to use new marketing techniques to earn more money. Many now forward-contract hogs and milk to packing plants and dairies or hedge on futures exchanges.

Their marketing doesn't have the flexibility of a grain farmer. One Iowa hog farmer I met brought the difference out vividly by asking, "Did you ever try storing a hog?" When the animals are ready, you have to sell.

When Dale Yahnke had cattle to sell, he would truck them to a terminal market like the South St. Paul stockyards and hope the buyers were hungry. These terminal markets are fading in importance, as the packing plants have moved out into the country. Witness Chicago, whose once-famous stockyards no longer exist.

Livestock farmers now sell at a local auction barn or directly to a packer. Dairy farmers take their milk direct to a dairy, while poultry producers go directly to the packer, as around 85 percent of the country's poultry and dairy business is contracted beforehand.

Sentinels of the Prairie

The grain that doesn't get fed on the farm ends up in what one poet called the "Sentinels of the Prairie." Grain elevators are located in most every farm community and often compete with the local church steeple as the highest structure around.

Elevators sprang up as railroads were being built, and served as the farmer's contact with the market. At the peak of elevator construction in the 1930s, farms were small in size and had no storage. The elevator was vital and trusted. I think it is sort of poetic that the manager of the Crystal Cooperative elevator, where Dale Yahnke sells his grain, is named Loyal Larsen.

Today, there are 15,000 elevators throughout the United States that take in not only grains but other crops that can be handled in bulk. When a farmer's grain comes in, it is weighed and a sample is taken; the rest is dumped into a pit, where buckets attached to a conveyor elevate the grain to the appropriate bin.

The elevator manager takes the sample and puts it in a dockage tester to remove the dockage (foreign material found in the grain). The clean grain is reweighed, and the amount of dockage is determined as a percentage of the grain's weight. The dockage is deducted from the gross bushels to give the net bushels delivered by the farmer. It is on this basis that the farmer is paid. As soon as this occurs, the elevator hedges the purchase on a commodity futures exchange to lock in a profit. Some elevators offer the farmer twenty days' free storage before he has to sell the grain he has delivered.

Once he has hedged, the elevator operator will try to negotiate a cash sale at a major market like Minneapolis or Kansas City. To do this, he appoints a commission agent, who acts on his behalf in selling the cash wheat to a buyer on the floor of the grain exchange.

Some people are not above cheating the elevator if given a chance. In a South Dakota case, seven men were involved in a scheme to use magnets and "double weighing"—putting the front wheels of a truck on the scales while another loaded truck was being weighed. This made the grain appear heavier, giving them more money.

Once the harvest is under way, the elevator begins to fill up quickly, and the railroad becomes important to move the grain out. Today, many farmers regard railroads with the same disdain that Frank Norris did when he wrote *The Octopus* decades ago. In parts of the farm country that the Burlington Northern (BN) serves, farmers tell me that the initials really mean "Better than Nothing."

Art Greenberg is a big, 6-foot 4-inch, 250-pound, pleasingly loud grain-and-potato farmer in Grand Forks, North Dakota, who jokingly asks for thirteen eggs for breakfast but gets a serious response from a waitress at the rustic Westward Ho restaurant in Grand Forks. Art's huge operations depend on timely freight; grain contracts call for delivery at a specific time, and failure to do so results in penalties and a bad reputation. He does not criticize the railroads for their size but for their inefficiency. One story Art likes to tell is about a shipment of commodities he made to the West Coast. He recalls asking a railroad dispatcher where his shipment was, and the dispatcher responded, "We know where it is, but we don't know how it got there." One North Dakota farmer feels the reason for the inefficiency is that railroad employees are more interested in their pensions and job security than in moving his grain.

Many farmers and elevators claim that rail cars are never available when they need them, and, when they do get them, the rates they get are worse than those given the big grain companies. Complaints are often heard that the railroads always make sure to have enough cars at attractive rates for the largest-volume shipper while the small guy needing five cars goes begging.

Another rural concern is over railroads abandoning little-used spurs to small elevators. In its 1975 farm policy statement, the National Farmers' Union called for a moratorium on rail-line abandonments until all economic and social impacts are evaluated.

Farmers in small towns are also worried about being abandoned. It is estimated that 1,000 miles of rails annually are allowed to grow weeds. While some farmers have openly protested, others have banded together to rescue rail lines.

In 1974, fifty small farmer cooperatives in Iowa got $1.2 million together to aid in roadbed improvement for the Rock Island Line, which was no longer "a mighty good line." The state of Iowa added another $1 million, as well. The money went to repair and renew 100 miles of track in an area of Iowa from which 90 percent of the grain sold goes for export.

Other elevator operators seemingly think "if you can't lick them, join them," and try to make their operations more efficient so as to keep the railroads interested in them. The Crystal Cooperative spent several hundred thousand dollars to put in unit-train loading facilities. A unit-train is a group of twenty-five rail cars having the same origin and destination, and because of the ease in handling these larger volumes, railroads offer a preferential rate. Thus, with a lower freight rate, the Crystal Cooperative elevator can better compete against an elevator that sends only five cars to a cash market. However, in January 1973 the Interstate Commerce Commission (ICC) ruled that railroads could devote only 25 percent (later reduced to 20 percent) of their hopper cars to unit trains in order to give the smaller shippers a chance at the cars. This order didn't work well because it applied to unit trains of fifty or more cars. One observer noted that the railroads formed unit trains with fewer cars, thereby avoiding the order.

Those elevators that can muster the capital to build the necessary facilities are doing so, while the big grain companies are constructing all new unit-train facilities. Cook Industries, for example, is spending $1.7 million for an inland grain-handling facility at Denison, Iowa, to load a 100-car train in six hours.

Railroads have always been a hot farm issue with both farmers and elevator operators, but became even more so during the large Soviet grain purchases of 1972. Exporters wanted to get their grain to port as soon as possible, while fertilizer companies wanted to get fertilizer to the farmers. Rumors of a black market in rail cars developed, with accusations that the big grain exporters were using cars as free storage at the Gulf while rural elevators had no cars at all.

Rail cars became so crucial to marketing that independent elevator operators in Iowa, Indiana, and Illinois accused eight large grain companies of forcing them to accept lower prices for their grain during times of rail-car shortages in order to get it shipped. The grain companies were able to do this because of the railroad cars they had leased. Cargill, the largest of the companies, owned or has leased a fleet of 3,000 rail cars.

One Colo, Iowa, elevator operator told the ICC that in the fall of 1973 he had a hard time getting rail cars to load grain that he had sold to Continental Grain Company. According to the operator, Continental offered to get him some cars, but it would cost him 5 cents a bushel.

In view of this situation, Senator Dick Clark (D-Iowa) asked the ICC to probe further into the matter, commenting, "As yet, we have no assurance that an inequitable distribution of rail cars favoring the major grain companies will not re-occur, blocking grain movement from the farm, forcing farmers and country elevators to sell grain to the major companies at below market prices."

Another transformation in the country elevator system is that they are becoming farm service centers. Instead of the farmer just coming to sell his grain, the elevator is gearing up to sell him fertilizers, seeds, and whatever else he might need. One-stop shopping has come to the prairies. In view of this expansion, one

crusty Fertile, Minnesota, elevator operator told me that he might change the name of the Fertile elevator to Prairie Plaza!

Shake, Rattle, and Roll

Once the Gilbey, North Dakota, elevator gets its rail cars loaded with hard red spring wheat, more likely than not they will end up at the North Dakota Flour Mill in Grand Forks, one of 148 flour mills in the United States. One hundred years ago, there were 11,000 such mills.

The North Dakota mill is the only state-owned-and -operated flour mill in the United States. This mill and a cement plant in South Dakota are the only state-run industries in our capitalist economy. It was built in 1918 as an outgrowth of the dissatisfaction farmers felt with the price they were getting for wheat. Back in the 1920s, the Farmers' Nonpartisan League, which reportedly had a lot of "anti-business doctrinaire socialists" in its midst, believed that the state should have all the means of production.

North Dakota legislators had another chance to examine the wisdom of the mill in 1970, when it was destroyed by fire. However, they chose to rebuild it, again under state control. It took a long time for the mill to reach the break-even point, but it is now an established part of North Dakota agriculture.

The fire enabled the mill to install all new machinery, making the North Dakota mill one of the most modern around. It, like other flour mills, has had to scrape to get by; the October weekend I visited the mill, no sweepers to keep down the dust were around, in order to save money.

It's confusing as hell to go through a mill, for the myriad pipes, tubes, and shafts make you feel as if you were in the boiler room of a ship. Sam Kuhl runs the mill with a lot of guidance from politicians, but he enjoys the work and demonstrated that when he took me on one of his dusty safaris on a Sunday morning.

The wheat that comes out of Pretty Prairie, Kansas, or Gilbey, North Dakota, goes through a milling process something like the words of that blond rock pianist and gyrator Jerry Lee Lewis's song, "Shake, Rattle, and Roll." Actually, the words are somewhat out of order as the process is more like rattle, roll, and shake.

There is really not much to it, even though it took man a couple of thousand years of milling to reach the current technology. Wheat comes in from the country, is dumped into a pit and then elevated. The North Dakota mill doesn't blend any wheat, but other mills mix the different wheats before milling.

The most sought-after wheats are those with high protein, like the spring wheats grown in North Dakota. Hard spring wheats have good protein—gluten, as in glue—which forms the hard crust in breads. Softer wheats grown in milder climes are lower in protein and milled chiefly into flour for cakes, cookies, pastries, and crackers. Durum is a hard spring wheat that makes a yellowish flour and is used for pasta.

Once in the mill, the wheat is shaken through screens to separate the grain from the rocks, bolts, sunflower seeds, sticks, and other dockage. From there, the wheat gets squeezed between two rollers like those on old-fashioned washing machines. Then this broken-down wheat kernel gets shaken through some 1,100 screens to separate kernel pieces into different sizes. About 75 percent of the wheat kernel becomes flour, while the rest, known as millfeed, gets fed to animals.

Of the flour produced in the United States, around 75 percent goes to big commercial bakeries. The rest gets packaged for family flour and other specialty uses, such as cake mixes. The flour intended for home use is enriched with thiamine, niacin, riboflavin, and iron as a result of the efforts in the early 1940s of a Dr. Wilder of the Mayo Clinic. South Carolina enacted the first enrichment statute in 1942, and other states soon followed. Bakery flour is exempt from these statutes, as bakers add these vitamins during dough preparation.

Some industry observers feel that enrichment came about as the heritage of one Reverend Sylvester Graham (who died in 1851), of Graham cracker fame. Histories of Reverend Graham's era would have you believe that he was the Euell Gibbons of his age.

Even though many of us, myself included, would consider the nineteenth century to be an age of natural foods, Reverend Graham did not see it that way. One past secretary of a milling trade association has labeled Reverend Graham a "natural foods crank and supporter of a long list of 'isms.' "

By observing the cracker to which the Reverend Graham gave his name, it is easy to surmise that he was against white wheat flour. He felt that white flour was harmful and that only whole-wheat flour should be used. Rumor has it that he thought white flour had an aphrodisiac effect and invented the Graham cracker as a counter-measure.

Reverend Graham espoused the idea that too many vitamins and other nutrients were taken out in the milling process. Enrichment put back some of what milling took out.

The fact that some flours were more yellowish than others also produced a hue and cry by winter-wheat growers for bleaching. Bleaching was a marketing tool at first, since it made flours whiter and they therefore appeared purer. Winter wheats have a more yellowish tinge than spring wheats, and because of the preference for a whiter flour—despite Reverend Graham's exhortations—southwestern flour mills began adding bleaching agents at the turn of the century.

During this era, the chief of the U.S. Bureau of Chemistry, a champion of pure foods, fought against bleaching agents, but was turned down by the Supreme Court in 1915. Bleaching went its merry way until 1946, when a study revealed that Agene, a nitrogen trichloride bleach, caused "running fits" in dogs. Agene was withdrawn and replaced by another bleaching agent, which we munch on today.

These images of the past flash through my mind as we finish our safari at the mill, our pants and hair somewhat whitened with flour. Sam points out that the mill, not by any means the largest in the United States, can mill the production of 1,000 acres of wheat a day. But due to the economics of flour milling, a resident of Grand Forks, North Dakota, can't buy at the supermarket any of the Dakota Maid flour made by the mill. It is too expensive to put the flour in 10-pound bags for the retail trade, so the mill concentrates on bulk business to bakeries and the like. "Freight is against us," Sam says. "Pillsbury in Minneapolis can make it cheaper than we can, and ship it in, and still make a profit." Pillsbury's larger volume enables it to cut production and transportation costs tremendously, leading to this seemingly illogical situation in Grand Forks.

From the mills, flour is shipped out in bulk railroad cars to bakeries and other food processors. Bakers like Continental (Wonder Bread) then bake up the 72 pounds of bread, buns, and rolls that the average American consumes each year. But because of our decreasing consumption, this quantity is down from around 200 pounds at the turn of the century.

To encourage our consumption of wheat products, flour-bakers like Pillsbury and General Mills have come out with Wheaties, Eggo French Toast, Klondike Pete's Crunchy Nuggets, and the like to stimulate our palates. Thus, we eat another 30 pounds of assorted baked goodies. In terms of cookies, Pillsbury tells us that we go to the cookie jar 21.9 billion times a year. Foods made from wheat have become products with colorful packaging, artificial colors, and extensive advertising campaigns. Costs mount until the cost of wheat becomes a minor factor in the final retail price. Reverend Graham must be shuddering in his grave.

The Crusher

Dale Yahnke harvests soybeans pretty much the same way as corn, maybe with a little more interest, as soybeans not only are a relatively new crop to American farmers, but their price may be the most volatile. Farmers like Dale grow fifty times more soybeans today than they did in 1962. Prices back then were around $2.50 a bushel, zoomed to $12 a bushel in 1973, but fell back to around $5 at the end of 1975. The United States is by far the leading producer of soybeans, with three times the yield of Brazil and five times the amount of the People's Republic of China, where the bean originated some 2,000 years ago. Soybeans seem to thrive in the United States more than in other countries. The importance of this fact led a researcher friend at the University of California at Davis to exult, "We've got the world by the oilseeds!"

The unprocessed soybean is not of much value—although you can buy toasted soynuts—but its by-products, soymeal and soy oil, have an almost unlimited range of uses. Soymeal provides the protein needed in animal foods and is used increasingly in making "meatless meats." The value of soymeal is easy to understand when you consider it is 45 percent protein, compared to the 8 percent of corn, barley, and other grains. The oil is found everywhere: salad dressings, ice cream, soap, paint, and margarine.

Once the co-op or elevator buys the beans, they, like corn, are hedged in the futures market and cash buyers come a-calling. About a third of the soybeans are exported eventually, bringing in an estimated $5 billion in foreign exchange, making them the leading U.S. agricultural export; beans are second to corn in domestic importance.

Sooner or later, the bean meets the "crusher." Time was when huge mechanical presses would crush the oil out of the bean, leaving the protein-rich meal. All soybean processors thereby got the name "crushers," but, like everything else, the mechanical process became too expensive. Now a chemical process using a petroleum derivative with the Flash Gordon–type name hexane separates the oil from the bean. But the term "crusher" stuck to firms like Anderson-Clayton, Archer Daniels Midland, A. E. Staley, Continental, and Cargill, which do most of our soybean processing these days. Decatur, Illinois, some 180 miles south of Chicago, is considered the crushing capital of the world. In fact, when prices for oil and meal are quoted, it is often on a Decatur "basis." Once separated, the two parts of the bean go their separate ways, the oil in special tank cars and the meal in hopper wagons.

Use of soybean oil in cooking has always been pretty well accepted, but when the oil became "hydrogenated" (hardened) into margarine, consumer suspicion and dairy-interest resistance set in.

The new margarine threatened dairymen, and in states like Minnesota and Wisconsin they lobbied for extra taxes and against the use of coloring in margarine. Stories of how the margarine of the 1950s resembled the first margarine developed in 1870 were passed around; it was an uncomplimentary comparison, since the first margarine consisted of a weird mixture of beef fat, milk solids, sodium bicarbonate, and an awful-sounding thing called "udder extract."

Margarine using soy oil got better, and, in something of a first, became more expensive than butter in the state of Minnesota in the latter part of 1974—due not so much to the extra taxes placed on it, but rather as a result of the demand. People now consume twice as much margarine as butter. Americans annually consume 50 pounds per capita of fats like butter, margarine, and vegetable oil, of which soybean oil has the lion's share.

The soymeal travels in its covered hopper car to an animal feed plant, where it is mixed with high-energy (carbohydrate) items such as wheat millfeeds, corn, or sorghum. These complete feeds are then shipped to hog, turkey, poultry, and cattle raisers, not to mention dog-food manufacturers and mink ranchers.

However, an increasing portion of the soymeal—which represents about 72 percent of the bean—never makes it to the animal-feed siding, but goes directly to a human-food plant. By grinding down the fiber in the meal a little finer, the meal can be used for direct human consumption in a number of ways. Regardless of the application, the goal is the same: to get protein to the body more quickly. Instead of feeding vegetable protein to animals to get animal protein, human consumption of soymeal avoids the animal entirely, saving time and resources.

I will be the first to admit that I thought my Seventh-Day Adventist neighbors a bit strange when I was growing up in Washington, D.C. They were always having artificial hamburger, pork chops, or some such thing made from soybeans. In fact, I can remember standing on our back porch, eating a hamburger, looking at them having a picnic, and wondering what "artificial" they were having.

Many food manufacturers have come up with a halfway house by utilizing the soymeal—now processed into textured vegetable protein—as a meat extender. This was particularly timely during the high meat prices in the past few years, as you could buy a pound of "Juicy Blend" or some such mixture of two-thirds ground beef and one-third textured vegetable protein for about 10 to 15 cents less than the cheapest ground beef.

Other products using textured vegetable protein have come on the market, and the TVP is no longer called "artificial" but rather an extender or analog (fake meat). You can find textured soy protein in pizzas, cookies, chili, stews, soups, and prepared dinners and in nearly every kind of convenience food, canned or frozen. The fall in meat prices in 1974 slowed down the growth curve, but Archer Daniels Midland, the world's leading producer of textured vegetable protein, is confident that TVP is going to be a "significant factor in the food of the future." It may be, for a consumer study done by Texas A&M in 1975 indicated that 75 percent of the first-timers who ate "soyburger" planned to use it again.

Beyond extending meat, efforts are under way to bypass the mixing of vegetable and beef proteins altogether. One company in Missouri now produces analogs that have textures and flavors similar to beef, ham, chicken, turkey, and shrimp. The company claims that the real advantage of the analogs is that they will be inexpensive, free of fat, high in protein, will not contribute to serum cholesterol levels, and will need no refrigeration. In November 1975, Food Fair Stores in Philadelphia began to offer its first 100 percent vegetable beef substitute. I doubt it was a bicentennial event, but rather evidence of increased interest.

Just as the dairymen fought margarine, cattlemen are not taking meat analogs lightly. The most interesting reaction is in Texas with its 13 million cattle, its cowboy tradition, and its longhorn steers. One cattleman in San Antonio pointed out that cattle eat forage that man can't utilize, use otherwise unproductive rangeland, and provide valuable by-products. Then he asked, "How can you really say, 'Get along, little soybean'? "

How Sweet It Is

The corn with which we are most familiar, the sweet corn that the Jolly Green Giant extols on the tube, makes up a very small part of America's overall corn production. Most of the corn we produce is like that raised by Gordon MacClean and Dale Yahnke. Gordon's is probably the more typical situation in that he feeds his corn to his own animals. Corn is the leading U.S. cash receipt crop and most important feed grain. The United States accounts for about 70 percent of world corn exports, and corn, like soybeans, brings in a lot of foreign exchange. In fact, the United States provides half the world's corn supply.

Dale Yahnke knows corn is in demand, and that's why he grows the yellow kernels. When he and other farmers find the price attractive—and it has been in recent years—they will truck it over to the nearest elevator or co-op. At the co-op, the corn will be graded No. 1, 2, 3, or 4 yellow corn, depending on the amount of broken kernels and dockage.

From here, it is the elevator's responsibility. As in the case of wheat and soybeans, the cash purchase is hedged in a commodity futures exchange, probably in Chicago. The elevator operator then calls his commission agent, and the bidding for the cash corn begins. Feed companies call to buy corn for the formula feeds; corn processors call to buy it to make corn oil and syrups; food manufacturers call to buy it for cornflakes; exporters call to send it to one corner of the world or another.

Of all these calls, the one I find the most interesting to follow is that of the corn processor, who, using newly developed technology, is making corn sugar a replacement for sugar from cane and beet. When I began to understand the switch, my concept of sugar growing had to change. Sugar, for me, comes from a tall, waving field of sugarcane, highlighted with a palm tree now and then. The grower wears a Panama hat and a white linen suit. But, alas, sugar from corn is now produced, likely as not, by a suspicious, tobacco-chewing farmer wearing off-color work clothes and a cap provided by a farm supply salesman. In recent years, high sugar prices have stimulated an interest in sugar users in finding a low-cost substitute for sugar from cane and beet (dextrose). Someone found the solution in Dale Yahnke's cornfield, with something called high-fructose corn syrup, which is now finding its way into canned fruit, jams, jellies, ice cream, table syrup, soft drinks, and beer.

Although ordinary corn syrup, like Karo brand, has been around for years, it could not substitute for cane sugar in many uses—for example, soft drinks. High-fructose syrup, however, is a direct substitute for cane and beet sugar. The process is a highly technical one, consisting of such things as "removing the pulverized endo-sperm through fine mesh cloth on rotating wheels." About 10 percent of the total U.S. corn production is used to make high-fructose syrup, to the dismay of cane- and beet-sugar producers in the United States and overseas. Archer Daniels Midland takes a whack at imported sugar by advertising its high-fructose syrup as the "All American Sweetener."

Industrial users are placing a lot of emphasis on high-fructose corn syrup, as evidenced by H. J. Heinz's seeking to merge with A. E. Staley Company, one of the largest producers of corn syrups. Heinz uses a lot of sugar; even ketchup is 10 percent sugar. But after having problems with the Staley acquisition, Heinz went after a smaller producer, the Hubinger Company.

It may be that one day they will have to move the New Year's Day football spectacular, the Sugar Bowl, from New Orleans to someplace in Iowa, the leading sugar-, that is, corn-producing state.

Chow Time

I am convinced that animals in the United States are fed just as well, if not better, than humans. Animal-feed manufacturers have nutritionists on their staffs to come up with better feeds, while the larger animal-feeding complexes in the country have their own consulting nutritionists. When a salesman with a new food item approaches a supermarket buyer whose stores serve 50,000 people, the promotional price is a chief determinant of whether or not the item is placed on the supermarket shelf. However, if you mosey into a 50,000-head cattle feedlot in Hereford, Texas, with a new feed, the feedlot manager is going to tell you, "I'll have to speak to my nutritionist." The difference between the two situations comes from the assumption that consumers can judge nutrition in foods, but cattle need a little help from their friends.

Whatever the case, the animal-feed industry in the United States has reached a high level of development. On the farm, farmers feed the grain they grow mixed with feed supplements they purchase to form a "complete ration." When Dale Yahnke had his livestock, he used this practice for a while but found it was cheaper to buy a premixed complete ration. Although a lot of speculation and trading go on in getting the feed to the mixer, once it gets to him, he has a processing charge added on, and then it is sold at a fixed price.

Today there are about 10,000 feed mills throughout the United States that buy grains from farmers and by-products such as wheat middlings, soybean meal, and corn gluten meal from processors. Because of the wheat-middling by-product available to them, most flour mills used this as a base to get into the animal-feed industry; the same holds true for the by-products of corn and soybean processors.

The feed ingredients are then mixed together with whatever vitamins and other elements a nutritionist feels are necessary for that particular ration. In the case of ruminant animals like cattle and sheep, three items are needed: protein for growth, energy for maintenance, and fiber as an aia to digestion. A complete feed will have all three.

Feed plants today are run by a very few people who push glowing buttons and use computers. Linear programming is used in selecting not only the right kind of nutrients for a particular kind of feed but also the cheapest mix. A pinch of this and a tad of that have been relegated to gourmet kitchens.

With feeding principles that have been refined over the years, a steer is ready for market in eighteen months; during one trip I made to Iran, I found some cattle took five years to grow to maturity, and even then there wasn't much to eat. Beef cattle account for 26 percent of the 120 million tons of feed we use annually and produce about a fourth of all farm income.

Most of the cattle feeding today takes place in family-owned and -operated corn-cattle farms in the Midwest, with around 1,000 head of cattle, or in the huge cattle feedlots in the West, particularly the

Texas Panhandle, which may have as many as 100,000 head. The trend is to larger feedlots. In 1962, 75 percent of cattle marketings came from feedlots with under 4,000 head; today, these marketings from smaller feedlots have fallen to 44 percent. Conversely, feedlots with over 32,000 head have grown in numbers from five in 1962 to seventy-three today; the giant of them all is the Monfort Feedlot in Greeley, Colorado, with over 200,000 head.

If you went to a convention of feedlot operators, the conversation would sound like that of a group of hotel executives, although more cowboy boots would be in evidence. The talk would center on occupancy rates, turnover, square feet allocated per head, feed palatability, and the investment climate, since many of the cattle-feeding programs originated as tax shelters.

Good growth rates can be attained in both indoor and outdoor feedlots. If everything goes right, a feeder can get one pound of meat for six pounds of feed, and on a good day will get two pounds of gain. As long as the meat on the hoof earns more than the cost of feed, both family and corporate feedlot can make money.

This was not the case in 1974 when meat prices were low—not, perhaps, in the consumer's eye, but in terms of this particular equation. The results were apparent in the big feedlots' annual reports; they paid more for the feed and labor than they got for the cattle they sold.

One way to cut costs is to let cattle eat grass for a longer period of time before putting them on a higher-cost grain ration. Many feeders are doing this not only to cut costs but also because of the consumer demand for leaner beef. Heavy use of grain causes the marbling effect—white specks—in meat, which is, of course, fat.

Hogs take up 16 percent of the feed produced each year and seem to thrive on nothing but corn and soybeans. Individual farmers account for about 90 percent of the 85 million pigs produced a year, an unusual circumstance in an age of increasing corporate agriculture. A jocular Iowa corn-hog farmer explained to me that this is because corporations don't like to get "squealed on." The hog is a better converter of feed than a steer, giving one pound of ham and chops for every four pounds of feed. The Corn Belt should actually be called the Hog Belt, since half the hogs in the United States come from here. Availability of good feed has enabled hogs to reach maturity in about eight months.

Most, if not all, hogs produced today are fed and raised indoors, which makes winter feeding easier, if more stinky. In Sidney, Montana, a farmer invited me to take a look at his new hog operation. Outside it was fifteen below zero, and as I stepped into the seventy-degree hog barn, the thick, pungent air enveloped and sank at least two inches into my skin. The memory is vivid, since I carried that aroma with me for some time afterward.

Most everyone's conception of a farm includes a rooster crowing and chickens scratching, but they have disappeared with the advent of modern poultry feeding. The scene of the farm wife throwing handfuls of corn out the door to scratching hens has been replaced by twenty-ton trucks with pneumatic equipment delivering the standard mixture of corn and soybeans to a conveyor belt that takes the feed to the waiting chickens. No longer does a chicken have the whole yard to roam. It is allocated one square foot in a modern chicken house, where the lights are kept on to encourage eating.

Chickens consume about 16 percent of the mixed feed produced annually. About 5 percent of the ration is usually alfalfa, and purely cosmetic in that it contains carotene—as in carrot—which gives the broiler or egg you buy that yellowish glow to the skin or yolk that is supposedly better than pale chicken. The Perdue Chicken, which is the most common in the New York market, has made inroads in that market because the company has convinced consumers that a yellower chicken is healthier. Color makes no difference nutritionally, but adds to the cost.

A rapid change has come over the poultry industry, for as late as 1959 nearly 60 percent of all broilers were grown by independent farmers. Today, about 85 percent of all chickens are raised under contract to corporations. Perhaps the ease of raising chickens accounts for this, for a three-pound broiler can be raised in eight weeks and will produce one pound of meat for every two pounds of feed. This ratio should improve, as animal breeders are working on featherless chickens; if feathers are eliminated, the chicken can produce more meat per pound of feed consumed. More research is needed, as featherless chickens—and this should come as no surprise—catch colds more easily.

In the modern "chicken coop," everything is mechanized, including the "harvesting." A machine zooms over the flock, grabs a chicken, and sends it off to a cage. Mechanization is necessary because 58 million chickens are processed each week. Perhaps more than anything else, it was the rise in poultry-feed prices that helped push the government to declare an embargo on soymeal exports in August 1973.

Another bastion of farm livestock feeding is the dairy industry, centered in Wisconsin, Minnesota, and New York. Corn is a major ingredient on the dairy farm, but is usually supplemented by oats, alfalfa, soymeal, and mineral supplements like the salt lick. Prepared feeds are also used, with 17 percent of total production going for dairy-cattle consumption. The milk cow, given proper water and feed, is a good producer, providing 100 pounds of milk for every 40 pounds of feed.

The thing that has shut down many a dairy farm is the unending, twice-a-day routine of milking that is necessary to supply the raw material for the 540 pounds of dairy products we each consume annually. Feeding is mostly mechanized, even on a small family farm of fifty dairy cows. Farmers have some storage for the milk, but require daily tanker-truck pick-up.

Half of the remaining 10 percent of the feed produced finds its way to turkey farms, located mainly in Minnesota and California, while the rest ends up feeding pets out of the bowl you leave on the kitchen floor. Pet foods are a growing business, with every feed manufacturer engaged in this $2.5-billion-a-year industry. Perhaps the most elaborate effort is being undertaken by General Foods, which has come up with dog food with egg, not to mention a three-course dry food that has meat-, liver-, and chicken-flavored chunks. Farmers can't knock it, for out of that $2.5 billion about $300 million is spent for the commodities that go into dog foods.

The Sting

Carl Sandburg once wrote that Chicago was the hog butcher of the world. That it was, in addition to being the cattle-packing center of the United States. The stockyards that fed the steaming packing houses are now parking lots and low-cost housing. Similar concentrations of stockyards and packing houses were found at other terminal markets like Indianapolis and Cleveland, but they, too, are a thing of the past.

Where it used to be economical to ship live animals for slaughter, you now ship frozen or chilled meat. The packing houses have moved out to the country. Swift, for example, is building its new plants in places like Sioux City, Iowa, and expanding in Guymon, Oklahoma, and Clovis, New Mexico. The world's largest cattle-slaughtering factory—as an Iowa Beef spokesman termed it—was recently started up in Amarillo, Texas. Between 1960 and 1970, the percentage of cattle purchased by packers at terminal markets declined from 46 to 19 percent, while direct purchases increased from 39 to 65 percent. The rest was purchased at auction barns.

A farmer or rancher with enough livestock to sell will get in touch with a buyer from a packing house, and they will agree on price and date of delivery. Large feedlots sell direct to the packer. If a farmer-rancher can't attract a buyer with his small volume, he will then pack up his cattle, hogs, or sheep and head for the auction barn. The rituals there are probably as old and elaborate as those of the Grange.

I remember visiting one of the newer auction barns in Edinburg, Texas, in the Rio Grande valley. Inside, the seats were arranged in two tiers, with the upper tier reserved for spectators and the lower tier with stuffed, theater-like seats for the buyers. To be a buyer, it seemed, you had to have on cowboy boots—those made from armadillo skin are the Cadillacs for the feet in those parts—and a big hat.

"Here we got a thousand-pound steer at forty-two, do I hear forty-three?" would bark the auctioneer, who would earn a commission for his efforts. Familiar with the wild gyrations of the commodity exchanges, I was expecting an uproar in response to the offer. The buyers sat motionless—almost. After about five minutes in the auction, I began to notice slight twitchings, and soon realized that faint nods and finger liftings were being made in response to the barks of the auctioneer. Watching these men for about an hour, I came away convinced that they were in a perpetual contest with each other to see who could make the least effort and still capture the attention of the auctioneer.

Sold, the livestock are loaded into trucks to begin their last mile to the slaughterhouse. When they arrive, they are settled into holding pens. It has always been the practice to hold livestock off feed prior to slaughtering, since the feed would only add a mess to the slaughterhouse floor.

Ramps lead the livestock into the slaughterhouse, where a fellow with something that looks like an electric billy club awaits with the "sting." An electric shock knocks the animal out, whereupon he is hooked on the "kill line" to be processed. Nothing is wasted, as the inedible parts go into leather, glue, pharmaceuticals, or back into animal feed.

The employees in a slaughtering operation get used to the blood, and I did, too, when I went through a slaughterhouse in Davis, California. One thing I couldn't adjust to was the job of one fellow who stood at the end of a long chute with his hand on something like a giant nutcracker. Every so often, a stripped skull tumbled down the chute. He calmly placed it in the nutcracker, split it open, took out the pituitary gland, which he placed on dry ice, and began the process over again.

When a 1,000-pound steer is slaughtered, you get only about 550 pounds of meat. With hogs, sheep, and chickens, the "dressing" loss is less severe but still significant.

The cleaned, slaughtered animals then go off to a fabrication line where giant saws and knives cut up the carcasses into preferred cuts. There has been union opposition to cutting up carcasses before shipping to their final destination, but the trend has been established and with some justification. The president of Lucky Food Stores has pointed out that handling carcasses from slaughterhouse to super-market adds about 6 cents a pound to meat costs. In the future, that which leaves the slaughterhouse will be that which is placed on the meat shelves in supermarkets.

6

FARMING
FOR FOREIGNERS

Although exports of grains have acquired a tarnished image of late, U.S. agricultural exports were begun almost as soon as the first settlers landed. The first recorded export shipment was in 1613, when 2,500 pounds of tobacco left Jamestown, Virginia, headed for what was then Mother England.

It was early in American history that grain became a pawn in foreign relations. Prior to the Civil War, strategists in the South felt that England would definitely recognize them in the event of secession in order to keep the cotton trade. However, as a result of crop failures there and in most of Europe, England was also interested in American wheat. Consequently, American wheat shipments went from 4 million bushels in 1860 to an average of 35 million bushels during 1861–63.

The importance of exports is evidenced by the fact that the United States exported around 90 million tons of grain during 1974—put another way, an amount equal to the corn production of Illinois, Indiana, Iowa, and Kentucky. When farmers go out to plow in the spring, they do so with an understanding that there will be an export market for their grain. Lester Wolverton says simply, "I don't mind farming for foreigners as long as they pay the price and say thanks once in a while."

As a means of protecting those spring-plowing farmers' incomes and earning foreign exchange, the government has provided a series of incentives to promote grain exports.

During the surplus years of the 1950s and 1960s, the years of "the farm problem," the United States subsidized grain exports, since the price of American grain was higher than that of the international market due to domestic price supports.

In the surplus years, grain prices were so low that few farmers could make a living on what the grain could bring on the free market. To help out the farmer, the government brought up the price the farmer got through supports in the form of loans. In those days, then, Uncle Sam not only had to pay the farmer to grow but also had to pay the exporter to export.

Since supports artifically raised the price of U.S. grain in comparison with the world market, there was no way to export profitably without government assistance. In 1964, for example, if the exporter bought price-supported wheat from a farmer for $2.30 and then tried to resell it at the world market price of $1.75, he would lose 55 cents per bushel. No one would export under those conditions, so the government stepped in with export subsidies. In the case just cited, the export subsidy would be the 55 cents the exporter would otherwise lose.

The subsidy program came to an end with the Russian grain sales of 1972. What had been a grain-surplus situation in the world became a shortage, and international prices rose to U.S. levels. The U.S. price became, in effect, the world price. The reason for the subsidy had disappeared, yet for a period of three months after the initial Soviet sale, while world and U.S. prices were at the same level, the USDA continued to pay the subsidy. Critics point out that some $200 million was paid out in excess subsidies.

The USDA must have been listening to some of the commotion, for in July of 1976, it got three large grain companies to pay the government a total of $1.6 million to settle claims that they collected too much in federal subsidies on the Russian grain sales.

The subsidies were not the only aspect of the sales to be scrutinized. To critics of the exporters, it was adding insult to injury when the exporters went to Washington to protect grain-sales profits under DISC tax benefits. A DISC is a Domestic International Sales Corporation, which a U.S. company may set up under legislation passed in 1971. The taxes on half the profits from receipts from export sales can be deferred, provided they are used in the parent company export business. Harry Byrd, the Independent senator from Virginia, couldn't see giving the exporters a DISC tax break and an export subsidy, too. "To apply DISC benefits to this sale would be a distortion of the purpose of the law."

Nevertheless, the grain exporters sought to get the DISC designation applied to these sales, but the Treasury Department contended that DISC did not apply. DISC will probably soon be withdrawn from agricultural shipments, as the world no longer needs prodding to buy our food.

As a result of this change, our Public Law 480 food programs are on their way out. PL 480 was created in 1954 as a means of exporting agricultural surpluses by extending credit terms and other considerations for foreign countries, particularly developing ones, in order for them to be able to purchase the commodities. Due to expire July 31, 1977, the program is being used politically more than ever now, as we shall see in a later chapter.

On Its Way

To make money in exporting grain, the faster you get it to water, the faster your transport costs fall. A common calculation used by those in the grain trade is that 50 miles of truck transport, 500 miles of rail freight, and 5,000 miles of ocean shipping run you about the same cost. It is no wonder one Minneapolis grain company finds it cheaper to ship feed to the Netherlands than to Indiana, for the grain going to the Netherlands travels mostly in huge ships by water, while grain may have to go in trucks by land to Indiana.

The elevator is the starting point for the export of Lester Wolverton's bushel of wheat or Dale Yahnke's beans. Exporting is not made easier by the fact that Lester's and Dale's bushels have to be translated to more manageable units of measurement. Harvests are now weighed in short tons (2,000 pounds) and then the number of bushels is determined; for example, a bushel of wheat is 60 pounds. Farmers sell by the bushel, but railroad freight is charged in short tons, the overseas buyer wants quotes in metric tons (2,240.6 pounds), and ocean-freight rates are charged in long tons (2,240 pounds). Pocket calculators notwithstanding, the different measurements lead to costly mistakes.

In spite of the confusion, the grain starts moving when the operator of the elevator gets a bid, and if it is high enough to leave a profit, away the commodity goes. From here on in, the grain seeks out water like one of those bifurcated branches that old-time dowsers used. Accordingly, the three big grain conduits are the Mississippi and Columbia rivers and the Great Lakes.

When the loaded rail cars reach the Mississippi—the primary grain-transport point—they are unloaded onto barges that are lashed together; each one holds about 1,000 tons. One flotilla of barges may hold the production of 20,000 acres of soybeans. A pusher tug then begins its long glide to New Orleans and the ships to take the grain to export markets. Louisiana ports alone account for a third of U.S. grain exports.

As soon as the grain meets the water, uncertainty begins. First, there is an active market for barges; their rates go up and down according to the market. So a crucial market decision is required to determine when to get a barge commitment. The larger grain companies have sought to minimize the risk by buying their own barges. But nature cuts even the most fully prepared down to size by inconveniently varying the speed and volume of the Mississippi. Old Man River can be parched and dry, making for unpassable shallow points, or totally flush, sending so much water down that the loading points become submerged or it's just too dangerous.

Having made it to the port by either rail car or barge, the grain must now wait for the ship to arrive. (The economics of waiting are such that you would rather have the barges and railroad cars wait for the ship than have the ship wait for them.) This circumstance was one of the causes (greed was the other) of the grain-inspection scandals of 1975. The revelation of bribes came as a surprise, although 111 different inspection firms were involved, making 4 million inspections a year in an industry that generates $12.5 billion in foreign exchange.

A ship would come into port still "dirty" from carrying fertilizer or petroleum, and instead of incurring the expense of cleaning out its holds and the wait this would entail, some grain firms found it was cheaper to pay the inspector $5,000 to certify the ship was "ready to receive grain."

Clues to this system were around for a number of years as complaints poured into the USDA and other agencies about poor-quality grain. Many discounted them by stating that the foreigners were on the wrong side of the market or didn't know anything about grain standards. The scandal came to light when a grain inspector demanded more than a ship captain was willing to pay, and the captain blew the whistle.

In addition to a ship-clearing inspection, the grain must also be represented correctly to go on its way. If the grain passes by the inspector, it waits in an elevator with a capacity of over 200,000 tons of grains, and when the ship arrives, it is discharged into a hold at a rate of 3,500 tons an hour. Here again, to keep their costs down, the big grain companies have purchased their own elevator facilities. These huge buildings serve not only as storage but as a place to blend grains to a customer's or contract's specifications. If a contract calls for a 4 percent allowance for foreign matter—damaged grains, dust, et al.—and the corn at hand has 2 percent, you can be sure that 2 percent foreign matter will be added. Similarly, if the grain is too low in quality, it will be upgraded by adding more of the good stuff.

In some of the bribery cases, shippers didn't bother to blend up or down, but merely paid an inspector to certify that No. 4 corn— poor stuff—was, in reality, No. 2—better stuff. And since No. 4 was purchased at a far lower cost than No. 2, a tidy profit was made.

As a result of the scandals and the diminished quality of U.S. grain shipped because of them, a Federal grain-inspection system will probably be instituted. Farm groups have petitioned for this system, figuring that foreign buyers would be willing to pay more if they knew good grain was coming. They are also concerned about the fact that in the past five years the American share of world soybean shipments has dropped from 95 to 70 percent as the buyers have gone elsewhere.

Some big exporters, like Cargill—of whom we will learn more later—dispute this claim and have stated that the poor-quality grain is more likely the result of a poor crop that has been difficult to handle at each stage. Complaints from overseas are attributed to the fact that foreign buyers are frustrated about having bought at too high a price. Walter Saunders, Cargill vice-president, added that in 1975 they screened and sold separately 250,000 tons of dockage thereby refuting claims that grains were adulterated.

Approval of "dirty" ships and the higher certification of lower-grade grain were but part of the problem. Short weights were also made on some shipments, leading to a $20,000 fine for the Bunge Corporation, which along with others had earlier been indicted in the scandals.

During Bunge's trial, an FBI agent testified that the scales had been manipulated at the company's grain elevator at the Port of New Orleans to record more grain going aboard ship than was really loaded in shipments to foreign countries. Some foreign countries don't have their own scales and thus had to trust the loaded weights. And even in those countries where accurate weights were available the contracts were written so that origin quality and weights were binding. This meant that even though the weights overseas might show a different amount received than was weighed at the time of shipping, the shipping weights in the United States would take precedence.

As a consequence of short weighing (loading less upon the ship than had been called for), the Bunge employees involved were left with grain to sell on the side. To make everything appear legal, false purchase records were fabricated for the grain, which was then sold on the open market. Credit for the sales was then distributed among the various Bunge offices involved. The sums involved reached into the millions. In addition to paying the fine, Bunge promised the court it would institute a $2-million surveillance program to make sure the situation would not happen again.

A further short-weighing scheme came to light in March 1976 when a Federal grand jury indicted three companies for conspiracy to defraud the government in connection with short-weighing grain-export shipments. The three involved were Archer Daniels Midland, Garnac Grain Company, and the St. Charles Grain Elevator Company. The indictment stated that the companies short-weighted ships by failing to load grain that was to be included in overseas shipments or by weighing the same grain twice. Also included in the indictment was the charge that the companies added inferior grain to overseas shipments when automatic sampling systems were not in operation. Grain inspectors purportedly found a concealed switch in the elevator control room that mixed inferior grain with higher-quality grains after inspection had taken place. The three companies pleaded no contest to the charges.

Most of the nonscandalous grain that finds itself sitting in a terminal export elevator has already been sold by a grain company to a foreign government's grain-purchasing agency—of which there seem to be an increasing number—or to a foreign grain company for resale to some party overseas. Some grain does get loaded on a ship and is sold afloat—that is, while the ship is actually on its way overseas. This was a common practice before telexes and telegrams. In those pre-Marconi days, signal flags at Land's End in England or some other strategically placed outcrop directed American grain ships to Antwerp, Rotterdam, or the Thames in accordance with the market in the various ports.

Strung Out

Although most U.S. exporters try to cover their sales overseas by hedging on a commodity futures exchange, the increased volatility of the international grain market has created an international resellers market. Sometimes considered a futures exchange for international sales, the resellers market has no locus but consists rather of phone calls and telex messages as buyers and sellers seek to limit their risk. The Italians were masters of it until a couple of bankruptcies in Italy shook, but did not kill, the market.

A typical transaction might involve the purchase of wheat in Gilbey, North Dakota, by an exporter. The exporter later feels that the market is going to fall, so he calls an agent in Italy to try to sell the grain FOB Gulf—this means in a rail car at some Gulf port. An Italian in Milan buys it, takes a profit, and resells it to a flour mill in the Netherlands. The flour mill feels wheat is going to go down farther and sells it to Poland's food-import agency. Another U.S. grain company knows the Poles are worried about the price falling, but they feel the market will rise, so they buy the grain and decide to take delivery. Some "strings" like this involve as many as forty paper transactions, which can all take place in a week's time. One trader I know, tired of those 4:00 A.M. phone calls, got an unlisted phone number.

The exporters and importers—not to mention the speculators—find this market attractive in that there are no regulations, no margin requirements, the market is always open, and your word suffices to get the business.

When the last piece of the "string" is completed, which is done, amazingly, with a minimum of paperwork, everyone gathers in their chips and settles the differences. On a string of ten transactions I once saw, the price within the string varied 20 percent, yet the initial sales price and the last purchase price were the same!

Although an article written in the USDA's foreign trade magazine defended the resellers market as a "help to equalize world prices," others take a dimmer view of all this paper-trading. For one thing, the resellers market has a tendency to distort the Federal reporting system, which records export sales intentions. In a resellers market, different exporters on a string may report sales, but when the string has played out, only one of the sales has materialized, yet a number of sales were reported. As a result, foreign demand as reported in government publications could be higher than it really is, causing domestic prices to rise.

In recent years, with the threat of an embargo facing exporters, and the 1973 decision to honor only half the existing export contracts after putting that year's embargo into effect, some exporters have been declaring larger sales than they have really made. Exporters figure that if they record extra sales and then the government allows only part of the sales, they can cancel the fictitious contracts and maintain the real ones. So, by looking at export commitments these days, you can't really tell what is going on. Secretary Butz admitted as much during the Midwest Conference of Democratic Senators in August 1975 by pointing out, "It is unlikely that all reported quantities will be exported. Our experience with this monitoring system suggests that sales are apt to exceed exports, sometimes by substantial amounts."

An interesting result of the paper-shuffling happened in early 1975, when statistics showed that the United States had purchased 590,000 tons of wheat from abroad, even though it is the world's largest exporter. What had happened was that foreigners who bought U.S. grain in 1974 had sold it back before it left the country.

The Bread Boats

Getting the grain overseas is probably as risky a task as covering yourself in the market. Twenty-five years ago, most exported grain moved in relatively small lots of 10,000 tons, generally as part of the cargo in ocean freighters or even in passenger liners. Today, grain is shipped in full cargoes with capacities ranging from 25,000 to 40,000 tons. Superships are also appearing on the scene, like the bulk carrier that transported 105,000 tons of wheat from Tacoma to India in the largest single consignment. While the loading on the U.S. end was accomplished without any problems, the ship had to unload five miles out on the other end, since Indian ports are not deep enough to accommodate such large vessels. The economics of using the big bulk carriers—"oboes"—are obvious, as freight costs per metric ton can be a third that of a conventional 15,000-ton vessel. Yet the overall costs are phenomenal, as a 75,000-ton bulk carrier might cost as much as $10,000 a day to operate—whether it sails or not. With sums like this common, it is easy to understand why a $5,000 bribe to a grain inspector makes economic sense.

Grain exporters have to know not only how to play commodity futures and the resellers market—not to mention the barge market—but also how to figure out what goes on in freight. Although the world trade in grain comes to 120 million tons, this represents only about 10 percent of cargo shipping. The big volume comes from oil, iron ore, bauxite, or coal, and their movement depends on situations other than droughts in Kazakhstan or bumper crops in Boon Valley, Iowa. You are therefore more likely to find the manager of an exporter's freight department reading *Business Week* than the *Farm Journal*. Because they are a breed apart, the high-strung behavior of an ocean-freight manager might be dismissed with, "Well he's a freight man."

Many major exporters have their own shipping firms—for tax reasons, based mostly in the Bahamas or Panama—to "fix" their freight for them. It irks American longshoremen that so much foreign freight is used; and, given the opportunity, the U.S. shipping industry, by refusing to load foreign ships, will pressure for the use of more expensive American bottoms in hauling grain.

American shipping, due to the higher wage rates paid to its seamen, has not been competitive with other shipping for decades, and thus finds itself unable to compete for cargo in an open market. Given a choice, the Soviets would have used no U.S. bottoms, but they had to accept some of the grain in U.S. vessels as part of the deal.

In the Soviet purchases of 1975, grain hauled in foreign vessels cost $9 a ton versus $16 a ton for American shipping. The Soviet purchases of 1972 cost the American taxpayer $55 million in shipping subsidies paid to owners of U.S. bulk carriers and tankers.

The freight manager has to guess at the course of the economy, for if the recession continues, rates will remain lower, even go down farther, and he need not worry about taking long-term time charters—that is, hiring a ship for a given time. In a declining market, exporters are content to fix freight for one voyage charter—for example, one trip from the Gulf to Rotterdam.

For exporters, profits often depend on freight costs, for the price difference between competing offers to sell grain with freight paid may be due entirely to differences in freight estimates used to calculate the competing price offers. An exporter with a good freight position would be able to sell grain for less than an exporter on the wrong side of the freight market. Due to the importance—and price volatility—of ocean freight, proposals surface every year for a futures market in ocean freight, but to date nothing has resulted.

The freight market also provides good clues as to who may soon be in the market for grain. Often, the first sign of Chinese or Soviet intentions to buy grain shows up in the freight market. The Baltic Exchange in London offers the best clues.

The final risk an exporter runs is that of currency fluctuations. Some analysts in the commodity trade ascribe the boom in American grain shipments not to Gordon MacClean's production techniques or to the Russian desire to eat better, but rather to the devaluation of the dollar in 1971 and 1973. By devaluing the dollar, foreigners were able to buy American grains for less of their own currency.

But all sales that exporters make are not to the Russians, nor are they in dollars. Accordingly, exporters devote a considerable amount of time to following international currency fluctuations.

If a sale for future delivery is made in French francs and francs are expected to fall in value relative to the U.S. dollar, the exporter will sell francs and buy dollars on the international monetary futures exchanges. Thus, a hedge in currency is made, similar to that in commodities.

Exporters also use currency futures to hedge their port costs. An exporter who has made a sale to West Germany knows he will have to pay port costs in deutsche marks in Hamburg at some future date. To "lock-in" those costs, the exporter will use currency futures to hedge deutsche marks.

The currency risks in international grain trading have become so large that a number of firms offer risk-management services to companies engaged in grain shipping. Their services, they state, will help cope with the "distorting effects of a fully dismembered monetary system."

Conceivably, an exporter could make poor decisions about buying the grain, about the barges, the resale, the ocean freight—but still come out fine by correctly anticipating currency fluctuations.

Buying Bread

Foreign buyers of U.S. grain have developed their own intricate techniques. None can do so well as the Soviets did in 1972, for none is so large. Furthermore, the element of surprise has been taken away, as, since 1974, big sales now have to be reported to the Federal government as they are made.

When the Soviets came around the first time, no one knew of their crop difficulties nor how much they wanted to buy. And when they went shopping they told Continental, Cook, Cargill, Dreyfus, and Garnac to be quiet about it; this group is quiet to begin with, so there was no problem. Having done all this, the Russians walked away with a bargain. They have actually had a lot of experience in buying U.S. grain, as one of their first purchases was in 1839, when Oregon farmers sent wheat to Russian settlers at Kamchatka, Alaska.

One disadvantage to U.S. exporters during the first Russian deal and with selling to many other countries is that the latter have central buying agencies that deal with several large sellers. American grain-selling and foreign-buying systems don't really mesh, so the United States was at a serious disadvantage in dealing with the Russians. This prompted calls for the United States to have one central selling agency, a proposal that continues occasionally to raise its head. Canada and Australia, both major grain exporters, already have such agencies, in the belief that the grain business should be in their national interest as well as in the interest of their producers. Some advocates claim a central agency is necessary if the United States is to avoid being picked off again.

The significance of the effect a centralized buying agency can have is brought out by the potential buying power of the People's Republic of China. For example, if the PRC were to increase per-capita wheat consumption by just two ounces per day, the resulting demand would cause an increase in excess of Canada's entire annual production of wheat. The Chinese realize this and are in a position to take advantage of the United States because its grain trade is divided among several competing firms.

Many countries around the world have adopted a common front in buying grains to feed their flour mills and processing plants, which may be privately held. To try to get as much competition as possible, the central buying agencies, with such acronyms as CONASUPO (Mexico), invite tender offers to be presented at a given time and place. The grain exporters submit offers, and the lowest bidder wins.

Knowledgeable traders within these agencies have learned how to play with this system over the years in the same way they have learned, if not developed, the resellers market. Knowing that tenders sometimes drive up prices, as traders anticipate new business, the agency may call a tender, reject all offers, and then quietly negotiate a purchase with a sole grain company two weeks later at lower prices. The permutations are endless.

As in the domestic grain business, once a deal is signed, it is inviolate. Despite the bad image that international grain trading has acquired in recent years, contracts, once made, are seldom broken. To facilitate trade, a number of standard contracts have developed over the centuries of international trade. The most commonly used are those of the Grain and Feed Trade Association in England, which has developed over fifty contract forms covering almost all possible grain shipments. In all these contracts, the arbitration clause to deal with disputes is among the most important. In view of all the uncertainty in the rest of the grain trade, these contracts are a sort of Gibraltar.

The rock shook, however, when the grain-purchasing agency of Turkey decided in May 1975 not to honor a contract for the purchase of 400,000 tons of wheat bought the previous October, since prices had fallen and the Turks wanted to renegotiate the price to lower levels. The shippers refused, the U.S. government protested, and the case went to arbitration at the Grain and Feed Trade Association in London. The Turks lost. .

The leading U.S. grain publication referred to Turkey's stance as an "act of piracy." The publication went further in its condemnation by stating, "If military action can be carried out to recover a ship [the U.S.S. *Pueblo*] and thus to signify that the U.S. government will not countenance piracy on the high seas, then some very firm and decisive steps are warranted to obtain satisfaction from Turkey on its contracts for American wheat."

Unfortunately for us, many foreign buyers felt the same way when the Unites States declared an embargo on oilseeds in July 1973 to stop domestic commodity prices from rising. The embargo broke contracts, leading to hundreds of arbitrations—not to mention strained relations. Maybe we set the precedent for Turkey.

Playing the resellers market and doing the tender two-step may not provide the market protection they need, so many foreign companies and countries are beginning to play the commodity futures market in the United States and elsewhere to hedge their grain purchases and sales.

But while some trade analysts regard this foreign interest as beneficial in increasing liquidity in futures trading, others regard it as potentially dangerous, since foreign interests could manipulate markets to their advantage.

The volatility in prices and the shortages of grain in recent years have, of course, been the main reasons for the foreign interest. Thus, it came as no surprise when, in 1974, the Minneapolis Grain Exchange received its first inquiry from a foreign country. A Japanese trading firm explained that it wanted to be "near the grain." Brazil's grain-exporting agency followed by setting up its own office at the Chicago Board of Trade.

Trade sources indicate that the Brazilians know what to do with futures. Brazil is the world's second-largest producer and exporter of soybeans, and what happens there affects the world market. Recognizing this, and with the government controlling exports by requiring licenses, Brazil's grain-marketing agency, COBEC, is in an excellent position to have advance knowledge of important government decisions in regard to commodity export policy.

For example, when the Brazilian government announced recently that an export tax on soybeans would be lifted, the market in Chicago fell, as most analysts saw that this would increase supplies of beans. Some market observers felt that COBEC had made advance short sales of soybeans, knowing that this move would be taken. As the rumor goes, COBEC sold soybean futures short—that is, made a commitment to sell soybeans at a given price at a future date—knowing that the Brazilian government's announcement would drive prices down. Thus, when the time arrived to meet the sales commitment, COBEC could "buy in" or cover its sales at lower prices.

This is but one example, and American brokerage houses have been quick to seize upon the growing use of futures by foreign grain traders. Witness Merrill Lynch, which, in addition to seeking foreign accounts through its overseas offices, issues basic how-to-trade-commodity booklets in French, German, Italian, Japanese, Spanish, Arabic, and Portuguese.

All this activity has caught the eye of legislators who were suspicious of the circumstances surrounding the Soviet wheat deal. This concern first surfaced in July 1973 during Senate hearings on the "Russian Grain Transaction." At those hearings, Senator Henry Jackson (D-Wash.) asked J. Caldwell, director of what was then the Commodity Exchange Authority (CEA), now the Commodity Futures Trading Commission (CFTC), if there were any indications of Russian futures activity, as had been heavily rumored.

Jackson was particularly concerned because a futures broker had written the Commodity Exchange Authority to find out if it would be legal for the Russians to use American commodity futures. "It would," responded Caldwell, but added he could not find any sign that they had used the market.

Questioning Caldwell further, Jackson asked, "Do you agree that persons making the size purchase the Russians made have a tremendous advantage if they go into the futures market?" Caldwell nodded in agreement but maintained that the Russians didn't use futures.

Some legislators and government officials feel that foreign interests could be beneficial to our futures exchanges, given certain conditions. Herman Talmadge (D-Georgia), chairman of the Senate Agriculture Committee, has stated that foreign hedging could be quite favorable. "If, for example, a foreign government purchased cash grain in this country at a fixed price and immediately hedged its purchase by selling futures, there might be a tendency to stabilize prices, since the selling hedge by the foreign country would tend to offset the buying hedge by the company or companies obligated to deliver cash grain."

David Hume, administrator of the Foreign Agricultural Service of the USDA, felt that foreign hedging should help U.S. agricultural planning, for, as he put it, "The FAS has encouraged importers of American commodities to buy for shipment further forward than they have in the past in order to facilitate agricultural planning here. It seems to us that orderly use of the futures market might help the process."

A commercial view of the foreign use of commodity exchanges came from Houston Cox, vice-president of Reynolds Securities, a New York brokerage firm, who said, "If foreign knowledge of crops and economic conditions is translated into their hedging activity, long or short, it will only make the pricing of our markets more reflective of the 'truth' relative to the real value of the commodity traded."

But a danger still exists, according to Senator Talmadge. Of particular concern would be a foreign country deciding to buy U.S. futures to hedge its grain needs even if they were to be filled from other countries. Under this circumstance, the futures transaction could be huge and bear no relationship to actual commodity transactions in the United States. This type of hedge would have the effect of pushing up the market levels unrealistically, since no corresponding cash transaction would be in the offing. Talmadge, therefore, warned, "The establishment and the holding of such a position and the demand for delivery on a large portion of it could result in disruption of our markets and severe problems for the farmer, processor, and livestock feeder."

Whatever the case, the new CFTC regularly monitors foreign trading. It can step into the market in case of an "emergency situation," caused by an action of the United States or a foreign government, that prevents the market from accurately reflecting the forces of supply and demand. If the CFTC sees that the futures market is behaving erratically, it can suspend all trading.

7

LET'S MAKE A DEAL

Most international dealings in grain manifest themselves as offers, tenders, resales, positions in the futures exchanges, and the like. However, most of the deals, and the dealers who arrange them, go unpublicized.

We have all heard of big wheeler-dealers such as Billie Sol Estes, Bobby Baker, Robert Vesco, Howard Hughes, and now Spiro Agnew, but there are hundreds—if not thousands—of less notable dealers wandering around the world in search of the perfect deal. The grain trade attracts a lot of dealers, since anyone can make representations of nontrademarked grains. All you have to do is pick up a phone and try to convince a grain company that you are for "real" and actually can be of some use. Furthermore, the volumes are so staggering that even a small margin per ton could net a dealer a good profit should the deal go through.

In one sense, it is tiring to be constantly bombarded with deals, yet it is also refreshing to see an individual hustling alone in an era of multinationals and big government bureaucracy. And because he operates alone, the dealer tries to convince you that he works quickly.

If dealers don't find a source of grain—which is unlikely in the grain trade—the grain trade can find them in the classified sections of most newspapers. A chief haunt is the Business Opportunities section of the *Wall Street Journal*. A typical ad reads:

"PETRODOLLARS"
Commercial interests of good renown requiring top-level and useful introductions in the Middle East in both public and private sectors should contact Box XXX, Geneva, Switzerland.

This ad means the advertiser has contacts in the Middle East that he is willing to exploit on your behalf, for a fee.

In my experience, dealers work three types of deals: the trading deal, the promotion deal, and the technical deal.

One of the most interesting trading propositions that several grain firms have received was from Kirby Jones of Alamar Associates, a Washington-based firm specializing in trade with Cuba. Direct trading with Cuba is still forbidden, but Jones offers American firms an opportunity to get to Cuba before the rush that will come when the blockade is lifted. When that day comes, the trade priorities will be agriculture and medicines, according to Cuban trade officials.

Jones, once George McGovern's press secretary, and Frank Mankiewicz, formerly Robert Kennedy's press secretary, did a lengthy press interview with Fidel Castro and struck up a good relationship with him and other Cuban officials. Building on this relationship, Jones formed Alamar Associates to channel proposals from American firms who want to do business with Cuba. He makes no promises other than to see that proposals are delivered to the proper officials. From there on, it is up to the Cubans—and the U.S. State Department—if any business results. To be sure, Jones seeks a fee for his services, but his credentials help him get the fee. He has become so much of an authority on trade with Cuba that he no longer has to go out and knock on doors. People come to him. Evidence of this is that the "establishment" American Management Association invited him to discuss U.S.–Cuban trade possibilities in February 1976.

Other trading deals fall far short of Jones's professional approach and usually consist of someone calling you from the Trans-International Company, or some such place, telling you that the bakers of Muscat need wheat, and if you can make an offer, he'll see to it that your offer is accepted.

One conversation with a trader of dubious qualifications went something like this:

"Hello, my name is Larry Fernsworth, and I understand that you export grains and other commodities."

"That's right," I replied, anticipating his next statement.

"I represent certain buyers in Iran and would like to get an offering of wheat."

I responded, saying, "I can do that, but what quality and

quantities for what delivery period?" I hung up when he said, "But isn't wheat, wheat?"

Trading deals can involve any commodity from soybeans to hemp to bailing wire, dry or liquid, in drums or bulk, but only in quantities of more than 50,000 tons, and the offer must be made immediately. One Chicago-based dealer stamps his stationery: "If it is International, Foltex is your one-stop service center." In most cases, you are being contacted because of your "fine reputation"—and bank account. Most trading deals are on the level, but you have to sort the good from the bad.

The promotion dealer may have learned that you are thinking of building a fast-food chain in Kuwait, a bicycle factory in Afghanistan, or a zoo in Qatar (which is actually going to be built—anyone have a special deal on crocodiles?). Or if you have not thought of these projects, the dealer will tell you that the government of Sandistan or a company in Petrolina wants projects like these and is looking for American "know-how"—which you have. The dealer graciously wants to help both sides get together, in a "spirit of international understanding"—for a small "consideration." The consideration is legitimate in that it is a sort of finder's fee. However, the dealer may use it to bribe someone later on.

"Considerations" have been getting a lot of scrutiny by the SEC of late, following disclosures of the payment of bribes to foreign buyers and officials. I, for one, was surprised at the SEC's reaction, since in many places the practice is an established fact of the grain business—or, for that matter, of any international business.

Finally, there is the dealer who comes to you with a project that he wants to build in Equatoriana—he needs funds and guarantees success. If you fail to understand how it will succeed, the dealer will explain that you should trust him. If you help in financing, then the plant to make marbles from camel hooves or hamburger from old tires can be built.

To pull any one of these deals off, the dealer must establish the proper image. The name of the firm is quite important and usually has "international" or "development" someplace in the title: Mideast Development Corporation, International Technical Specialties Incorporated, African Import Services. The best I have seen is a dealer in oilseeds who set up a firm called Yollobusha International in Gibson City, Mississippi.

Also vital is your location. In order to lend prestige, no dealer would set himself up in Peoria, Illinois, but prefers places such as Beirut, Panama City, Tangier, Zurich, Hong Kong, or—for some reason I can't figure out—Newport Beach, California, where there seems to be a preponderance of dealers.

An accent is of particular value; Arabic and Greek are best, although French will do. If you are an American dealer, you should have foreign associates, as does Spiro Agnew's dealing firm, Pathmark. One Middle East dealer offers his services by handing out a card showing how he is related to important government officials. Titles are useful, with every dealer being called the president, or at least the executive vice-president, of his respective firm. One dealer in Latin America liked to point out that he was a member of the Spanish nobility. Graced with the knowledge of the Almighty, another dealer had the title "broker-futurist" stamped on his business cards. There also seems to be a plethora of generals flying around making deals. Why not? Promotion is an important concept of military life. One dealer I heard of said that he could make a commodity sale go through to a Far East country, since his secretary was the mistress of an influential general.

Once, in Venezuela, I met a really good dealer who had the best image going. Born in Switzerland, he had carved out the good life by putting grain deals together between the United States and oil-rich Venezuela. He had bought a Mercedes from the departing Swiss ambassador and had two telexes—one tucked away in the hall closet at home so he would not miss any midnight opportunities. Few clients visited his office, as most of his dealings were by telex. His two-room office was sparsely furnished and had only one phone. But he kept up his image by never answering the phone, which sat on his desk. His secretary came in from the other room each time it rang, and asked the caller to "wait while I transfer you."

Another dealer in the New Orleans area who specializes in grain deals and who has numerous "contacts" in the Middle East—he says—set up shop in the basement of a $250,000 home. You walk downstairs, and phones are ringing; ribbons of long telexes hang on the walls with headings such as Rome, Paris, Tehran; secretaries call over to say that Felix is on the line from Hong Kong; an erect man with a very British bowler sits patiently in the reception area; and the head man, named Olympus Rabat, tells you he can give you a half hour before he has to catch a plane to Istanbul via Zurich.

The most confusing image I ever encountered was in Bahrain, an island sheikdom in the Arabian Gulf. (You have to be careful to say Arabian Gulf while in Arab countries, and Persian Gulf while in Iran, or you might lose the deal.)

I was in Bahrain on a trip to see if a market for fresh produce from Iran existed in several of the Persian Gulf states. While talking to a government official in Manama, Bahrain's steaming capital, I was overheard by another fellow who said he had a deal for me. He gave me an address and told me to be there at 6:00 P.M.

I got there on time, excited that a real deal—my first—was in the making. The address turned out to be a dress shop that catered to the wives of British officers then stationed in Manama. Yes, my dealer owned the shop and would be down in fifteen minutes.

Sitting down to wait, I was approached by a stout British lady who came up to me and asked, "Do you have a thirty-six D bra?" Regretfully, I said "No" and excused myself, feeling that one of us was dealing in the wrong commodity as, befuddled, I left the shop.

Equally confused was a trader of a well-known firm who was asked to provide offers of soybeans in response to a letter written on the stationery of the National Lottery of Honduras.

Having the proper social graces is also an important part of being a successful dealer on the international scene. If you can afford it—but most cannot—you throw parties for a thousand of your closest friends on Grand Cayman Island, serve Beluga caviar and champagne, provide fireworks, and hand out linen handkerchiefs as mementos. The minister of finance of Higher Octania always seems to be the guest of honor.

Short of that, you should exhibit good taste when the buyer or the seller takes you out to dinner. When you find yourself buying, watch out. On a business trip to Mexico, I took a dealer to dinner who immediately ordered two Chivas Regals for himself—at $8 a shot. Conversations at these functions center on just how polo players are rated, the dealer's contacts in Singapore, who went to the Canton trade fair, how hard it is to find parts for one's Mercedes, the corruption and disarray in bordering countries and what a gracious hotel the St. George's in Algiers is.

One dealer I met had good taste but very little to back up his dealings. He wanted to get into a $50-million wheat deal, but in checking his bank account I found that he had $75 and had recently had his car repossessed.

The thing that sets the good dealers apart from the others is information, the kind that you can use to put deals through. "If you get your price below five hundred dollars a ton, we've got the deal." Another important point in the dealer's relating information is his timing; some feel that if you rouse a grain trader out of a sound sleep at 2:00 A.M., he will assume that the dealer must really be onto something (he is: you).

Some dealers try to demonstrate their knowledge of a situation by sending out a newsletter. It is usually marked "confidential," even though it goes to 5,000 addresses. The usual approach is to have you get acquainted with the newsletter and then you call on the dealer for consulting services.

The dealer's chief goal, however, is to make you believe he "knows." Part of the trick in reaching this goal is the use—and misuse—of certain key words. The accompanying Dealer's Dictionary provides a look at dealer semantics and their reality, which I have experienced on a number of occasions.

Many dealers are honest, fair, and can be helpful in providing a businessman with the information and contacts he needs in making a sale. Others just get in the way and make you pretty cynical about the whole lot.

In one case, in Brazil, a multinational company hired a dealer to serve as its agent in the central area of the country to get offerings of grain. The company hired this dealer because it felt—or was made to feel—that it needed him to make contacts with government officials. These same government officials later admitted that they could not stand the dealer, but felt—or were made to feel—they had to work through him because the foreign company thought highly of him.

One way of separating the good dealers from the bad, as many firms have found out, is to offer commissions rather than retainers. To make money on a trading deal, then, the dealer will have an interest in the deal's going through. On a promotion deal, a good technique is to offer the dealer stock in the new company rather than a set payment. As a stockholder, he will have a stake in seeing the promotion through.

Most deals, alas, have a way of never reaching completion. Perhaps this is the reason we use the derogatory term "big deal!" to refer sarcastically to a happening of little significance.

But dealers will continue to exist. Some deals do get put through, and, what the hell, they sometimes bring intrigue and excitement to

DEALER'S DICTIONARY*

Dealer's Choice of words	How They Are Explained to You	What They Really Mean
I have contacts	Dealer knows someone to put deal through.	Knows another dealer.
I'm "in" with a "high" government official.	Knows "touchable" bureaucrat who makes purchase decisions.	Friend of his partner's cousin who works on 27th floor.
I would like your cooperation.	10% of sale price for dealer.	20%.
Inside information.	Information that will help you outbid competition.	Information supplied by competition.
100% financing available.	Amount other party will make available to put deal together.	Amount you have to put up to close deal.
My partner is ruler's cousin.	Family members get best deal.	Youngest of ruler's 75 cousins; eldest works for competition.
Make my staff available to you.	Professionals who will work night and day to put deal through.	His driver will take you to bank to cash checks.
If you had more time, we could go to my country place to relax.	Successful deals have enabled me to buy country home.	His mother's house where he goes when money runs out.
Petrodollars.	Dollars that oil producers have to buy your goods.	Money you supply to buy gas for dealer's car.

*Reprinted with permission of Miller Publishing Company.

an otherwise dull grain transaction. As one trader for a major commodities firm told me, "Look, I know that most of the guys who call and claim they are the Pope's cousin are not going to put the deal through. But one of these days it will happen, and when it does, I'll leave the soybeans to the cows."

8

OMNIVORE

Despite the efforts of the Agricultural Communications Council, urban-rural forums, and the like, farmers and consumers often have to view each other through the prisms of big business and big government. Consumers feel they pay too much for food; farmers complain they don't get enough. A lot of the problem lies in the complicated marketing system we have developed that takes an agricultural commodity and transforms it into a product. "Freakies Breakfast Cereal" doesn't have much resemblance to the grain from which it is made.

But in the view of some consumers and public-interest groups, increasing food costs are but a symptom; they feel the real reason why food costs more and farmers' commodities fetch less is the increasingly larger grain-marketing and -processing firms. Leading the criticism against bigness in the grain industry are public-interest groups like the Agribusiness Accountability Project based in Washington, D.C., and farm groups such as the National Farmers' Organization.

A group of U.S. senators have also begun to question bigness in food through the introduction of a bill calling for an annual "index of competition" in the food industry. In introducing the bill, the Food Industry Anti-Trust Act of 1975, Senator John Culver (D-Iowa) commented, "Until we enlighten ourselves . . . we will not learn why consumer prices are high and farm prices are low." To the critics of bigness in food, practically anyone along the way in the bushel's trip from farmer's field to consumer's plate is a nefarious middleman who gets his cut "off the top." This category includes not only the big five grain-merchandising firms (Cargill, Continental, Cook, Dreyfus,

Bunge) but also processors like Green Giant and Swift and super-markets like Safeway and Winn-Dixie. Large farm cooperatives are also given low marks because they are "too big" to represent their farmer members. Secretary Butz, in describing the Agribusiness Accountability Project's former director, Jim Hightower, called him an "economic jerk," due to Hightower's tendency to conclude that bigness is bad in any sector of agribusiness. At the same time, Hightower and his research group, supported by several foundations, have picked up support in the Congress, notably from former Senator Fred Harris of Oklahoma and James Abourezk (D-S.D.). The latter calls Hightower "a dedicated David in the struggle against corporate 'Goliaths,' bent on taking over agriculture." The project does make all involved in food marketing appear to comprise an omnivorous beast that is "situated between farmers and consumers ... in a position to set food prices, to determine food quality and even to control food supplies."

People within the food-marketing industry agree that the firms involved are large and powerful, but they are also efficient. As one executive of a Minneapolis-based commodity firm explained, "It can't be all that bad. We've got more food in this country than anywhere else. Americans overeat on our low-cost foods, and it earns us a lot of foreign exchange. The critics want to change this, but what are the alternatives?"

Farms as Firms

"A few farmers going broke each year is one of the most healthy things there is," according to a statement in early 1975 by Kenneth Frick, administrator of the USDA's Agricultural Stabilization and Conservation Service. Frick made the statement because our free-enterprise system gets better by sorting out the inefficient farmers. Many firms have felt the same way—that is, they can bring their efficiency to bear on farming, where a lot of inefficiency and dated techniques still exist.

Accordingly, big corporations like Purex and United Brands have gone into farming, but Tenneco (with 1974 sales of $4 billion) has been one of the few that have made a success of it. Some corporations have had the same problems as collectives in the Soviet Union—namely, how to stimulate an employee to put in the long hours and the attention needed to make farming a success. In John Kenneth Galbraith's terms, corporation farming can't provide the "self-exploitation" required to make a go of it, thus the reluctance of some firms to get into it. In addition, the larger the farm, the greater the management skill needed to operate it. Few corporations have been able to provide this skill.

Cargill, perhaps the biggest private agribusiness in the world, engages in grain merchandising, flour milling, poultry raising, and other agribusiness areas, but has chosen not to get into farming itself. One advertisement it uses might give a clue to why it has not: "Times change. Methods change. Equipment changes. Even the earth itself changes. But one thing remains the same. The indomitable spirit of the people who till the soil. We hope that never changes."

But an agricultural consultant at Chicago's largest bank, Continental Illinois, feels that the family farm is doomed to be replaced by a strictly business operation. This operation may be run by a family, but on a more businesslike basis: Capital will continue to be substituted for labor. More corporations will also enter farming. This consultant also contends that as farming becomes just another business, it will lose its historical uniqueness. Thus, when election time comes, the "farm vote" will be a meaningless term.

In those cases in which there is not an outright entrance of corporations into farming, the American Agricultural Marketing Association feels the farmer will lose a lot of power by farming by contracts which commit him to sell to one buyer. In so doing, the farmer will lose the opportunity to sell to the highest bidder.

By 1985, 75 percent of agricultural production will be cornered by contracts, according to the association. If this does happen, one of the last free supply-and-demand markets will have disappeared. For with a farmer's production committed at a certain price, market fluctuations are reduced, if not eliminated. Instead of being his own boss, the farmer will become the employee of whomever he has contracted his grain to.

To many proponents of family farming, these predictions are tantamount to burning the flag on the Fourth of July. Accordingly, legislators like State Representative Lane Denton of Waco, Texas, have sought restrictions on corporate farming. Denton introduced bills to that effect after learning that most of his dinner was produced by big business.

Denton was upset that corporations like Greyhound produced the turkey that he ate, or that Smithfield ham is brought to you by ITT, lettuce by Dow Chemical, potatoes by Boeing, and fruit juice by Coca-Cola.

However, Denton's bills never got out of committee. One bill would have required corporations to divest themselves of their farming interests within ten years. The other piece of legislation would have prohibited manufacturers, wholesalers, and retailers from entering the production of food and fiber. Similar proposals exist in other states, with a prohibition against corporate farming already in existence in North Dakota and Minnesota.

The Starting Five

No discussion of the grain trade is possible without mention of the big five grain-merchandising firms in the United States—or, for that matter, the world. The quintuplets—Cargill, Continental, Cook, Dreyfus, and Bunge—are either accused of being among those responsible for high food prices or praised for keeping food prices as low as they are. In looking at their operations, I have to agree with a friend of mine who stated: "Bigness is not necessarily better, but then neither is bigness badder." While these companies have been making big profits, they also take big risks.

With the Soviet grain sale of 1972, the public was made aware of some of these firms for the first time, even though Continental Grain has been around since 1839. It's been estimated that these five firms control 90 percent of U.S. grain exports and 70 percent of world grain exports. Accusations have been hurled at them in recent years ranging from manipulating the distribution of railroad rolling stock, to keeping down farmers' prices, to using U.S. tax dollars to develop competition for U.S. farmers overseas, to cheating in grain inspection and weighing.

The circumstances surrounding the Soviet grain sale in 1972 were seen by some as a conspiracy by these firms to hide from farmers that the Soviets were buying. But they never tell the farmers or other exporters anything, anyway.

The big exporters all operate in basically the same way. In addition to their domestic offices, they have sales offices and agents around the world. Direct-line telexes tying the various offices together spew out hundreds of messages providing details of sell-and-buy orders, deals, crop conditions, and political analyses. All belong to the major commodity exchanges and have diversified into every aspect of the grain business from flour milling to baking.

These firms have all been accused of being useless middlemen who do nothing except raise prices from the time they buy the farmer's grain to the time they sell it. But their logistics of railroad cars, barges, elevators, terminal storage, and ocean shipping are unparalleled. They have been the leaders in concepts such as the unit train—up to 150 cars loaded with grain that clickety-clack nonstop to a port in about half the time of regular trains. And all have sales reported to be near or exceeding $1 billion.

Each has hired top officials from the USDA to serve as its executives in the same way aerospace and defense contractors hire admirals and generals from the Pentagon. Earl Butz came to the USDA as a member of the board of Ralston Purina; Butz's predecessor, Clifford Hardin, took up his vacated seat at Checkerboard Square.

They are well-managed firms that have a lot of influence, so much so that the Federal Trade Commission began investigating these five and other large grain traders for possible law violations in early 1975. In response to fears that these exporters didn't really serve the interests of America—three of the top six (Bunge, Garnac, and Dreyfus) are foreign-owned or -controlled—a bill was introduced in the House to place grain exports under government control.

Hyde Murray, minority counsel for the House Agriculture Committee, feels that some sort of control is necessary. "Their interests and ideas are not always in line with those of the United States. They're afflicted with the same kind of schizophrenia as the international oil companies."

The USDA has now gotten a better hand on what the exporters are doing by having them report export commitments of 50,000 tons or more when the sales are made. Prior to June 1973, exporters filed export declarations only at the time of shipment. Reports of actual shipments were made available usually within forty-five days following the end of the month of shipment. The delay between filing and announcement was the amount of time it took to organize and transmit the information.

Cargill, the biggest of the exporters, is located in Minneapolis. With sales of around $5 billion a year, Cargill maintains an operation with 50 domestic offices, 100 grain elevators, 33 terminal elevators, 2,000 railroad cars, hundreds of trucks, and 5 ships. Cargill is the largest soybean processor in the world and also engages in anchovy fishing in Peru and seed and feed production—not to mention flour milling and salt and fertilizer production. All this activity is controlled by the Cargill and MacMillan families, who have 85 percent of the stock in the company, whose net worth is around $350 million.

The company began in 1864 near Conover, Iowa, and now operates out of a château-like building on the outskirts of Minneapolis. Although well-managed, Cargill is so large that on one occasion another agribusiness company was able to buy grain from Cargill's commodity division, and turn around and sell the same grain to Cargill's feed division, and make a tidy profit on the "scalp."

Despite its secluded headquarters, Cargill has made an effort to be more open to the public, sending out its executives to conventions and meetings with the press to explain that it does not monopolize the grain trade but fiercely competes to see how it can "get grain to the Gulf for ⅛ of a cent a bushel cheaper than the other guy."

Late in 1975, it was revealed by the *Des Moines Register* that the U.S. government, through the Overseas Private Investment Corporation (OPIC), helped Cargill receive $3 million in loans and guarantees to finance soybean-processing facilities in Brazil, Dale Yahnke's chief competition in selling soybeans for export.

An OPIC spokesman said that Cargill got the loan because it stipulated that Brazilian soybean products would not be exported to the United States. However, the meal and oil produced by the new plant would compete in the world market with American soybean by-products. In effect, American farmers' tax dollars went to help the competition.

The American Soybean Association has been infuriated by this state of affairs since 1972, when Brazilian soybeans really began to appear in the world markets. The association felt it made little sense for the U.S. government to help finance a Cargill soybean venture in Brazil through OPIC.

No less controversial among farmers, Continental Grain Company, the second-largest U.S. grain exporter, has been called the "complete breadstuffs company." Begun by the Fribourg family in Belgium in 1839, the firm is now headed by Michael Fribourg, the great-great-grandson of the founder. A hard worker, Fribourg courted the Russians throughout the 1950s and 1960s, until his persistence paid off in 1972 with his big sale to the Soviets. Continental's first sale was for $460 million and was concluded by Fribourg after a mammoth, thirty-eight-hour negotiating session with Nikolai Belousov, the Russian buyer.

"Conti" moved its operations to New York in the 1920s and, according to industry insiders, has annual sales of $3 billion. In addition to its rural purchasing operations, Continental has at least a hundred companies in the corporate structure, including Orowheat Bread, Polo Frozen Dinners, and Hilbun Chickens. It is further diversified into shipping and metals.

Like other multinationals, Continental transcends political boundaries in its dealings to maximize its returns. The trade embargo prevents it from selling U.S. rice to Cuba, but its European subsidiary sold 100,000 tons of Italian rice to Cuba in December 1975. This infuriated Representative John Breaux (D-La.), whose district includes many of Louisiana's rice growers. Breaux was hopping mad that a U.S. grain company's subsidiary was able to sell Italian rice and make a profit, while 600,000 tons of Louisiana rice sat unsold in warehouses. Breaux referred to the Treasury Department's granting of a license for the sale as "blatant favoritism towards multinational corporations." Licenses to trade with Cuba are hard to come by and were instituted in the early 1960s as a means of eliminating trade with Castro.

Although an American company, Continental acts as the exclusive agent for the Australian government in selling Australian wheat to South America, often in competition with American wheat.

Continental made Walter Cronkite's "Evening News"—probably the first time it had ever been on television—when Cronkite questioned the propriety of Assistant Secretary of Agriculture Clarence Palmby's having been a member of a U.S. team that went to Moscow on April 8, 1972, to negotiate grain sales, even though he was considering employment with Continental. Palmby, incidentally, springs from Blue Earth County, where Dale Yahnke farms. On June 8, 1972, Palmby announced he was going to work for Continental, the biggest seller in the initial deals. Earl Butz later admitted it might not have been a good idea to take Palmby along.

In a financially secretive grain industry, Cook Industries of Memphis is probably the most open. Since it is a public company, it is obligated to reveal its financial data, which, like those of the other grain companies, are quite impressive. In 1975, Cook reported gross income of $302 million, which, even considering inflation, is impressive, as in 1971 it was only $92 million. This growth has been propelled by its president, Ed Cook.

An avid free-trader like all the other entrepreneurs heading the big grain companies, Cook is upset with trends in the United States. "The worst thing that's happening in our country today is the overriding obsession for a riskless society. Safety, security, to hell with all that. That's a helluva way to run a country. They've got that in England and look at them."

Possessing a logistics network as extensive (except maybe in storage) as Cargill's and Continental's, Cook, too, has come under considerable scrutiny. Some coverage has been given to the fact that Carroll Brunthaver, who as a USDA official worked on setting the subsidies for the first Russian sales, is now a vice-president for Cook. Brunthaver pulls no punches in pointing out the value of the American export firms. "The aggressiveness and competitiveness of individual marketing firms within the United States has done a much better job of pricing, moving and marketing U.S. grain in competition with other origins."

Following Cook in grain exports from the United States is Louis Dreyfus Corporation, headquartered in Paris. It is perhaps one of the more secretive exporters: When the House of Representatives held hearings on the Soviet grain sales in 1972, Dreyfus was the only exporter that chose not to appear. Nathanial Samuels, the new chairman of Dreyfus and former New York investment dealer for Loeb Rhoades, recognizes that exporters have a bad public image and seems more active than his predecessor in trying to improve it. Prior to joining Dreyfus, Samuels served as Undersecretary of State for Economic Affairs in the Nixon Administration.

Bunge-Born follows Dreyfus in importance in U.S. exports, but, worldwide, Bunge may be even larger than Cargill, as it handles 20 percent of the world's grain shipments. Bunge is headquartered in Argentina, and its size may be gauged by the ransoms it pays. Early in 1975, two of the Born brothers were kidnapped by Argentine terrorists but were released unharmed sometime later after payment of a $63 million ransom. After it was paid, the Argentine government called for an investigation—to find out where the $63 million had come from.

Not much is known about Bunge. Reportedly, it is owned by a

Curaçao holding company held, in turn, by Bunge-Born of Argentina. It got its share of public scrutiny when it, too, hired away one of the USDA officials who went to Moscow to negotiate the first trades, Clifford G. Pulvermacher, to head its Washington office.

Bunge acquired an additional black mark by being one of the few firms directly charged in the grain-inspection scandals. Of all the exporters, Bunge is the only corporate farmer, as it operates First American Farms, which farms 40,000 acres of soybeans in Walton County, Florida.

Other grain firms that continue to grow in importance are Archer Daniels Midland (ADM), located in Decatur, Illinois, and two Minneapolis-based firms, Peavey and International Multifoods. ADM had 1975 sales of $1.8 billion and is the second-largest soybean crusher behind Cargill.

Dwayne Andreas, the dynamic chief executive officer of ADM, has made quite a reputation through selling soybeans and giving some untimely political contributions. During the preliminary stages of the Watergate investigation, it was discovered that the $25,000 cash contribution Andreas made to the Nixon campaign ultimately turned up in the bank account of Bernard Barker, one of the Watergate burglars. Andreas ultimately gave $122,000 to the Nixon campaign, but also gave around $75,000 to Humphrey.

A free-trader like all the major exporters, Andreas worked on one of the first Russian commodity deals in 1954. Butter was in surplus, and Andreas wanted to sell them 100,000 tons, but the deal fell through when the Secretary of Commerce refused the sales to the Russians at a price substantially below what the American housewife was paying. Things have obviously changed, for the Russians enjoyed the wheat we sold them in 1972 at a price lower than domestic buyers paid, since the Soviet purchases pushed up domestic wheat prices drastically.

Although the big grain firms, particularly the "starting five," remain secretive, free-trading risk-takers, they have benefited from the public treasury over the years. In the era of grain surpluses, these big firms got government money for storing grain and received a large part of the $4.2 billion in export subsidies for wheat that the United States paid out between 1949 and 1972.

Keeping Them Honest

Farm groups have watched closely while the starting five and friends got most of the export business, but a movement is afoot to expand the cooperatives' role. In spite of the fact that cooperatives handle domestic sales of 40 percent of the nation's grain, they have only 6 percent of American grain exports.

One step has been the organization of Promark, a pool-marketing program for wheat adopted by Far-Mar-Co, the nation's largest regional grain cooperative, in October 1975. The purpose, of course, is to give farmers more control over what they grow and sell and how much profit they gain. Participating farmers pledge a certain proportion of their wheat acreage to the co-op venture. Far-Mar-Co then estimates how much grain this is likely to yield and commits itself to supplying wheat to both foreign and domestic customers. Lester Wolverton likes the idea, as it will "keep the big boys honest."

Far-Mar-Co directors are ebullient over the idea, as it will "effectively exclude the profiteering middlemen." Far-Mar-Co will take none of the profit; instead, profits from the sales of grain, less expenses, will be divided equitably among the participating farmers.

Following the announcement of this plan, a statement was released by the Farmer Co-operative Service (FCS) urging farmers to act through their cooperatives to establish a single producer-owned export organization. At present, 6 percent of exports is split among five smaller co-ops.

Noting that this single organization would have an advantage over the big exporters by controlling grain from the time it is produced to the time it is shipped, the FCS stated that the organization would "act as a barometer on the efficiency of the major grain exporters and reflect the earnings back to producers." But most people in the grain trade can't see the several cooperatives agreeing on such a cooperative export scheme.

Despite the good sense that a cooperative makes to farmers, farmers make co-op activities quite difficult. While they may own only a small percentage of the cooperative's equity, they do own 100 percent of the crops they sell a co-op. Thus, they want the highest return on their initial sale, rather than on the resale to a domestic or foreign buyer. The head of the FCS pointed out that for this cooperative-marketing program to be a success, farmers must be willing to accept the fact that they are turning pricing and marketing functions over to the export cooperative and cannot hold onto their grain after the cooperative makes an export commitment.

This commitment, however, requires faith in the cooperative concept, which some farmers and many consumers have lost in recent years. Several farm cooperatives have grown to such size that critics claim the cooperatives have gotten as big, self-serving, and corrupt as the big agribusinesses. The biggest in order of size are Associated Milk Producers, Inc. (AMPI), Land O'Lakes, Farmland, Agway, Gold Kist, Dairylea, and Farmers' Union.

In organizing cooperatives, there is one tremendous tool in a little piece of legislation passed in 1922 called the Capper-Volstead Act. This act allowed farmers to come together in marketing associations. Without this act, farmers in such organizations could be considered in violation of antitrust laws. If farmers who operate as independent businesses were denied the right to form cooperatives, they would have no alternative but to sell their products through middlemen, except for whatever they could sell directly at a roadside stand.

However, an increasing number of charges have been leveled at cooperatives of late, including accusations that they have become politically corrupt, that they no longer serve their members, and that they restrain rather than foster competition.

More public attention was focused on cooperative activities when it became known that AMPI—Associated Milk Producers, Inc., headquartered in San Antonio—had persuaded the government to increase milk price supports in 1971, allegedly in return for the pledge of a campaign contribution to Richard M. Nixon's 1972 presidential election campaign. The whole affair showed that this cooperative knew how to exert as much power in achieving its ends as any large corporation. John Connally, while Secretary of the Treasury, once remarked to Nixon, "They're doing some things that I think are a little strong-armed tactics."

While AMPI's long-term goal was a single milk cooperative, their immediate aim in 1971 was higher milk price supports. AMPI first began to ingratiate itself with the Nixon administration in 1969, with a $100,000 cash contribution. But when this didn't get them the presidential attention they sought, they then pledged $2 million to Nixon's 1972 campaign. At the same time, they gave money to other candidates, which reportedly infuriated the presidential counselor Charles Colson.

AMPI lobbied in Congress as well, and in early 1971 got 118 representatives and 29 senators to sponsor bills to hike price supports. The administration wasn't listening, however, and on March 12 stated that the price would be maintained at $4.66 per hundred pounds—AMPI wanted $5.21.

After all AMPI's efforts, the organization was shocked by the administration's decision, but the decision also strengthened its resolve and led it to seek support from John Connally and Murray Chotiner, a Nixon friend, and to offer Chotiner a $60,000-per-year retainer from AMPI. On March 21, AMPI officials met with Nixon, whose economic advisers had previously told him not to increase the supports. At their meeting, Nixon rambled on about their backing, the value of milk ("it has a certain soothing effect"), and handed out some presidential cuff links ("since your wives will wonder where you really were today"). The meeting ended with no commitment on Nixon's part.

Later that same afternoon, Nixon called a meeting on price supports and invited John Ehrlichman, Connally, Clifford Hardin, George Schultz, and other top advisers. After Connally had given a rundown on the political realities of supporting rural America, Nixon stated, "I could not veto any price support bill. Not because they're milkers, but because they're farmers. And it would be just turning down Middle America, uh, where we need support." Everyone agreed, and as they got up to leave, Ehrlichman joked, "Better go get a glass of milk [laughing]. Drink it while it's cheap."

On March 25, Secretary Hardin announced that the price support would be raised to $4.93 from the $4.66 previously announced. Hardin later testified that the new support was "based entirely on a reconsideration of the evidence." Whatever the case, the dairy cooperative had made a good investment—for the $632,500 it eventually contributed to the 1972 campaign, dairy farmers got literally tens of millions of dollars in extra income. But to AMPI's surprise, on February 1, 1972—about a year later—the Justice Department filed an antitrust suit against AMPI in spite of its generous campaign contributions and the umbrella of the Capper-Volstead Act.

Some corporations have also sought shelter under the Capper-Volstead Act. Ralston Purina, Wilson & Company, and other poultry contractors once formed their own co-op, the National Broiler

Marketing Association (NBMA), asserting that they were "producers." Eventually, the Justice Department filed an antitrust suit against the members of the NBMA, asserting that they "have been engaged in a combination and conspiracy to fix, maintain and stabilize the price of broilers." In August 1975, however, a Federal judge ruled that NBMA members were engaged in the production of agricultural products as defined within the meaning of Capper-Volstead.

There is no doubt that cooperatives are becoming more powerful. To better gauge the extent of this power, the Federal Trade Commission (FTC) performed a major investigation of the nation's 4,800 agricultural marketing co-ops and concluded that, for the most part, they do not possess inordinate marketing power.

The FTC began looking into the cooperatives when it felt that the Capper-Volstead Act, while exempting co-ops from antitrust provisions, did not provide them with a "carte blanche to monopolize and restrain trade." Furthermore, the FTC felt that if wrongdoing were found, the co-ops, like any other business, should be prosecuted under the Sherman-Clayton Antitrust acts, and not by the USDA, which bears the responsibility for co-op "supervision."

In a staff study by the FTC, milk co-ops were found to control more than 70 percent of the milk supply in metropolitan regions spread from Ohio to Colorado and from the Gulf of Mexico to the Great Lakes. The report went on to state that milk co-ops "manipulate the market" through a variety of devices, including encouraging limited production and controlling surplus supplies. Co-ops are aided in this through Federal price supports—like the increase AMPI sought in 1971—and Federal marketing orders. Marketing orders set the minimum price that buyers must pay for milk in about sixty metropolitan regions across the United States. The FTC points out that much of this legislation grew out of the "distress of depression agriculture," but its primary concern in looking at the power of the milk cooperatives is the effect on the consumer.

At the November 1975 National Agricultural Outlook Conference, the National Consumers Congress called for a redefinition of the antitrust exemptions of the Capper-Volstead Act so that cooperatives could be maintained as moderate-size entities large enough to take advantage of modern marketing techniques but not so large as to monopolize major regions of the country.

Representative Peter A. Peyser of New York, the nation's third-largest dairy state, is also worried about the effect of those co-ops on the dairy farmer, and accordingly in 1975 introduced a bill that he called the "Dairy Farmers' Bill of Rights." The intent of the bill, according to Peyser, is to ensure that the big dairy cooperatives do not take advantage of their members—or of smaller cooperatives, for that matter. The bill is still pending. The result of the FTC study and bills like Peyser's could be to change the Capper-Volstead Act and to push for Federal and state legislation to modify marketing orders.

The cooperatives involved responded, "Why us?" In the case of the dairy cooperatives, the managers point out that the combined sales volume of the four largest co-ops is less than one-third the volume of the four largest dairy corporations (Kraft, Pet, Carnation, and Borden).

Bemused by the whole affair, the editors of *Farm Journal*, America's oldest such publication, addressed its farm readers by stating: "City people liked farmers best when you all wore straw hats and produced cheap food. Then farmers were real team players in the American marketing system. Now that strong coops have some muscle in the market, the push is on to bring back the good old days."

But the most stinging criticism of the move against co-ops came from the president of the National Council of Farmer Cooperatives, who wondered at the logic of the FTC investigators who believe "that small and harmless coops are O.K, but that it's these other bastards that are big enough to do the farmer some good that you have to crack down on."

Making Dough

Although bread has been eclipsed by dairy products and meat in terms of per-capita consumption, it somehow remains emotionally the favorite food. This tie to our daily bread has led to a lot of scrutiny of the milling and baking industry and its increased concentration. About twenty-five milling firms now account for 90 percent of commercial flour production, and of these, nine national companies account for 60 percent. It is not the nefarious competition of the big boys like Pillsbury, Multifoods, and General Mills that is causing a continuing erosion of small mills, but the decline in flour usage. Interestingly, while most of the grain-exporting and -mer-

chandising firms are privately owned, milling and food manufacturers are public.

Paralleling the increasing concentration in flour milling has been
the decline in the number of bakeries. The last census of manufacturers, done in 1972, showed that the number of bakeries declined 44
percent from 1958 to 1972. The fellow who really suffered during
this time was the corner baker, who had accounted for 10 percent of
sales but now has a negligible percentage of the $6-billion bread
industry. Taking his place has been the wholesale baker—like ITT-
Continental (baker of Wonder Bread)—which now accounts for 85
percent of bread sales.

According to *Milling and Baking News,* these trends toward
concentration have not led to possible price fixing of your cupcakes,
but rather to more vigorous competition. *Milling and Baking*
contends that the survivors of the bread industry shakedown will be
stronger and better able to compete with each other.

Some withdrew from the foray voluntarily, like General Mills,
whose sales are now in excess of $2 billion. In 1965, it made the
decision to close nine of its seventeen flour mills and to devote more
attention to marketing than to production. Having begun as a flour
miller, it became a consumer products company. Most millers have
expanded—or, as an economist would put it, integrated forward—into
different products made from flour. General Mills figures—and has
proved—it can take its expertise in marketing Wheaties and use it to
sell electric trains and postage-stamp albums. A consumer advocate I
know added slyly, "By the way, did you notice that General Mills
now makes the Monopoly game?"

Another rapidly growing, diversified grain company is International Multifoods, headquartered in Minneapolis. Now an $800-
million-a-year concern, Multifoods began as New Prague Milling in
1892. Atherton Bean, Multifoods' soft-spoken but dynamic chairman,
is the grandson of the founder. Like all successful businessmen, Bean
has his motto, which in his case reads: "Beware of the easiest way."

The largest flour miller in 1970, Multifoods began to pick up
additional businesses. Some came when their owners got too old to
continue a line, so Multifoods picked them up. They bought Mister
Donut in 1970, when the old management, which they supplied with
dough, could no longer continue without outside assistance.

Responding to claims that the millers have been ripping off
consumers by making inordinate profits in selling flour, one industry

executive pointed out, "If the money is so good, how come we aren't building new mills, buying old ones, instead of investing in consumer goods?" This does not mean to say that there are no profits—or that the millers would turn them down—in their basic business. In its 1974 annual report, General Mills couched its increasing food profits in the following Madison Avenue-ese: "The dramatic rise in world demand for virtually all grains and ingredients resulted in supply shortages and skyrocketing prices during the crop year, presenting increased opportunities in grain handling and merchandising for companies with elevators and other facilities necessary to serve such activities. General Mills was in a position to serve this need."

Pillsbury has also been buying up one new business after another. Perhaps the most fascinating to contemplate was its attempt to pick up Weight Watchers via the acquisition route. Industry analysts state that one reason sales of flour and bread products have fallen off is that consumers consider them fattening. Thus, by combining Weight Watchers with its dough-and-pastry business, Pillsbury could profit not only by fattening you up, but also by helping you take it off. General Mills already does both by having its Counterweight program.

The largest-volume flour miller at present is the Peavey Company, also located in Minneapolis. An old-line milling firm, Peavey has, more recently, expanded into new areas, including baking, through the acquisition of Catherine Clark's Brownberry Ovens. What makes this acquisition interesting is that Peavey is one of the few millers that have gone into baking breads, which seems a logical step if you make flour. Frank Lindblom, a Peavey executive, feels that the milling industry will remain competitive, even though "possible agglomerations of mills will not be uncommon" in the future.

In spite of increasing concentration, the milling industry has not drawn much Federal scrutiny. The most significant legal issue facing one miller, General Mills, and three cereal food manufacturers, Kellogg, Quaker Oats, and General Foods, is a complaint issued by the Federal Trade Commission alleging that the four comprise an illegal oligopoly of the ready-to-eat cereal industry.

The four control 90 percent of a business that in 1970 brought in around $700 million in sales. To my mind, the issue here is not that of concentration, but the power of advertising. After all, the four companies created the "breakfast cereal"; it did not exist before, as did, for example, bacon and eggs. Yet the concept of a breakfast cereal has become so institutionalized that it is almost as American as applie pie. Kellogg's president, W. E. LaMothe, dismisses the complaint "as an ivory tower theory held by some economists that, where an industry is concentrated, anti-competitive conditions exist."

Changing consumer preferences have eroded the corner bakery. Consumers now shop in supermarkets, which can offer a larger variety than the corner bakery, and usually the consumer does not want to stop at a number of stores when one will suffice. Thus, the baking market has become concentrated in the hands of companies such as Continental, which has 12 percent of the nation's bread market and serves as the acknowledged price leader. The wholesale bakers hold the lion's share of the business, with four firms accounting for around 35 percent of the action nationally.

The FTC, in a staff study released in September 1975, gave the baking industry a good report card, saying that, as a whole, there was "no profiteering during the economic turbulence" in 1973 and 1974. The rise in bread prices, the FTC found, was related to a rapid rise in flour prices. In addition, retailers' gross margins on bread widened to 6.2 cents per one-pound loaf during calendar 1974. The FTC found that some bakers operated at a loss during this period, evidenced by the number of baker failures—thirty-three for bakers with less than $10 million in assets, compared to twenty-four the previous year.

If you recall, it was the American Bakers' Association that screamed so loudly that wheat exports would drive the price of a loaf of bread to $1 if allowed to continue unabated in late 1973 and early 1974. Some cynics felt that with the $1-a-loaf cry having prepared us to pay $1, the retailers could easily charge 80 cents a loaf. But when wheat prices began to fall in early 1975 and the price of bread didn't, the government's wage-and-price-monitoring agency wanted to know why.

Accordingly, the Council on Wage and Price Stability sent letters to the eight leading firms—ITT-Continental, American Bakeries, Campbell Taggart, Nabisco, Sunshine Biscuit, Interstate Brands, Keebler, and Borden Food—which control over 50 percent of the market, asking them to furnish price and cost information on raw materials, labor, wrapping, and "other significant items."

In reality, many bakers were forced out of business by the cost-price squeeze since 1974, while others, depending on whom you listen to, went out with a little help from their larger baking competitors. In 1973, the U.S. Supreme Court ruled that Continental, baker of six million loaves daily with sales of almost $1 billion annually, had used unfair methods to compete with two local Denver bakers and had damaged them in the amount of $3.8 million. Two years earlier, Continental had been named in a $45-million antitrust suit brought by five independent bakeries. Continental had also been involved with three other bakers in a price-fixing suit in Seattle in the early 1960s, which scheme had reportedly cost Seattle bread eaters around $30 million.

Price-fixing allegations were not directed solely at Continental. In 1974, Rainbo Baking of Tucson, a subsidiary of Campbell Taggart, the second-largest wholesale baker, with annual sales of $590 million, was indicted by a Phoenix grand jury for conspiring with three other bakers to fix bread prices at high levels; it eventually pleaded nolo contendere. Campbell Taggart became involved in another price-fixing conspiracy in 1975, when two of its subsidiaries and three other bakeries were fined a total of $276,000 by a U.S. District Court in Baton Rouge, Louisiana, for having fixed prices in the sale of wholesale baked foods in four South Central states. The companies and their executives pleaded nolo contendere in the case.

Sit-Down Lunch

While crop, dairy, and hog farming will remain family enterprises, cattle and chicken raising are being done more and more on a corporate basis.

Confined feeding of cattle has long been recognized as the quickest way to ready cattle for market. After all, having the cattle in a confined area means they don't waste energy—and weight—in getting to their feed. An Amarillo acquaintance feels the preponderance of feedlots in that area makes it the "sit-down-lunch" capital of the world.

Family feedlots—clustered mainly in the Corn Belt—began to fade in importance as the commercial feedlots grew, until by 1972 Texas outranked Iowa in numbers of cattle fed. Scores of new feedlots began to emerge in the Panhandle as a whole new crowd began investing in agriculture: Bankers, doctors, lawyers, dentists, et al began to participate in the ownership of No. 1 Okies—the term for prime feedlot cattle.

A new type of agricultural institution appeared: the Wall Street Cowboy. This new breed of cowboy saw cattle feeding as a tax shelter. Federal regulations permit ranchers, even the Wall Street variety, to take a tax deduction for grain bought in one year even though the grain isn't fed to the cattle until the next year. Under this regulation, an absentee cattleman could often shelter his nonfarm income until his cattle were sold, at which time he would hope to be in a lower tax bracket or to have another shelter. Joan Baez and other celebrities, not to mention your run-of-the-mill Wall Street crowd, poured billions into such tax shelters and distorted the cattle market.

Advertisements in various business journals for these tax-shelter feeding programs were directed toward readers in the 70 percent tax bracket. For most of these investors, the prime motive was the immediate tax saving rather than an anticipated return on the investment.

It became difficult for a farmer-feeder to compete with this new cowboy. Whereas the farmer-feeder got his cattle for his investment, the tax-shelter feeder got not only his cattle but also a tax break. As a result, the outside investor was able to outbid the farmer-feeder in buying feeder cattle and was willing to resell the cattle at a lower price.

A report issued by the USDA Packers and Stockyards Administration summed up the situation: "This is a case where the displacement of a dispersed, family-type of farming by the growth of industrialized agriculture has been subsidized by the Federal Treasury." Cattle feeders will admit that this has caused changes in the feeding industry, but insist that if the tax-shelter programs were eliminated, there would be reduced agriculture production, with price increases. The big feedlots are here to stay; witness the entrance of Cargill into cattle feeding with the purchase of a large Kansas feedlot.

A similar displacement of chicken farmers by corporations has also occurred, which has brought the price of chickens down dramatically, as large-scale production has decreased costs. About 85 percent of the broiler industry is now fully integrated from hatching to processing. The main producers are Holly Farms, Wilson, Armour, Kentucky Fried Chicken, and Cargill. In fiscal 1975, Holly Farms marketed over 550 million pounds of broiler meat, compared to the 200 million pounds processed by Colonel Sanders' crowd.

Holly, which holds 7 percent of the market, owns its own breeder chicken flocks and hatches over three million chicks per week. The chicks are placed with independent farmers for about eight weeks, until they reach the desired weight. The company mills and delivers the feed to the growers and, when the chicks are ready, collects them and sends them off to their processing plants, which slaughter three million chickens a week.

Much has been made of the status of the independent farmer who raises the chickens for these big firms. While some of the arguments are valid, others are emotional. Jim Hightower, for example, attacked the system by pointing out that in 1974, when supermarket prices for broilers were as much as 90 cents a pound, chicken farmers were getting only 2 cents. The broiler industry, however, maintains it did not keep all of the differential to itself; 75 percent of the price of a chicken is feed, which it—and not the farmer—has to buy.

Nevertheless, a lot of acrimony exists over the integrator-farmer relationship, with the major farm organizations seeking legislation to protect the bargaining rights of the chicken farmers, who are, according to Crawford Smith, an Alabama contract farmer, "the only slaves left in this country."

Ralph Nader's Center for the Study of Responsive Law came out with a report in 1972 that stated that the days of low-cost poultry may soon be over as the concentration in the industry increases. A "technological rigor mortis" would set in as firms freed of competitive pressures in pricing put more attention on corporate-risk reduction than on product improvement. The report continued: "The Pillsbury chicken may soon rival the NBC peacock as the nation's most ubiquitous TV fowl." This prediction didn't hold, as Pillsbury, which entered the poultry business in 1962, was out in 1974, after sizable losses. Ralston Purina, another billion-dollar firm, also found broilers rough going and bowed out of the fray in 1972.

Packing Them In

Meat packing is also a concentrated industry, and has been for quite some time, as any reader of Upton Sinclair's *The Jungle* can attest. Cartoons depicting the beef trust appeared as early as 1880. Several meat packers had become so powerful that in 1917 President Woodrow Wilson directed the Federal Trade Commission to investigate the meat-packing industry to see if there were "monopolies, controls, trusts, combinations, conspiracies or restraints out of harmony with the law and public interest." An FTC report released in 1919 alleged that Swift, Morris (merged with Armour in 1923), Wilson, and Cudahy had used collusive practices by allocating market shares and fixing prices among themselves. A consent decree was issued in 1920, upheld again as late as 1960, undoing some of the vertical integration and prohibiting them from retailing meat or having any ownership in stockyards or in newspapers and journals carrying market information.

Big firms are not packing them in as they used to, but there are still fewer buyers of livestock than there are sellers. The biggest buyer of them all is Iowa Beef Processors (IBP), which prides itself on being the largest meat packer in the world. IBP comes in for its share of criticism, but Currier Holman, IBP's controversial chairman, is philosophical about it, always quoting a Chinese aphorism: "The taller the tree stands in a wood, the harder the wind tries to blow it down."

From rather humble beginnings, Iowa Beef's sales are now in the area of $1.8 billion. Its newest packing plant in Amarillo is called a "factory" and can kill, cut up, and package 20,000 head per week. The choice of Amarillo as the site of the "world's largest packing plant" coincides with a shift of cattle feeding away from the family feeders of the Midwest to the larger commercial feedlots of the Panhandle. IBP likens its production method to "taking beef apart like Henry Ford puts cars together."

Of growing concern to consumer and farmer groups alike is the trend of packers to acquire custom feedlots. Among the seventeen firms that made or proposed such acquisitions in 1972 were the top four and the sixth- and eighth-largest fed-cattle slaughtering firms. Together, these firms account for more than 60 percent of the fed cattle slaughtered in Iowa, Arizona, and New Mexico, and 50 percent of the fed cattle slaughtered in Texas, Oklahoma, and Utah. Farmer-feeders fear that they won't get competitive prices under these circumstances.

A bill was introduced in the House by Representative Neal Smith of Iowa in July 1975 to prohibit packers or chain stores from engaging in custom feeding in their own feedlots. The NFO strongly supported the bill because of the leverage it would give the feeder. According to the NFO's Washington office chief, a farmer-feeder who has to sell cattle on a given day might not be able to get his price, since the packer would be able to slaughter his own animals instead of buying from farmer-feeders. Secretary Butz opposed the bill on the grounds that there is too much government interference already. The NFO claimed Butz's opposition was in line with his "consistent defense of big agribusiness corporations."

Iowa Beef is setting up such a custom-feeding subsidiary, stating that "this subsidiary will be expected to stabilize and supplement the supply of raw materials needed by the parent corporation as a whole." IBP does point out that in addition to purchases from commercial feedlots or its own feedlots, cattle may be contracted on a joint-venture basis from farmer-feeders and cooperatives.

While several antitrust cases are pending against packers, supermarkets have also come in for criticism in meat-price fixing. Mayor Joseph Alioto of San Francisco, testifying on food-chain pricing activities before the Joint Economic Committee of the Congress in December 1974, said that at the turn of the century 5 packers controlled producer prices. Today, however, there are 2,000 packers; but instead of independent stores, there is now a tremendous concentration of chains, which puts pressure on producers' prices.

Alioto gave as an example A&P's buying meat for its stores on Tuesdays. The prices of these purchases get reported in the "yellow sheet," a daily trade market letter that most buyers read to learn about current prices. Winn-Dixie and Safeway read about A&P's purchases on Tuesday and use them as a guide in buying meat the next day. Alioto commented, "You don't have to be particularly intelligent to see that staggered buying is an effective means of stabilizing prices and literally setting the pace for all of the beef producers throughout the country."

In 1975, cattle feeders in California won a $32-million judgment in their favor against A&P when a jury found it had conspired with others to fix wholesale beef prices. Safeway made an out-of-court settlement with California cattlemen in a similar case.

In December 1975, five hundred cattle feeders in fifteen midwestern states charged ten large supermarket chains and two other defendants with violations of the Sherman Anti-Trust Act. The suit, which has yet to be tried, brought by a group called the Meat Price Investigators Association, charged that in 1973 the defendants—Safeway, A&P, Kroger, Winn-Dixie, American Stores, Food Fair, Grand Union, Lucky, Supermarkets General Corporation, the National Association of Food Chains, and the National Provisioner (publisher of the "yellow sheet," which gives daily meat prices)—conspired to pay low cattle prices to farmers and to charge high prices to consumers. The suit was directed at the supermarkets because the plaintiffs felt that the supermarkets were putting a squeeze on the packers, and this squeeze resulted, in turn, in lower prices to cattlemen.

The lawsuit alleged that the defendants fixed prices at artificially low levels, charged noncompetitive and artifically high prices for beef, cut up the market geographically among themselves, and eliminated price competition among themselves by employing the "yellow sheet" as a device to communicate the price paid in different parts of the country.

In a detailed story the *Wall Street Journal* did on the "yellow sheet" in 1974, the business daily's reporter found out that no one questioned the "sheet's" integrity or its desire to quote prices accurately. However, the *Journal*'s investigation did find instances in which buyers tried to jimmy the market, unknown to the "sheet's" reporters. One Chicago meat broker said, "They've got a hell of a lot of people lying to them." And these lies help determine the prices we pay for our meat.

To try to give an alternative picture of the market, the USDA had "beefed up" its meat-reporting service. The power of the "yellow sheet" remains intact, however, as the Department of Defense (the country's fourth-largest meat buyer) and other agencies buy "at the sheet."

Some industry spokesmen want the licenses of people giving false market information revoked, but others feel that this is unrealistic. After all, they point out, it's the same story as a stockbroker's trying to get rid of his stock before the public finds out it's going down.

Paying the Bill

While certain segments of the food-marketing chain are picked out for scrutiny from time to time as being too large and wasteful of our gastronomic dollars, supermarkets—or, more properly, food retailers—receive the bulk of the investigations. Much of the responsibility for the rise in food prices by 37 percent in the period from January 1973 to July 1975 is placed on supermarkets, for it is in their aisles that we come face-to-face with food prices. My neighbor was less restrained. "We get ambushed in the aisles." And, of course, the aisles are the last stop before the kitchen for Dale Yahnke's corn and soybeans and Lester Wolverton's and Gordon MacClean's wheat.

Food retailing in America has come full circle. When the first settlers came, the general-store concept was begun. One merchant would handle everything from meat to grains to vegetables. General stores and then corner groceries sprang up everywhere. As communities grew in numbers and in buying power, specialized food retailers sprang up as well: the butcher-baker-candlestick-maker syndrome. But the automobile and the high cost of labor speeded the development of the self-service general store: our supermarket. Like a general store, it had everything, including something the little store didn't have: volume. Charm was too expensive to keep, except maybe in places like Gilbey, North Dakota, where you can still find a general store.

There is volume in food retailing, as Americans spend around $125 billion at the 250,000 retail food stores, of which 42,000 could be called supermarkets. A good supermarket could account for $4 to $5 million in annual sales. Nationally, the top twenty chains generate about 40 percent of all sales, but in given communities the concentration of sales by four of these supermarket chains is much larger. In Washington, D.C., Seattle, Portland, and Denver, for example, over 70 percent of the food retailed is sold by four chains.

The corner grocery faded as people moved away from the central city and as supermarkets could offer lower prices. Mom and Pop faded from American food retailing. Depending on whom you listen to, we are now either wrapped up in another of the omnivores' high-cost tentacles or enjoying the "most efficient food retailing system the world has ever known," as one enthusiastic supermarket executive termed it.

Supermarkets are a forum for sales, packing in as many as 10,000 items in the hope that consumers will buy them. The vendors who sell their goods compete fiercely for shelf space. The Poultry and Egg Institute complained recently that advertising pressure exerted on the consumer has forced the food retailer to give fourteen times more shelf exposure to cereals than to eggs. The institute, in an analysis of "facings" in Kansas City, found that cereals were given 420 linear feet, compared with only 30 linear feet for eggs. The battle goes on in other items as well.

Supplier pressure to move goods has brought on allegations of bribery and kickbacks in the supermarket industry. It also gives the supermarket a tremendous amount of leverage with suppliers who try to outbid each other for shelf space.

In October 1975, A&P was charged by the FTC with unfair price cutting for milk and dairy products sold in its stores. In the course of its investigation, the FTC alleged that A&P had falsely told Borden that another Chicago dairy had offered it lower prices to supply its two hundred Chicago-area stores with milk and milk products. Borden wanted to keep the business, so it came back with an even lower price.

The FTC judge ruled that because of this deal A&P was able to offer Borden products at a lower price under its own label than competing stores could offer Borden products. This practice was "anti-competitive and discriminatory" and thereby a violation of the Clayton Anti-Trust Act, the judge ruled.

One of the increasingly popular items sold is not food, but time. Supermarkets are stocking more and more convenience foods, which are expensive, draw complaints from consumers, and whose prices have little relation to raw agricultural prices. The USDA found, in November 1975, that only 36 percent of the convenience foods studied (for example, frozen dinners, cake mixes) had a cost-per-serving advantage over their home-prepared or fresh counterparts. Reflecting this trend, the USDA found, 80 percent of the "new-generation" convenience foods were more expensive than if they were prepared from basic ingredients.

To get customers in to look at (and buy) their wares, super-markets engage in expensive, non-price-competitive practices, such as trading stamps, parking lots, fancy interiors, carry-out and check-cashing services, music, and carpeted aisles, to mention only a few. It came as no surprise when members of Senator William Proxmire's staff compared Safeway and A&P prices in the Kansas City area in October 1974 and found that of 3,959 items checked, Safeway and A&P had identical prices on 2,969, or over 70 percent.

Hubert Humphrey, in addressing William Mitchell, president of Safeway Stores, on this point, commented, "When you and A&P compete, you come down the skids together, like two skiers coming down the slopes—just like twins. You come down there and your prices hang together." Safeway and A&P are the two largest food retailers in the United States.

Mitchell, however, disagreed with Humphrey's assessment by pointing out that Safeway is only one among 250,000 food retailers, and the industry as a whole earns less than 1 percent on sales. Mitchell added, "From the profile presented by the industry, it should be self-evident that strong, effective, anti-inflationary competition is the name of the game in food retailing.

Many doubt that statement. During Mayor Alioto's testimony before the Joint Economic Committee, he pointed out that from February to July 1974, cattle prices declined, yet only in July was any price decline noted in the supermarket. Alioto added that "the economic behavior in this industry cannot be explained by supply and demand and collusion is one of the options that explains it." Ann Brown, chairman of the Consumer Affairs Committee of the Americans for Democratic Action, agreed in noting before the Joint Economic Committee that on Thanksgiving Day, 1974, the four Washington, D.C., chains all charged 55 cents a pound for turkey.

The FTC has been watching food retailers for a number of years. For example, from 1941 to 1955, Safeway was convicted of six criminal violations of the Sherman Anti-Trust Act.

The FTC expects to find out more about the pricing policies of the chains in a study it is conducting on food-marketing and competitive practices in Jersey City, Little Rock, Washington, D.C., Detroit, Atlanta, and Denver. The FTC requested corporate data from twenty-five firms, but Safeway, Giant, and Winn-Dixie refused to hand it over. In December 1975, a Federal judge ruled that the chains must supply all the requested information.

The FTC had earlier made the statement that if the chains were broken up, "at least $1.25 billion could be saved by consumers." The FTC made this claim after receiving some of the supermarket-profit data, which showed, for example, that Safeway boosted its profits by 51 percent during the first nine months of 1974, compared to the same period in 1973. In the same period, Kroger had an increase of 94 percent.

However, one industry analyst discovered the interesting fact that the net profits of all food chains amounted to $700 million, so if you saved $1.25 billion by breaking up the chains, all the supermarkets would have to go out of business.

Supermarkets realize that they are in for it and have been trying to cut their costs before the FTC cuts them up, as some industry executives fear. One place they have begun to carve is in labor, where an industry survey found that sales per man-hour showed lower results in 1974 than in 1968.

Another area where some supermarkets are looking to cut costs is that of the route salesman. This is the fellow in the little panel truck who delivers bread, cakes, or snacks to supermarkets on a daily basis. For this effort, the route salesman gets a commission on what he "delivers," but the concept of "deliver" has taken on a new and more expensive meaning. Some supermarkets have such a large volume that a tractor-trailer delivers the merchandise; however, even though the route salesman has had nothing to do with this large shipment straight from the bakery, he stills collects his full commission. Retailers want to change this system, even though the baker pays it, because this cost ends up being part of the price of the baked goods.

The major innovation supermarkets are proposing to reduce costs—and about which they are facing consumer resistance—is the Universal Product Code (UPC). This is the little square with stripes and numbers you see on an increasing number of food packages. An electronic scanner reads the code, which describes the product and relates it to a price stored in a computer memory bank. The supermarket industry wants to eliminate stamping prices on each product in order to better control inventory, but consumers fear they will not be able to determine the prices of products or be sure they are being charged accurately.

Reflecting consumer concern are bills introduced by Senator Frank Moss (D-Utah) and Representative Benjamin Rosenthal (D-N.Y.), allowing the use of the UPC scanners for inventory purposes but requiring item-by-item pricing. Moss asks how, it you don't have item-by-item pricing, the consumer can compare prices between stores or with previous purchases. Some consumer groups feel that the UPC is just another attempt by the large supermarkets to victimize the food buyer.

Some supermarkets, however, are helping consumers to find the best buy, even though it means selling less of a high-margin item. Red Owl, a chain of 450 food stores in the upper Midwest, has instituted a "Price Guard" program to educate buyers as to what they are paying for. They encourage buying whole fryers and cutting them up yourself, and using your own sugar on cereal instead of buying the presweetened stuff. They point out that by putting on your own sugar, you save, since the cost is less than half the presweetened version.

Other supermarkets have tried less substantive programs, such as one Los Angeles market, which advertised it sold merchandise "at our low prices plus 10%." In November 1975, the California attorney general issued a complaint charging the chain with false advertising, stating that the term "our low prices" was misleading because it did not refer to a wholesale price but to a fictitious price that led shoppers to believe they were buying products at some special "wholesale" price.

The concern over prices has changed the supermarket industry in recent years, as trading stamps have been replaced by discount pricing. The next few years should also see a continued movement into what have been termed "hypermarkets," which combine a grocery supermarket with a department store—the general store rises again. Some feel such a combination will provide much of the growth that supermarket firms are looking for, without putting as much pressure on food prices.

The outcome of our involved marketing system and the controls exerted on it by large corporations and small farmers alike is reflected in the accompanying farm-retail spread. The continuing issue is going to be: Are these spreads between consumer and farmers justifiable? Maybe not justifiable, a supermarket executive confided to me, but inevitable.

FARM-RETAIL PRICE SPREADS IN 1975
FOR GRAIN-BASED FOODS

Food Item	Retail Price	Marketing Costs°	Farm Value	Farmer's Share of Retail Price (%)
Beef per lb.	$1.35	$.46	$.89	66
Pork per lb.	1.09	.38	.71	65
Broilers per lb.	.59	.24	.35	59
Eggs, grade A	.78	.24	.54	70
Milk per ½ gal.	.65	.31	.34	52
Butter per lb.	.91	.29	.62	68
Bread per lb.	.36	.30	.06	16
Rice per lb.	.47	.33	.14	29
Salad & cooking oil (24 oz.)	.71	.49	.22	30
Margarine per lb.	.62	.48	.14	22

Source: Adapted from several USDA sources.

°These include processing, transportation, wholesaling, and retailing.

9

OMNIVORE IN ACTION:
A CASE STUDY

How a lot of small, grain-based food industries became a few large industries is a fascinating, if not sad, process. While many people don't associate beer with grain, the fact remains that barley, rice, and corn are the essential ingredients in this well-known industry, which buys about five hundred million dollars worth of grain each year.

The changes that the beer industry has undergone in America parallel those in other grain-based industries: Small family operations grow into huge companies; the inefficient fall by the wayside; processes become more mechanized; packaging ends up costing more than the raw material; advertising grows in importance; and in the end only a few big firms are left. Conspiracy? Probably not—just capitalism at work.

Where Are You Now, Miss Rheingold?

In early 1975, a collectors' fair was held in Minneapolis, and some of the many items the collectors traded back and forth were beer cans. Now, that struck me as funny—there always seem to be plenty to pick up alongside the road without having to go to a fair. But close observation revealed that the cans traded back and forth bore such names as California Gold Label, Meister-Brau, Peoples, Rahr, Heurich, Monarch, and Ballantine. Also being traded were Miss Rheingold posters—Miss Rheingold was the famous symbol of New York's Rheingold beer when it was at its peak of popularity.

All the companies that brew those brands have gone out of

business, and although other brewers have picked up some of the brand names, the original cans are indeed collectors' items. In all probability, some of the four hundred existent brands will soon become collectors' items, too, for in the American brewing industry, although a greater volume of beer is being sold, fewer brewers are doing the selling.

In fact, from the time I drank my first beer in the darkened back seat of my friend's jalopy in 1959 until the present, perhaps four hundred brewers have gone out of business; in 1973, seventeen brewers left the scene. A sad 1974 departure was Jax beer, whose mild taste was a memento of my honeymoon in New Orleans. The departure was certainly sadder for Jax, for while my honeymoon memories date back only to 1967, Jax beer went back to 1890.

The president of Coors predicts that we will have only three brewers by 1990—and Coors will be one of them. The question now is: Can the sixty regional brewers survive? But surviving is not enough, states Fritz Maytag, president of San Francisco's Steam Beer Brewing Company, the nation's smallest brewery: "I don't see the real reason for small and regional breweries unless they produce something interesting." Beer connoisseurs contend that what black bread is to baking, and granola is to cereals, Steam Beer is to brewing.

The beer industry is undergoing the same consolidation that has occurred in baking, milling, supermarkets, lawnmowers, and just about everything else. Budweiser, Schlitz, and Pabst now dominate the industry, with about 50 percent of the total market; add three more brewers (Miller, Coors, and Falstaff), and you have six brewers accounting for two-thirds of all the beer sold in the United States.

That leaves about one-third of the market to the other sixty regional brewers. The size differentials are staggering: Nationally, Budweiser produces a thousand times more beer than Spoetzl brewery of Shiner, Texas, yet both compete for the same Texas drinkers. But among the regionals the urge to stay on has strengthened in the face of the increased competition and power of the majors. "We are rather sick of reading our obituaries almost daily," states F. X. Matt II of the West End Brewing Company in Utica, New York, brewers of Utica Club.

The regionals feel their chances are good, for beer demand continues to grow at around 4 percent a year, and they think they can get part of the increasing market. Americans, on the average, consume an annual 19.4 gallons per capita. As we would expect, freewheeling Nevada's per-capita consumption is tops, 30 gallons; and Mormon Utah's is at the bottom, 12 gallons. Regionals, however, realize that they, too, must keep up-to-date, keep their suds "tasty, not just automated," as one regional brewer put it, and at times get some help from the government to prevent questionable marketing practices and to enact tax legislation favorable to smaller brewers.

Several regional brewers claim that the majors have gotten where they are through illegal marketing methods. Accordingly, there are a number of lawsuits pending against the majors. In reference to the lawsuits, the majors feel the regionals' problems are due to their old techniques, and that these, not the majors' marketing strategies, are responsible for the growing concentration. One executive of a major was quoted as stating: "The regionals are going out of business on their own, they don't need our help."

America and Beer

The beer industry today, with its high-speed canning lines, slick advertising, and recycling problems, seems unrelated to the slower-paced, nostalgic past that most breweries emphasize with such devices as the slogan "Good Old-Time Flavor," the horse-drawn beer wagons, and the old, baroque labels that adorn cans and bottles. The turn of the century is the most highlighted period, but beer began in America long before that.

Discounting the fermented mash American Indians made for centuries before the arrival of the Europeans, the first beer in America was made in 1612 by Dutch settlers in New York. This first brewery was also famous as being the birthplace of the first white child born in New York, who, not surprisingly, was later to become a brewer. Twenty years later, in 1632, Peter Minuit established the first public brewery in America, on Whitehall Street. Public drinking was introduced with the opening of a tavern in 1643. Realizing the revenue potential of beer, the Dutch put an excise tax on it in 1644.

The Dutch left and the English came, but beer continued as a popular drink. During the Revolutionary era, James Madison, hoping to displace "ardent spirits" with a more moderate beverage, stated that "the brewing industry would strike deep root in every state in the Union."

Advocating beer became a temperate, if not patriotic, act. In

1792, New Hampshire passed an act to encourage brewing, stating: "The manufacture of malt liquors in this state will tend to promote agriculture, diminish use of ardent spirits and preserve the morals and health of the people." This sentiment is still apparent; witness the Olympia Brewing Company's stationery, which carried the statement: "Beer . . . a light refreshment beverage of millions of temperate people."

With the consolidation of the colonies, larger and larger breweries began to go up. What was eventually to become the Ballantine Brewery began in 1805. Lager beer was introduced to America in 1840 by John Wagner, operating a small brewery in Philadelphia. From this time on, the more familiar names in brewing come into the picture: F & M Schaefer in 1842, Pabst in 1844, and Miller in 1855. Less well-known, but still operating, smaller breweries also began in this period: Jacob Leinenkugel began to make his regional Chippewa Falls brew in 1867: Oregon's best-selling beer, Blitz-Weinhard, was first brewed in Portland in 1866; and Stroh's of Detroit began its "fire-brewed" beer in 1850.

The revolutions of 1848 in Europe were the catalyst that sent a whole new wave of settlers—including German brewers—to America. By 1850, there were 430 breweries in America, compared to 140 in 1795; in 1860, there were 1,270 breweries in existence throughout the country. German was the recognized language of the trade; H. L. Mencken in his study of the American language points out that not only did the Germans give us beer, but they left us its vocabulary as well: biergarten, lager beer, bock beer, not to mention Oktoberfest.

In order to help finance the American Civil War, a revenue law passed in 1862 placed a $1-per-barrel tax on beer. This prompted the brewers in the United States to join together to resist the measure, and the United Brewers' Association was formed. The association contended the tax was unwise because "to a large element of the population malt liquors partook of the nature of a nutriment, or 'liquid bread,' and constituted a necessity of life."

In 1864, the association formed a "permanent agitation committee" to further the goals of the brewing industry. A variant of this committee must still be around, for the actions that the Brewers' Association took in fighting Vermont's new antilitter legislation led Vermont's governor, Thomas P. Salmon, to state: "The Brewers' Association and the other big guns in the industry are sending their troops to beat little Vermont into the bulrushes."

Although the creation of this association represented the nationwide interests of brewers, it was not altogether a "national" organization: English became an official language of the association only at its twelfth convention, in 1872—and then was used only in alternate years. Beer associations have since become more American; the secretary of the first association was named Johann Katzenmayer, while the present executive secretary of the Brewers' Association of America is one Bill O'Shea.

It was at that twelfth convention in 1872 that the president of the association eloquently, if not immodestly, reviewed the importance of beer. "What effect has the introduction of beer had on mankind? The continued spread and use of beer has gradually changed the habits and mode of living of people in the minds of most rational men so that wherever this drink has been introduced and adopted, the social condition of the people has become more animated, improved and pleasant."

The last three decades of the nineteenth century brought new technology to the industry and witnessed the demise of the backyard brewery. Brewers began to get process-oriented. The final step in modernization was probably Louis Pasteur's *Études sur la Bière*. Published in 1876, it revealed the mystery of fermentation in yeast and how it could be controlled in the brewery. The first brewery school was opened in 1888, and big brewers brought innovations to the industry. Ironically, Pabst Beer, which in its present-day advertising likes to hark back to the good old days and old-fashioned methods, was probably the most advanced brewer of its day. A 1903 brewery trade publication described the Pabst brewery as "one of the largest and most complete establishments in the country . . . laboratories for analyses, experiments . . . are other features of the establishment which is virtually a varied industry community centering in one special industry."

The same publication credited Adolphus Busch with ensuring the success of Budweiser by "inaugurating the system of push and enterprise which has since characterized its management."

By 1900, there were 1,760 breweries in existence, but some consolidation had occurred, as this number was down from 2,200 in 1880. Even though improved production and management techniques produced more beer more cheaply, the Prohibition steamroller brought the industry to a halt. Many brewers never came out of it; others, such as Coors, survived by making malted milk or ice and "near beer." There were only 756 brewers left in 1934.

The modern marketing era of the beer industry probably began in 1939, when Jinx Falkenberg became the first of many "Miss Rheingolds." Something other than the intrinsic taste and qualities of beer began to be advertised; image became important, if not paramount.

Bigger Brews Yet

In spite of, or more probably because of, their already commanding position, the majors are intensifying their capital expenditures, packaging, and advertising budgets to gain an even larger share of the beer market. Sales of the big three brewers have grown at a rate of 12 percent a year for the past ten years, and with overall demand growing at 4 percent, it is obvious that part of these advances have come out of the brew kettles of regional brewers.

Miller and Schlitz plan to build huge new breweries within fifty miles of each other in New York State, while Budweiser is planning a new facility in Fairfield, California, outside San Francisco. Pabst's new facility in Pabst, Georgia, went full brew by the end of 1974. Each of the breweries can produce at least two million barrels of beer annually, and at an investment cost of $40 to $60 per barrel, the amounts involved are significant.

Miller—owned by Phillip Morris—has set up a $200-million investment program for the next five years. What makes the staying power of the big brewers more impressive is that Miller is expanding even though it lost $2.4 million in 1973. Anheuser-Busch has stated it will spend $600 million in expansion over the next three years.

The automation of the new breweries is overwhelming. A canning line at a Schlitz plant can put out 1,800 cans per minute. Automation has cut back on labor requirements, as well. Schlitz likes to point out that in their old Milwaukee brewhouse they need twenty-four men per shift, compared to two men per shift at their new Winston-Salem plant. One reason that Rheingold had such a hard time in New York was that beer from such modern out-of-state plants as Schlitz's cost less to produce than New York–brewed beer.

To further enhance their position, the big brewers are becoming self-sufficient. Coors builds 75 percent of its packaging equipment and 90 percent of its brewing equipment. Schlitz is to build three new can plants costing more than $100 million, with Milller building a $16-million can plant in Milwaukee. This emphasis on packaging is highlighted by the fact that 87 percent of the beer consumed in 1973 was packaged, compared to only 25 percent in 1934, when draft beer and the local tavern predominated. Packaging is important as a marketing tool; the old but reassuring brown smoke bottles with the label you scraped off with your fingernails and returned are disappearing, replaced by aluminum cans that are thrown away.

The big brewers are also integrating themselves more directly into the grain picture. Breweries are now beginning to contract grain to be supplied directly. This has been the case with Colorado farmers for several years, as Coors has made growing contracts for grain. But a decline in beer demand led Coors to back out of some contracts in early 1976, according to trade sources. Barley farmers were able to sell the barley for livestock feed, but for less than they would have gotten for beer.

Anheuser-Busch is contemplating similar direct contracts with grain growers once its planned $20-million malting plant gets underway in Moorhead, Minnesota. These steps worry some barley growers, who watch as fewer, yet stronger, buyers come looking for their grain.

To match these steps in becoming self-sufficient in brick and mortar, the majors spend millions on advertising. Anheuser-Busch spent around $20 million on advertising expenditures in 1973; it spent $12 million on television alone, compared to $1.5 million for Rheingold. Schlitz spent about the same as Bud overall, but put a total of $15 million into television.

The message we get from the advertising is not what the brew tastes like, but, usually, what it does for your self-image. According to the television commercial you watch, immediately before, after, or sometimes during drinking a major brand of beer, you: ride a camel, sail a boat, drive a motorcycle, or are magically transferred to the crime- and inflation-free Gay Nineties.

This self-image advertising approach became somewhat of a necessity for the national brands. Because they were brewing and selling beer in many locations, they could no longer emphasize any regional aspect of their brew, such as the use of local raw ingredients—for example, the water of a given area.

Today, few of the national brands comment on their ingredients except to say that they are of good quality. Water is not usually mentioned, for this still remains the province of the regionals, who use it to the utmost. Some effervescent examples are: Olympia, "It's the Water"; Grain Belt, "The Wonderful Water of Diamond Wells"; Coors, the largest and most successful regional, "Brewed with Pure Rocky Mountain Spring Water"; and not to be outdone by anyone, Leinenkugel of Chippewa Falls, Wisconsin, "Brewed with the Purest Spring Water in the World."

Keeping Pace

In view of the capital expenditures by the large brewers, the regionals recognize the challenge facing them, and through a combination of modernizing and expanding their operations, developing regionally based advertising, making better-tasting beer, and using court action, they are determined to stay in business.

Lee Birdsong, president of Pearl Beer of Texas, points out that "regional brewers can survive in our industry today, providing they modernize their older, more labor-intensive plants in order to stay competitive." And Anchor Steam became the last U.S. brewer to bottle beer; up to three years ago it produced only draft, but began bottling to keep pace.

The modernization of plants and expansion of markets are being used by the more aggressive regionals as a way to break into the major brands' market. The results of these efforts are mixed and lend credence to the statement that the regionals don't need the help of the majors to go out of business.

Rheingold was a very successful eastern brewer with most of the New York City market when it decided to go national and expand to the West Coast. In 1953 it bought two breweries on the West Coast, and four years later had to start selling them off. Rheingold's mistakes in the West became part of a how-not-to-do-it marketing book entitled *Mismarketing*. Then, after taking its lumps out West, Rheingold began to have troubles at home. A New York friend of mine felt Rheingold's greatest mistake came in dethroning Miss Rheingold in 1962. After her departure, Rheingold had to establish a new identity, which its most recent owners, Pepsi-Cola and Chock Full O'Nuts, have not been able to do.

But Miss Rheingold was not necessarily the only good image going. Consider the Theodore Hamm Company of St. Paul, Minnesota, which, in addition to the catchy phrase "From the Land of

Sky Blue Waters," had a bear. The bear was a good choice, since Minnesota law prohibits women in beer advertising. The bear became quite a good sales tool for Hamm's until Heublein—a leisure-food conglomerate—bought the company. When the acquisition occurred, the bear was caged in Heublein's ill-fated effort to make Hamm's a national beer. Then, when Heublein later resold Hamm's back to its distributors, incurring losses of several millions, the bear was again allowed to prowl Minnesota billboards.

Where Rheingold and Hamm's failed, and almost bankrupted themselves in their attempts to expand to new markets, other regionals have had success. Coors is the best-known example, in that from its one brewery in Golden, Colorado, it has become the best-selling beer in ten of the eleven western and southwestern states in which it is distributed. And Washington's Olympia successfully entered the midwestern market and subsequently bought Hamm's.

A lesser-known, but nevertheless successful, expansion program is that of the National Brewing Company of Baltimore, probably better known as the brewers of Colt 45 Malt Liquor. National, which ranks fifteenth nationwide in beer sales, dispels the stereotyped image of regionals' being "too set in their ways." Introduced eleven years ago, Colt 45 is the world's leading malt liquor and is sold in all fifty states. And on a recent trip to Panama, one traveler noticed a Tocumen Airport vending machine neatly dispensing Colt 45 alongside two others for soft drinks and milk. Under terms of an agreement with the fourth-largest brewer in England, Colt 45 will be produced and marketed in that country. Beyond this, Milwaukee brewing purists probably shudder at National's two new beer products: Malt Duck and Apple Malt Duck. The significance of Colt 45's success is highlighted by the fact that Budweiser's own malt liquor entry was somewhat less than successful.

Although expansion into new areas and new products has undoubtedly helped some regionals prosper, a greater marketing tool has been their advertising. Their emphasis on their use of local ingredients is but one tool. If Budweiser goes out and proclaims itself the "King of Beers," some of the smaller breweries make a point—and sales—by being the pawns.

Schell's Beer of New Ulm, Minnesota, has one of the best campaigns playing on a lack of size. Example from a radio spot: "Schell's is number one in New Ulm. I mean Schell's is so big in New Ulm, we built a brewery there. Think about that, willya?" Another well-received campaign involved Schell's "Really Big Prize Sweep-stakes," which consisted of "a deluxe all-expense-paid trip for two to exciting New Ulm (population 13,051) for a night." The trip involved a round trip by Greyhound bus to New Ulm, a room with a bath at the Grand Hotel, a visit to the statue of Herman the Great, and a ten-course dinner (salad, two bratwurst, potatoes, and Schell's beer). This approach has attracted many younger drinkers to Schell's fold, for they want to identify with something small. A similar program has worked for the Spoetzl Brewery of Shiner, Texas. Their sales manager feels "the role of the underdog has been a mainstay for our brewery . . . the average person is fascinated with the operation and wants to be part of it. Call it togetherness."

What the somewhat larger regional brewers bring out in their advertising is not so much their relative size as the fact that they are part of the region. Rainier Brewing Company of Seattle gears its advertising to the life-style of the Pacific Northwest; Grain Belt of Minneapolis points out that "The Best Things in Life . . . Are Here"; and Anchor Steam prides itself on being part of the tradition of San Francisco.

But expansion and catchy local advertising aside, the regional brewer will tell you that it is the individual taste of his beer that keeps his suds in front of, and inside, the drinker. F. X. Matt, brewer of Utica Club, emphasizes, "I could write a book on what I feel the appeal of our beer is." However, some critics of American beer have been hard-pressed to write a complimentary paragraph.

They claim that it has gotten to be blander, particularly among major brands, so as not to offend anyone—a complaint similar to that leveled at American television. These brewing gurus have stated that the blandness has come about partly due to the fact that U.S. beer makers use only one-fourth the hops—the ingredient that gives beer its bitter taste—that European brewers use. But, queries *Modern Brewery Age*—the industry's trade journal—if the European version is superior, why is only less than 1 percent of the beer consumed in America imported?

Regional brewers say their beer is tastier than the nationals' for the reason that, since they aim at a certain market, they don't have to go bland to appease everyone. Matt of Utica Club says that "modern beers have pushed 'lightness' to the point where they are what we call 'empty.' It's fine to make a light beer . . . but it must have character."

Not awed by the monied clout of the majors, Leinenkugel's president relies on his beer's flavor to get him through. "Instead of putting our dollar in advertising, we put it in the bottle." Fritz Maytag is even stronger in his opinion of the lack of taste in most beers today. "To many brewers the product they make is money, not beer."

Recently, several newspapers and national magazines have had stories on beer tasting. In the reports I have seen, expert drinkers had difficulty distinguishing any particular beer from any other. Since I always shy away from experts, I invited some of my more beer-bellied friends over for a beer tasting one Saturday night.

Over the objections of the liquor store owner that we were breaking up six-packs, we bought four imported, six regional, and four major brands, two boxes of Saltines to "cleanse the palate" between sips, and set to tasting. The imported brands were clearly discernible, but trying to figure out the regionals from the majors proved a little more difficult; in fact, my palate was right only 40 percent of the time in determining one domestic brew from another. My friends had an equally poor percentage. I don't think our test will clear up the taste issue.

Taste is dwarfed as an issue by the legal sparring going on between the regional and national brewers. The most burning issue is that of the national brands' pricing policies. Jerry Hoffberger, president of National Brewing, is quite upset at their tactics. "With their tremendous economic power, these brewers can enter a market, promote their product with 'price-offs' until they have killed the local competition, after which their prices return to normal."

To this argument, the national breweries state that their plants are more efficient, enabling lower prices. Not so, states our Mr. Matt of Utica Club. In a letter to the Federal Trade Commission, Matt conceded that "if Schlitz and Budweiser can honestly produce beer more economically than we or other brewers can, there is no reason why we should be allowed to stay in business." However, Matt's figures show that this is not the case.

Echoing Hoffberger's contention, Matt feels that the majors sell their beer at a lower price in New York to undercut competition, while their products sell at higher prices in New England, where they already have most of the market. Matt feels that the consumer is getting a bad deal on this and that the FTC should require the nationals to charge no more in areas of "shared monopoly" than they do in their lowest-price areas. Other ways that Matt feels the nationals infringe on fair competition include their special discounts and total control of distributors—that is, the brewery and not the distributor sets the price.

In a recent decision in this regard, the FTC ruled in 1973 that Adolph Coors—the nation's fourth-largest brewer—had engaged in a policy of fixing and maintaining prices at both the wholesale and retail levels, had used illegal methods to cajole draft-beer accounts to carry Coors exclusively, and had imposed illegal territorial requirements on its distributors. A Federal Appeals Court upheld the decision in 1974. Coors still maintains, however, that its actions were justified because of the perishable nature of its beer, which, unlike other beers, deteriorates when not refrigerated.

The FTC investigated illegal practices in New York State during open hearings held in August 1975 in Syracuse on the topic "How have the marketing practices of the large brewers affected the national and local brewers?" The results of that meeting have yet to be disclosed.

Regional brewers point out that the New York situation is not an isolated case. Pearl Beer of San Antonio, Texas, has a suit pending against Budweiser and Schlitz for violations of Federal anti-trust laws. In one portion of the suit, Pearl had asked the court to impose an injunction against what it claimed were illegal price cuts. In a written ruling, the judge refused to overturn the price cuts but went on to state that the two leading brewers seem to have "tampered with and consequently restricted" their wholesalers' pricing policies in a possible violation of anti-trust laws. Both Budweiser and Schlitz have denied the charges in this case, which will be tried soon.

In a Midwest lawsuit that was settled in late 1975, Grain Belt Breweries of Minneapolis contended that Budweiser and Schlitz used illegal pricing methods to force it to close its Omaha brewery in 1972. Budweiser and Schlitz were ordered to pay substantial damages to Grain Belt as a result of the ruling.

The regionals had hoped that one of these cases would be ruled in their favor. One Eastern regional brewer is so incensed at the action of the majors that he suggested I entitle this section "Bigness Is Not Greatness." While some regional brewers have claimed inaction on the part of the government in redressing some of the above grievances—one regional brewer in New York even offered to hire and pay an investigator to work for the FTC—they have also criticized the government for too vigorous activity in other areas.

In the antitrust area, the Justice Department has held a tight rein on brewers that want to buy other brewers. In 1963, the Justice Department ruled that Budweiser could not acquire Miami's Regal Brewing Company, and this, to a large extent, discouraged brewers from trying to acquire existing plants. In a more recent case, a U.S. District Court in 1971 required the Pabst Brewing Company—the number-three brewer—to divest itself of the Milwaukee Blatz brewery. These decisions have meant that for a brewer to expand, it must build new facilities.

Most regional brewers feel that this policy is the correct one to apply against the majors; the problem, the regionals contend, is that the Justice Department applies it against them also, and they don't have the cash to build new plants. Edwin Coombs, president of Seattle's Rainier Brewery, contends that one of the reasons for the steep decline in the number of regional brewers has been precisely this policy, which has prevented mergers and acquisitions among smaller and medium-size brewers, which might have made possible more vigorous competition with the giants. A recent example of this was the attempt by Grain Belt Breweries to purchase the Theodore Hamm Company in 1972; "No go," said the Justice Department, since Grain Belt is already the leading brewer in Minnesota. Nationally, however, Grain Belt ranks only twentieth in dollar sales. These types of rulings, Coombs contends, make for a "short-sighted and harmful policy."

August Busch III, president of Anheuser-Busch, contends that the FTC ruling turned out to be a blessing of sorts for his brewery. Commenting on the need to expand via new breweries, Busch stated: "That new production is a helluva lot more efficient than what would have been bought." He therefore feels Bud was helped.

To help bring specific legislative needs before lawmakers, the regional brewers have their own trade association, the Brewers' Association of America; the other trade association is the United States Brewers' Association, to which both the majors and regionals belong. The regionals' association constitution states that one of the purposes is to "take such steps as may be necessary to preserve the Small and Regional brewers of the American Brewing Industry." While the executive secretary of the Brewers' Association of America, William O'Shea, is reputed to be a hard worker and a staunch advocate of the regional brewer, he did sum up the difficulties facing regional brewers by predicting in a magazine article in 1973 that by 1980 only a dozen brewers would be left in the United States.

One of the association's main programs at present is to gain excise-tax relief for small brewers. Several states have already enacted relief, but no Federal help has come as yet. Representative D. D. Rostenkowski (D-Chicago) has introduced a bill in the House to lower the Federal excise tax per barrel of beer to $7 for the first 60,000 barrels for brewers who produce no more than 2 million barrels of beer. This bill would affect about forty-four brewers out of the five dozen regionals left today. The majors would continue paying $9 a barrel. The majors have gone on record in support of this legislation, for even more scrutiny would probably be brought on their operations if these forty-four brewers went out of business.

One piece of legislation that both regionals and majors are vigorously fighting, even though it would yield benefits to the smaller brewers, is a requirement to "ban the can." Most brewers feel that the mandatory use of returnable containers is discriminatory and anti–freedom of choice. The trend toward nonreturnables has been significant; in 1958, 42 percent of beer containers were nonreturnable, and if this trend continues, 80 percent will be disposable by 1980.

Gerald Meyer, president of Grain Belt Breweries of Minneapolis, contends that the reintroduction of returnables would affect the majors considerably more than the regionals in that they would have to transport used bottles longer distances than local brewers. In effect, national brewers would have to overhaul a one-way distribution system.

Outlook

In all likelihood there will be an even greater concentration of power among the larger brewers. We are not alone in this phenomenon, however, for in Britain the number of brewers has fallen from 840 to 163 in the last thirty years; one analyst predicts that there might be only fourteen brewers left by 1980. Do these parallel trends mean that we will be faced with perhaps a few multinational brewers in a few years?

Grain Belt's president was not so pessimistic. Additional brewers will go out of business, he said, "but I would guess that at least twenty-five or thirty breweries will survive and be prospering nicely within the next ten years." He gave me this statement in September 1974; in February 1976, Grain Belt closed its doors forever.

One ardent Leinenkugel drinker in rural Wisconsin summed up the feelings of many regional brewery aficionados by stating, "If Leinenkugel goes, it won't be merely the brewing industry that has been diminished. It will be all of us."

10

YOU CAN DEPEND ON U.S.—OR CAN YOU?

While the major food issue in the United States is how to bring grain prices down, in other areas of the world the issue is how to get enough food—period. The United States has always had more than enough food and has been, until recently, a dependable donor or seller of food. Everyone looked to the United States, which produces 25 percent of the world's grain and contributes more than 40 percent of the grain moving in international trade. In recent years, things have changed, as food exports incited consumer fears of more inflation and diplomats began to use food as a political weapon.

Food for Peace and Other Reasons

In the early 1950s, after the Korean War, and with World War II a poignant, but nevertheless fading, memory, American farmers turned their full attention to producing grain. They did such a good job that something had to be done with the surplus. Accordingly, Public Law 480 came into existence in July 1954 to provide a humanitarian means of disposing of our surplus. PL 480 enables poorer countries to buy U.S. surplus commodities on easy credit terms, in most instances paying with their own currencies. The local-currency payment came under Title I of the program, with other titles relating to credit sales for dollars, and outright relief, such as the food supplies that went to the drought-ravaged Sahel, the southern margin of the Sahara, in 1974.

From 1955 to 1973, $22.3 billion in agricultural exports were sold under the PL 480 program, which represented about 20 percent of agricultural exports during that period. India was by far the largest recipient, getting $5 billion worth of commodities, mostly wheat. The U.S. was mostly alone in this food-on-credit effort; in 1972, for example, the U.S. provided 75 percent of all bilateral and multi-lateral food aid. The United States got a lot of kudos for the program, but it was not pure altruism.

Food for Peace got rid of surpluses but also developed markets for hardcash sales, thereby expanding trade and helping to drive out competition. Far from being a program that involved only idealistic bureaucrats, it also served some political ends. One Washington journalist felt the "food aid business in Washington spawns intrigues, rivalries, and a cast of characters which sometimes seems to be drawn from an Agatha Christie mystery novel."

A lot of U.S. companies wanted a piece of the action, which in 1964 reached $1.6 billion, the highest yearly total in the program's history. Shipping executives, grain companies, and foreign diplomats all ran around Washington trying to get the most out of the program, which in 1973 was extended to December 31, 1977.

After the food had been shipped overseas and the United States had been paid in rupees, bahts, or lempiras—"funny money," it was derisively called—some use had to be found for all this "soft" currency. In India, the Peace Corps was run on all those millions of rupees we had. Elsewhere, American business found good uses for these monies also, so much so that Ronald Muller, co-author of *Global Reach*, an exposé of multinationals, cites some aspects of PL 480 and corporate interlock as "instances in which private and public interests are almost indistinguishable."

Monies from PL 480 sales were lent to Cargill and Ralston Purina to develop their feed business in South Korea. According to a Ralston Purina spokesman, "We wouldn't put capital into that market without this arrangement. . . ." Dan Morgan, a food writer for the *Washington Post*, has called PL 480 a "come on" for later cash deals.

South Korea, which, after India, has received the most PL 480 foods, has changed her tastes and diet considerably as a result. More protein is now used, as is wheat. According to Clayton K. Yeutter, former Assistant Secretary of Agriculture, PL 480 turned Korea from a "zero" market for U.S. farm products to a market worth $700 million annually. South Korea, which twenty years ago had but a handful of bakeries, now has 7,000, as bread has supplanted rice to a great extent. Yugoslavia, Brazil, Taiwan, and Japan have also gone from heavy dependence on food aid to being all-cash customers.

In addition to building new markets for U.S. farm products, PL 480 helped to eliminate competition. The United States won Iran's vegetable oil market from the Russians through Food for Peace in 1968–69. The first sales were on credit, and then cash was required. The same thing occurred in replacing the Australians in Iran's wheat business. Many claim that the zoom in U.S. agricultural exports from $2.3 billion in 1955 to $21 billion in 1974 is linked to the market-development efforts of Food for Peace.

Since the United States was a steady and low-cost supplier, many countries slackened their own agricultural-development efforts. One University of Montreal scholar felt that even though PL 480 was "on balance positive," agricultural production had fallen off in Colombia, Pakistan, Indonesia, and South Korea because of it. I remember when I was working in a Peace Corps marketing program in the Sabana de Bogotá, an extremely fertile high-mountain plain, a farmer asked me if I could help market his wheat. He grew it with little assistance from the government and felt it was a good hedge against the fluctuating prices of the vegetables that predominated in the Sabana's agriculture. We went around to the buyers, but they all had American wheat and rejected us, saying, "It's better than yours." The farmer went back to vegetables the next year.

Sometime in the early 1970s, Food for Peace began to serve a useful political purpose as well. Vietnam and Cambodia began to receive American rice as our involvement there grew and their agriculture declined. Many called it "Food for War."

In Chile, Salvador Allende wanted to establish a Socialist state, which American companies like ITT wanted to stop. Columnist Jack Anderson discovered and published the fact that ITT was willing to contribute "up to seven figures" to stop Allende. Food for Peace money began to dry up for Chile; in 1972, credit sales came to only $3.1 million, but the year after Allende's fall, credit sales had risen to $41 million. Chile was severely hurt by this situation. During the last year of Allende's rule, a friend of mine, Lorin Parks, was an agricultural economist with the Ford Foundation in Santiago. He recalls that a black marketeer once came to his door offering *one* potato hidden in his coat.

Pakistan's food-credit line went up when it served as an

intermediary in Nixon's China breakthrough, while Egypt, Syria, and Jordan were granted $50 million in food-buying credits by Secretary of State Henry Kissinger while he was trying to solve the Middle East crisis. Food for Peace was also used as leverage to get South Korea to cut its textile exports to the United States. The administration let it be known that South Korea would have a more difficult time in obtaining PL 480 credits if it did not voluntarily cut its textile exports. A domestic food program, food stamps, helps keep Puerto Rico in the U.S. fold; Puerto Rico now ranks with California, New York, and Texas as the biggest user of food stamps, as 60 percent of the island's three million residents qualify.

Congress has not always been in agreement with using the Food for Peace program for political purposes. In December 1974, Congress passed a measure prohibiting the administration from using more than 30 percent of the Food for Peace funds for political objectives. Senator Dick Clark (D-Iowa) wants further limitations, as "the door is wide open for continuation of the flagrant political manipulation which has plagued the Food for Peace Program in the past."

Hubert Humphrey was particularly upset that during fiscal 1974 over 50 percent of the commodities shipped under the "soft-currency" provision of PL 480 went to Cambodia and Vietnam. And, Humphrey felt, if the 30 percent limitation on the political uses of food had not been enacted earlier, the administration would have shipped two-thirds of the PL 480 commodities to Southeast Asia, the Middle East, or to other countries, such as Chile, where the Department of State had made special foreign-policy commitments.

Humphrey also wanted more emphasis put on agricultural development by countries accepting PL 480 commodities. In several cases, countries have used the foreign exchange they saved to bolster their defenses.

In January 1975, during South Vietnam's last hours under the Thieu regime, Secretary of State Henry Kissinger proposed that South Vietnam be "reclassified under another PL 480 provision making it get 'humanitarian' assistance, thus obviating the 30% limit imposed on December 31, 1974." The Senate Foreign Relations Committee rejected the thought. Kissinger, however, beat back an attempt to have Egypt excluded because of its higher per-capita income, as its friendship was crucial to Kissinger's peace-making attempts in the Middle East.

Congress passed a bill, which was signed by President Ford in

December 1975, stipulating that Food for Peace go primarily to countries with per-capita incomes of less than $300 per year. However, allocations as to which of the poorer countries actually get the aid are made by high administration officials, dominated by a very political Kissinger. The bill calls for $3 billion in food and development aid through 1977.

The Food for Peace program underwent a tremendous change when the Soviets came a-shopping in 1972. Surplus stocks were wiped out. Food aid that had reached 18 million tons in 1965 was down to 6 million by 1975. And food-aid exports that were governed by our surplus situation now got caught up—along with commercial sales—in our own inflation.

Cutting the Pipeline

Despite Earl Butz's testimony to Senator Henry Jackson's committee (Permanent Subcommittee on Investigation of the Committee of Government Operations) in the summer of 1973 that the huge Russian wheat sales had little to do with rising food prices, few believed that. At the time, Butz stated, "The total effect of the price of wheat is centered almost altogether in bakery products, which have little to do with what Americans consider to be a high standard of living."

But soaring prices of soybean products finally forced Butz to declare an embargo on June 27, 1973, prohibiting further exports of soybean meal. The grain trade was shocked and confused; the embargo led to five hundred arbitrations of the Grain and Feed Trade Association (GAFTA), which is the main arbiter of international grain trading. Ministers of large importing countries of American foods met to discuss the implications. They were angry, since they were paying the consequences for the Russian purchases and they had been steady customers for years.

The administration took the action under the Export Administration Act of 1969, which was used then to stop the export of hides. The Russian sales seemed the catalyst to send food prices higher in an overheated economy. Senator Jackson pointed out, "There is such a thing as an inflationary psychology. When grain prices go up and flour prices go up and pork and beef prices go up, there is a tendency as we saw in 1972 for everything to go up."

Fear of a repetition of the 1972 sales came in 1974 when the

Russians came to buy corn. When the U.S. corn crop didn't look so good, Ford pressured Cook and Continental to cancel contracts of wheat and corn with the Soviets. Butz wanted the sales, as did farmers, but consumers had more votes. The Consumer Federation of America had earlier accused the government of furthering détente and the U.S. balance of trade at the expense of consumers.

Arthur Burns, chairman of the Federal Reserve System, also urged caution in making further grain sales to the Soviets before the Senate Agriculture Committee in the fall of 1975.

The chairman of the American Bakeries Company pointed out in a *Wall Street Journal* article that the Soviet grain sales "depleted U.S reserves, wheat prices rose, feed grains rose in sympathy, meat prices rose with feed grains, certain vegetable and fruit prices rose with wheat prices; high food prices brought on wage increases."

Hubert Humphrey was more direct, stating that he was going to watch Butz like a "suspected burglar" in the next few months to make sure that he didn't let the U.S. crop go to the Russians, jeopardizing U.S. consumers and humanitarian commitments.

By this time, Butz had had enough, and he lashed back at his critics. "Some people who don't know wheat from the chaff are drawing ridiculous conclusions about the effects of selling grain to Russia."

Although the prime reason for the 1973 embargo and 1974 cancellation of contracts to the Soviets was related to the U.S. domestic situation, the increasing use of commercial food sales as an instrument of foreign policy began to creep into discussions. Burns, in his Senate testimony of September 1975, had some reservations. "From a moral standpoint, I would not like to use foodstuffs as an instrument of foreign policy. And, yet, in the kind of world we live in, we are the granary of the world as things stand, and if the Arabs have a monopoly on oil, for every practical purpose, we have a monopoly on grain." Burns found himself, like others, "oscillating between human, political and nationalistic considerations." One legislator was more direct in stating, "We hold the world food mortgage and are in a position to foreclose."

Meanwhile, steady customers of U.S. foodstuffs didn't know if they were going to get the goods or not. Delegations from around the world began flowing into Washington seeking assurances. Even Mexico, our good neighbor to the south, sent a delegation in September 1974; they were reassured that the United States would continue to supply the $1 billion in U.S. foodstuffs Mexico imports every year.

The Japanese were the most concerned, as they have been by far the largest importers of U.S. foodstuffs, importing $3.1 billion worth in 1975. So dependent on imports is Japan that one cynical Japanese stated, "There is no longer such a thing as Japanese food, just Japanese cooking."

Fearing the direction the United States would take, the Japanese began buying foodstuffs, particularly soybeans, from Brazil. After the U.S. embargo in 1973, a Japanese trade mission visited Brazil and reportedly offered to buy the entire soybean crop of Rio Grande do Sul (where 60 percent of the soybeans are currently grown) for the next ten years. The embargo scare, not to mention the shortage mentality, led Brazil to expand her soybean production rapidly, reaching 11 million tons in 1975 (production had been only 4.5 million tons in 1972). Argentina got into the act, and its soybean industry representatives, along with those of Brazil, were invited to visit Japan in the fall of 1973.

Japan, at least, could buy ahead and store food; but what of such countries as Morocco and Tunisia, which can store only 3 percent and 18 percent, respectively, of their annual consumption, and which rely on U.S. foodstuffs? A further problem is that storage conditions in many developing countries are poor, as a University of California Food Task Force found. During 1962–64, the storage losses in India came to 5 million tons, or about 1 million tons more than the total food imports for that period. Recognizing this problem, Senator Robert Dole (R-Kans.) introduced a bill in 1975 to exempt foreign-owned reserves from export controls. Dole's bill would allow foreign countries to buy grain in advance and store it in the United States until they are ready to ship it. Pointing out that half the nation's 190 million tons of storage (more than the 1975 Russian grain crop) goes unused, Dole added, "If foreign interests could utilize this storage, it would enable this country to maintain its abundant storage capacity as well as retain a great many jobs for American workers."

Kissinger and Calories

While American foodstuffs had always been involved in our foreign policy, 1975 marked their entry into the diplomatic arena in grand style as another tool of the peripatetic Henry Kissinger.

Kissinger's own public entry into the world food picture came when he addressed the delegates to the November 1974 World Food Conference in Rome. Kissinger, however, played a significant role in the U.S. preparation for the conference, for it was his man, Edwin Martin, U.S. Coordinator of the World Food Conference, who coordinated the U.S. effort, even though Secretary of Agriculture Butz "headed" the U.S. delegation. Kissinger got more deeply involved in the food situation in response to criticism that the State Department did not pay enough attention to the foreign-policy ramifications of grain trading at the time of the 1972 Soviet grain sales. Thus, when the third moratorium or embargo was placed on export sales in the fall of 1975, it was the State Department, not the Agriculture Department, that was calling the shots, or so it seemed. The moratorium was called to evaluate the U.S. harvest and also as a tool to exact a long-term deal with the Soviets.

For a while, America's foreign food policy appeared to resemble the Abbott and Costello routine "Who's on first?" The Department of Agriculture would say "Export," while the State Department would say "Export—but not just yet."

As a result of this confusion, markets slumped to the point where one indignant Arkansas soybean farmer stated that the moratorium on sales to Russia and Poland—Poland became involved, as well—caused farmers in that state to lose $100 million.

The Poles became the innocent victims in these transactions, for on September 12 a USDA announcement read: "Poland gets priority to buy U.S. grain," yet two weeks later, Poland had to wait until after the United States and the Soviets had reached some sort of agreement. One U.S. official stated that the Polish embassy had sent diplomats to talk to Polish-American groups, warning them the administration was going to "starve their relatives in Poland this winter." Poland's need for U.S. grain served as an added impetus for the USSR to conclude the agreement.

Markets now became affected by diplomatic considerations and language. In response to a question asking whether exporters had been banned from making sales, a State Department official replied, "Exporters had not been asked to refrain from making sales; it was a matter of the Poles being asked not to buy."

The Polish sales ban began to highlight the increasing conflict between the State and Agriculture departments. One State official stated: "Defense policy is too important to be left to the generals and agriculture policy is too important to be left to the Department of Agriculture." In fact, it was reported that Butz learned of the Polish embargo only after it had been imposed by State. Senator Dole of Kansas did not like this switch, either, and sent Kissinger and Butz a telegram on September 23 inquiring, "When did export controls become the prerogative of the State Department?"

In delaying sales to the Soviet Union, the administration had several goals: Tie the Soviets to a minimum purchase each year so as not to "disrupt" markets; secure at least a third of the shipments on higher-priced American ships; and attempt a grain-for-oil swap.

To reach these goals, the Ford administration picked a State Department official, Undersecretary of State Charles W. Robinson, to go to Moscow to see what could be done. After several weeks of negotiations, Robinson obtained an agreement that the Soviets would buy 6 to 8 million tons of American grain each year through 1981, provided U.S. harvests were at least 225 million metric tons. The Robinson agreement also included a letter of intent under which the Soviet Union would provide the United States with 64 million barrels of oil a year, at below OPEC prices, with the hope of more later on. In addition, the Russians agreed reluctantly to ship a third of the grain on American vessels for $16 a ton, compared to the going international rate of $10 a ton.

After the signing of the Soviet accord, other countries sought similar assurances from the United States. In November 1975 the Japanese received a written promise from Secretary Butz that the United States would guarantee to sell them 14 million tons of grains and soybeans annually over the next three years. Poland then came around for a five-year agreement.

Butz—quietly—and farm groups and grain companies—more vocally—were opposed to these guaranteed sales. William Kuhfuss, president of the American Farm Bureau, stated: "The State Department has used farmers as political pawns in its diplomatic game through its manipulation of the marketing of agricultural commodities." Fritz Corrigan, chairman of Peavey, declared that there "is no more reason to believe the government's involvement in grain trading today will work any better than it has in the past, where the record shows it failed miserably." Warren W. Lebeck, president of the Chicago Board of Trade, was afraid that increasing government controls would "bungle America's new super strategy"—selling food abroad in a competitive market. And Edward Cook, in testimony before a Senate Agriculture Committee meeting in January 1976, stated that the 1975 moratorium on grain sales to the Soviets and Poland had cost the American economy $1 billion. The moratorium, Cook stated, led the Soviets to buy elsewhere and sent prices skidding.

Representative John Melcher (D-Mont.) had a more germane comment when he sent a telegram to Kissinger asking him under what authority the State Department had embargoed sales to the Soviets which were used as leverage in the negotiations for a grain purchase agreement. The answer came back sometime later, saying that there was no legal authority. The State Department moratorium was in effect an ad hoc sort of thing, but there is a movement afoot to formalize government control of our food supplies.

One such effort was contained in a bill introduced in 1975 by Representative James Weaver (D-Ore.) to make the Commodity Credit Corporation the sole marketing agent abroad for U.S. grains and soybeans. Weaver felt his bill was our "answer to OPEC," adding, "there is no reason we should keep paying extortion prices for foreign oil, while selling wheat to the same countries at bargain prices." Weaver reasoned that the United States could set its grain prices wherever it wanted to, becoming, in effect, the price leader, and giving other exporting nations the chance to raise their prices correspondingly. Weaver also felt the big grain-exporting companies weren't nationalistic enough and did not always work in the interests of the United States.

Weaver got a lot of publicity about his bill and responded to a question asking if the United States ought to use food as a weapon, "We can just let it be known that we don't intend to be the breadbasket for Russia and the Arab world unless we get a return for grain comparable to that for oil." Weaver's bill did not pass, due to opposition from farmers and grain companies that preferred no government role whatsoever.

A Cargill vice-president, William Pearce, opposed the bill as unrealistic, damaging to commercial and political relationships, and discriminatory against poorer nations. He further pointed out that the analogy between OPEC and grain producers was false, since grains could be grown everywhere.

Other companies did not agree. Corn Products Corporation (CPC), the billion-dollar firm that produces Mazola corn oil, Karo syrups, and Skippy peanut butter, put out a series of advertisements headed: "The Arabs have the oil. America has the corn." CPC pointed out that, in a sense, "American farmers are the Arabs of corn," as close to 50 percent of the world's corn is grown in the United States.

On a more strategic level, the Central Intelligence Agency has been studying what exactly can be done with food in a strategic sense. In a study made available in the spring of 1975, entitled "Potential Implications of Trends in World Population, Food Production and Climate," the CIA makes no bones about the fact that as "custodian of the world's exportable grain, the U.S. might regain the primacy in world affairs it held in the immediate post–World War II era."

The CIA study allows that food can serve as a weapon to achieve political ends only to a point. After that, "there would be increasingly desperate attempts on the part of the militarily powerful, but nonetheless hungry nations, to get more grain any way they could." The study adds that "nuclear blackmail is not unconceivable."

While no one wants the manipulation of food supplies to go that far, the United States has used its leverage effectively in recent years under the direction of Henry Kissinger. This fact was perhaps best expressed by a confident county extension agent in Central Kansas. "Look around you. See these wheatfields. They'll get us closer to détente with the Russians than Air Force One ever will."

Many observers feel that U.S. grains—and the Soviet need for them—were a factor in the Russians' sideline stance during the U.S. negotiations for the Egyptian-Israeli accord. The United States is also using grains as a means of reducing tariff barriers in the Geneva trade negotiations, with Japan as a case in point. And many officials had suggested that the way to get the Russians out of Angola is to threaten them with a cutoff of grain sales. The most recent use of grain politics, of course, was the Soviet-American grain pact of 1975, but the longest has been the trade embargo on Cuba.

The United States placed the embargo on Cuba soon after Castro entered Havana on New Year's Day, 1960. At that time, the rationale was to cut trade to gain some leverage against Castro. The State Department hoped the embargo would make the Cubans more amenable about settling the United States' $1.8-billion claim for expropriated property and about allowing freer migration and home visits, and that it would dissuade Castro from exporting the revolution.

The Cubans, who depended on the United States for most of their grains, were hurt by the embargo initially, but a visit to Cuba in October 1975 convinced me that they have managed to get by quite well.

In early 1975, relations between Cuba and the United States were improving. Castro returned $2 million in ransom money given to hijackers of a Southern Airlines plane; Senators George McGovern and Jacob Javits visited Cuba; and Luis Tiant's parents were allowed to come to the United States to see their son pitch in the World Series.

Food was already being considered as a peacemaker between the two countries. A leading Brazilian weekly, *Manchete*, carried a full-color picture of McGovern and Castro licking away at ice cream cones, with the headline PEACE BY ICE CREAM.

Trade relations were relaxed somewhat, in that overseas subsidiaries of American companies were allowed to trade with Cuba under certain conditions. A bill was introduced in the House by Representative Jonathan Bingham (D-N.Y.) to lift the embargo, and on September 23, William Rogers, Assistant Secretary of State for Inter-American Affairs, said, "We have put a policy of permanent hostility behind us. We are ready to begin a dialogue with Cuba." Hubert Humphrey announced that he was going to go to Cuba in January 1976 and hoped he and Castro could go fishing together. Things were moving.

I met Kirby Jones in Minneapolis in the spring of 1975 and helped put together a proposal, which Kirby then sent on to Cuba. Things moved fast and by October I was on my way to Cuba as part of the first American trade delegation in fifteen years. Although the embargo was still in effect, what interested us and other American grain companies was the almost $1 billion worth of food that Cuba imports every year.

After we had arrived, drunk our complimentary daiquiris, and with a very warm welcome had our first meeting, we saw how illogical Cuba's trade patterns had become. Rice was imported from the People's Republic of China, thirty-five shipping days away, instead of from New Orleans, which is three days distant. Soybean meal came from Rotterdam and had probably been crushed from U.S.-grown soybeans. The Cubans, in effect, were paying double freight. U.S. beans went to Rotterdam, were crushed, and then were sent to busy Havana harbor. Wheat came from Canada, as did flour, some of it milled by subsidiaries of such American companies as Multifoods. Frozen and chilled broilers came from Bulgaria and Denmark, while vegetable oil made the long haul from the Soviet Union. Corn came up from Argentina.

All this food business had originally belonged to the United States and had been embargoed in the hopes of diplomatic gain. The Cubans admit that the initial cutoff hurt, and that they now have to pay higher transportation charges. However, during my visit, there seemed to be enough food; eggs were no longer rationed, and milk was almost free. Good-tasting bread was available in the stores, and plenty of food was in evidence as I and 2,000 exuberant others watched the Las Vegas–type floor show at the Tropicana nightclub. Cubans enjoy food and are well aware of its political usefulness. In one meeting I had with a member of the staff of Carlos Rafael Rodríguez—reported to be Cuba's Kissinger—I went into a discussion of concessional food sales under the PL 480 program. Midway through my discussion, I was interrupted with the comment, "What does the *yanqui* want in return? Nothing is free."

By the same token, the Soviets must gain something important by paying for the Canadian wheat that Cuba imports. This commitment must be quite firm, for during the week I spent in Cuba, no interest was shown in purchasing American wheat.

With Canadian, Japanese, Dutch, and British businessmen all around Havana, it was apparent that the embargo was now isolating the United States more than it was isolating Cuba. It was time for a change.

Members of my delegation were not the only ones to recognize this. At the same time I was in Havana, John Breaux, a Louisiana Rice Belt congressman, was there promoting Louisiana rice. After Breaux's four days in Havana, he stated: "The U.S. embargo on trading with Cuba is no longer effective and no longer in the best interests of the United States." Breaux also expressed the rice industry's concern for markets, since the trade it had with South Vietnam and Cambodia ended when the Communists finally took control. It had not been lost on rice farmers that three of the best rice markets—Vietnam, Cambodia, and Cuba—had been closed due to foreign-policy decisions.

In view of this situation, it seemed that rice offered the best opportunity to test the waters on at least a partial lifting of the embargo. The logic was not difficult to understand: Rice is in surplus in the United States and is not really an essential food that would produce the knee-jerk reaction that wheat does when it is exported. In addition, the states that produce rice, particularly Texas and Louisiana, have strong political voices in John Tower and Russell Long, respectively.

Probably the best indication that the Cubans are not affected by the food embargo came when they led the "Zionism is racism" issue at the UN, and when they funneled some 10,000 troops to Angola; in the old days, the manpower would have been needed for the sugarcane harvest. The Cubans knew that these two actions would push back talks on lifting the embargo, but their food needs no longer depended on the United States.

Both Cuban actions stifled the momentum that had been building up to lift the embargo. Representative Bingham withdrew his resolution, fearing the ire of his constituents, while Senator Humphrey decided his scheduled trip in January would be "inappropriate."

When I left Cuba in October, the Cubans sent us off with the message that we would see each other again soon. But the Cuban trade officials, as well as the American grain traders, realized that it was up to Kissinger and Castro how quickly our next meeting would come about.

The United States has come in for a lot of criticism overseas for cutting anyone's food supply. Dr. Addeke H. Boerma, the outgoing director-general of the United Nations Food and Agriculture Organization (FAO), commented, "The world will judge nations on their willingness to give food to nations in need much more than it will judge those nations which might withhold oil." Libya, not impressed by anything the United States had done with its food money—including supporting over half of the FAO's budget—proposed, in December 1975, that the United States be thrown out of the organization. And a group of seventy-seven developing countries has issued complaints that U.S food aid in the past has been ineffective in promoting real development and has too often been used as a means of pressure.

Earl Butz responded to this criticism with a veiled threat of congressional reduction of funds allocated to UN organizations if they became politicized. Morihisa Emori of the Mitsubishi Research Institute commented that "Japan lived on rice once and could live on rice again" if the United States decided to pressure Japan too much.

The Soviets receive their share of criticism as well for coming in and out of the market and seemingly getting first crack at America's food. Both the Soviets and the complicity—or cunning—of Kissinger came in for some barbs in the following comment from *Eurofood*, a well-read and respected London-based newsletter:

Once upon a time, last November, there was a convocation of many people in Rome. They talked about the Great Hunger. Everyone agreed that there was a Great Hunger, even the mighty Kissinger. The cupboard was nearly bare, he told us. A typhoon here, another failure of rains there, and there shall be famine in the land. And unimaginable disaster would visit mankind.

But wait, help was at hand! The Great American Farmer could save us with his golden corn, and fill the begging bowls of the world full again ... provided the wise men of the Middle East with the inconceivable riches helped to pay.

And Kissinger said, "Let there be World Food Security. Let us all join together to make sure that when the cry of hunger is heard, the golden corn will be in mountains of plenty close by."

The Great American Farmer did then grow more corn, and the rains did come and sun did shine, and there was a mighty harvest, and the cathedrals of the prairies began to fill again with corn.

But lo! From the east there rode a stranger with many guns and checkbooks. "Give me grain," he said, "for I am the Great Grain Stealer."

And the men of Chicago said one to another, "Let us give to the Great Grain Stealer, for when he goes we shall have Action such as we have not had these three years past."

And the men in Washington said, "Let us give to the Great Grain Stealer, for our vows of Republicanism do not allow us to pay for storing grain."

And Kissinger said, "Let the Great Grain Stealer have grain, for if he is well fed and happy he will tell the World Security Conference and all shall know that I am a star."

And so it came to pass. Once more the cupboard was bare, and unimaginable disaster visited mankind.

Ready Reserves

Much of the world's food reserves are due not only to the efforts of American farmers like Gordon MacClean and Dale Yahnke, but also to America's storage facilities and how much grain we keep in them. World food reserves in case of poor harvests were one of the chief items of discussion at the Rome Food Conference and the subsequent follow-up meetings.

Prior to the Soviet grain sales in 1972, the United States was, in effect, the food warehouse of the world, but that situation has changed dramatically. In 1969, for example, world grain reserves were seventy days of consumption, but by 1974 they had fallen to twenty-seven days. People who laughed at William and Paul Paddock's book *Famine 1975!* now began to read it to see what clues it held to the world's precarious food situation. At the conference in Rome, it was estimated that one out of every eight people in the world suffers from malnutrition.

Prior to the conference, one of the most actively debated concepts was the one set forth in early 1973 by Dr. A. H. Boerma, then director-general of the FAO. Boerma wanted adoption of the idea of "minimum world food security." Under the FAO plan, all governments would be asked to hold certain minimum levels of food stocks with which to meet international emergencies. The governments of participating countries would consult regularly to review the food situation, judge the adequacy of existing stocks, and recommend necessary actions.

The U.S. Chamber of Commerce issued a statement favoring concessional food sales in emergencies, but added that it didn't want the United States to have any formal role in a food reserve program, since such a program would depress prices and, in turn, discourage production. Instead, the organization felt that each country should establish its own reserve food supply for domestic use, trade, or aid purposes.

Secretary Butz shared this view, stating, "We must get over the idea that there is something evil about reasonable rises and falls in food supplies and prices."

Responding to a proposal for an international reserve run by a committee representing several countries, the USDA felt that in some instances developing countries might convince the managers of the reserve that they needed grain, when in reality the reserves would be replacing a sale that could be made commercially.

For example, an African nation suffers a poor crop and receives donated grain from the reserve, even though it has enough foreign exchange to buy through commercial channels. Taking an example closer to home, it would be like giving food stamps to people who had plenty of money to pay for food.

The USDA's concern with maintaining a reserve went back to the first Soviet wheat deal, in which the U.S. consumer, not to mention the farmer, fared so poorly. A USDA official commented that the Commodity Credit Corporation, which has the responsibility of storing surplus grains, and its grain reserve program had made it possible for the Soviet Union to enter the world market three times in the past dozen years to buy large quantities of grain at relatively low costs when her own grain crops were poor.

Since grain was in surplus, the Russians enjoyed bargain-basement prices; however, since the purchases cut the surplus, the market prices went up afterward. This did not concern the Soviets, since they had already bought; but the rest of the world had to pay the higher prices.

It was with this background that the U.S. delegation went to Rome. Other Americans at the conference, like Hubert Humphrey, wanted the U.S. to be more positive in making a commitment to establish a grain reserve. Frequently quoting the biblical story of Joseph's convincing the pharaoh of Egypt to store grain for famine years, Humphrey pointed out that his proposed legislation would provide for government acquisition at times of surplus. Sales of these surpluses would occur only in times of short supply.

Responding to critics prior to the November 1974 conference, Humphrey stated: "I don't know how you taxpayers are willing to put up with the Pentagon's demanding we have reserves of tanks and ammunition when at present we don't have enough food in reserve to feed the armed forces." Humphrey's plan called for stocks of 7 million tons of wheat, 600,000 tons of feed grains, 1.4 million tons of soybeans, and 1.5 million bales of cotton.

While on a governmental level the U.S. was reluctant to talk reserves, one enterprising individual in Provo, Utah, was making large sales of food reserves for the individual family. Rainy Day Foods was organized to produce an array of dehydrated grains, fruits, and vegetables packed in airtight cans. With catchy advertising leads such as "You buy automobile insurance to protect yourself. Why not food insurance?" the idea caught on, while headlines proclaimed poor crops. In June 1974—before the Rome conference—sales were only $100,000 a month, but by March 1975, sales had risen to $1 million a month. George Murdock, president of Rainy Day, remarked, "I hate to say it, but our customers are preparing for the worst." He added, "Selling is getting easier because of the threat of world famine or world economic chaos."

A competitor, Self-Sufficiency Products, started up in Minneapolis and really poured it on as to why you should buy their foods, citing crop failures, depression, war or rebellion, natural disasters, riots, power crises, illness, and, finally, economic collapse.

No real specifics came out of the Rome conference, although a lot of vituperative comments were directed at the United States. The food shortages that were discussed at the conference were, of course, the results of overpopulation, poverty, and agricultural mismanagement, and could not be overcome by reserves alone. The conference ended with a general consensus that food production should be expanded and accelerated, food distribution and financing should be improved, the nutritional quality of foods should be enhanced, and a system of reserves should be created.

However, immediately after the Rome conference, Phil Campbell, then Assistant Secretary of Agriculture, echoed Butz's recalcitrant stance on reserves. "There's no more justification for the government to store six months' to a year's supply of farm goods than there would be for the government to store goods such as automobiles, dishwashers, clothes, steel, building materials, or fuel."

This recalcitrance of the USDA was not surprising, for prior to 1972, it had been criticized for the high storage costs of surplus grain. But after the Rome conference, the USDA found itself being called on to get back in the reserve business.

Some senators (among them Hubert Humphrey, George McGovern, Jacob Javits, and Mark Hatfield) also went to the conference with the hopes of getting the administration to pledge an extra million tons of grain aid to needy nations during the first half of 1975. President Ford turned down the request, leading some congressmen to charge that the United States was putting commercial sales ahead of food relief. The National Farmers' Organization felt this made the United States appear "just as stingy and mercenary with its food as the Arab countries are with their oil."

U.S. proposals for a reserve began to appear in the spring of 1975—and it was Kissinger, not Butz, who was making them. Kissinger gave the outline of the U.S. reserve plan to a Kansas City audience in May 1975. This, no doubt, pleased Morton Sosland, editor of the influential *Milling and Baking News*, who had earlier stated that the Department of Agriculture should move to Kansas City in order to get closer to the farmers.

Kissinger wanted an international system of food reserves, based on the following points: that they be large enough to meet potential shortfalls; that everyone have a fair allocation; that each participating country be free to determine how its reserves are maintained; and, finally, that the system encourage an expanded and liberalized trade in grains.

In October 1975, a specific proposal came from Assistant Secretary of Agriculture Richard Bell, en route to Moscow to negotiate a grain agreement with the Soviets, who stopped in London to address the International Wheat Council. This reserves plan called for holdings in excess of normal working stocks, estimated to be 10 percent of national production. Based on this criterion, a reserve of 30 million tons—25 million of wheat and 5 million of rice— would be about right. The responsibility of holding the stocks would be shared among the participants. The criteria for determining individual responsibility would take into account the historical roles of the participants. The cost: $4.5 billion, to be shared by both producing and consuming nations who participated in the plan.

Some grain specialists at the London presentation felt that, in presenting the plan, the United States was motivated as much by domestic political conditions as by any effort to thwart hunger. One dealer felt that the Ford administration was merely trying to appease cost-conscious consumers before the 1976 elections.

Some U.S. farmers have mixed feelings about having a large grain reserve. On the one hand, they want as little government involvement in grains as possible; but, recognizing the strategic value of a reserve in times of shortage, Lester Wolverton was moved to remark, "They got us over a barrel, but we got them over a bushel."

11

Over There

A curious news item that appeared in June 1975 reported that bread prices in the United States had shown the sharpest rise of anywhere in the world for the previous year. This could mean that we were paying too little before, or too much after, the rise. But whatever the case, Americans have always produced the most food and have spent less on it (as a percentage of disposable income) than anyone else around.

In 1970, the Japanese spent 34 percent of their disposable income for food, while the West Germans were allocating 27 percent and the Soviets 50 percent for their food budgets. The corresponding figure for the United States was 16 percent. Put another way, in December 1975, while a government employee was munching on a sirloin steak costing $2.14 a pound, a Japanese industrialist was spending $16.54. Things were a little better in Bonn, but the German auto worker had to pay $4.23.

The reasons for these differences are all unique to the individual countries. What is common to them is that, like many developed countries, they still come to the United States to buy their groceries—or at least a good part of them.

Land of the Rising Son

The Soviet Union has gotten much, if not all, the publicity concerning U.S. export sales, but Japan has for a number of years been the leading buyer of U.S. commodities. Japan assumed this position as a result of the intricacies of its geography, population growth, pollution problems, and adaptation to the Western life-style. All of these factors led the Japanese to buy $3 billion worth of U.S. agricultural commodities in 1975.

Japan is not really that large, occupying a land area the size of California, but its population numbers a little over 100 million. Population growth, however, seems to have been contained at manageable levels; currently at 1.2 percent per year, this growth rate is the lowest in Asia. This is not surprising, as abortion has been legal since 1948, and a program to promote contraception as an alternative to abortion has been active since 1952.

Of more significance to Japan's food needs and its demand on Gordon MacClean's wheat is its mountainous terrain. Although this makes for out-of-sight postcards, it also makes for poor and sparse cultivable land. Only about 15 percent of the land area is suitable for modern agriculture, and even this has to compete with housing, highways, and golf courses.

As a result of this pressure, the price of farmland has risen 3,000 percent since 1955, to the point where the average selling price is $18,160 per acre. Although the average Japanese farm is quite productive, having the highest rice yields in the world, its small size (averaging 2.8 acres, compared to 385 in the United States) makes its long-term prospects dim.

A visit to any auto showroom or electronics store will provide convincing evidence that Japan is an industrialized country. But the industrialization has its price. The acrid smoke you breathe as you walk down the Ginza is not so insidious as the mercury that is poured into the Sea of Japan. Fish pick up the mercury, which is eventually transferred to humans. The Japanese have always been the biggest fish eaters in the world (56 pounds per capita annually, compared to 15 in the United States), but they have been told by the government to cut back on fish consumption, due to the high mercury levels. Some stop-gap measures to satisfy the Japanese demand for fish have been taken, like the live eels that have been shipped by air from the Chesapeake Bay.

The Japanese have taken to Western ways, to the chagrin of the older generation. Going with Western-style clothes is the desire for Western food. Since the United States began relief shipments of flour and wheat to Japan in 1947, consumption of bread has risen to twenty times that of the immediate prewar period. Bread has always been a foreign item in Japan, and the present word for it, *pan*, is also the Spanish word for "bread"—Spanish sailors reportedly introduced the term four hundred years ago.

The relief shipments of wheat and flour were distributed through a school lunch program, where, from an early age, kids got used to the taste. Although the quantity of rice consumed is still ten times that of wheat, the trend is unmistakably toward more flour use.

Japan now has 6,000 bakeries and, at last count, 127 Mister Donut shops, franchises of Minneapolis's Multifoods and the largest chain in Japan. McDonald's has some three dozen carry-outs as well, as the demand for meat has increased.

Putting all of these factors together, you have a country that has become the world's largest importer of food, being only 50 percent self-sufficient in its food needs. In 1974, Japan imported 24 million tons of food—a figure that represents 26 percent of the domestic food consumption of the United States.

So, when it's dinnertime in Japan and the family sits down to sake, bean curd, soba (buckwheat noodles), rice, bread, coffee, lobster tempura, and tuna sashimi, only the rice and sake may have been produced domestically.

If recent Japanese purchases are any indication, more meat is also finding its way to the dinner table. A 1975 U.S. livestock auction involving the sale of three boars brought $100,000 from Japanese buyers. Beef is at such a premium that 130 cattle were air-freighted from Moses Lake, Washington, to Tokyo in 1975. And the largest retail supermarket in Japan is working with a U.S. grain organization in the construction of a feedlot.

The improved diet—in terms of protein—has literally made Japan the land of the rising son (and daughter), as babies born since World War II are about three inches taller than their fathers.

The Japanese are proud of their nutritional progress but are concerned that so much food is imported. Imports are inevitable, for, as one Japanese economist noted, "If we try to grow all our food at home, we will be paying $7 for a loaf of bread, $10 for a gallon of milk and $15 for a can of corn."

High prices, however, are preferable to no food at all, a situation that many Japanese feared when the United States levied its 1973 export embargo, since the Americans provide 15 percent of Japan's wheat, 96 percent of their soybeans, and 82 percent of their barley. When your major supplier lays an embargo on you, you get worried.

The immediate thought of many Japanese was to stockpile in

preparation for future embargoes. This idea of stockpiles also came up when Clayton Yeutter, then Assistant Secretary of Agriculture, traveled to Japan in 1974. The Japanese questioned whether Yeutter's motives in talking about stockpiles were other than altruistic. It was reported that Japanese agricultural officials suspected that the American government was attempting to increase the global demand for U.S. farm products, and thereby to drive prices up.

But even stockpiles run out, and so the Japanese government, in order to feel more secure about their food supplies, has embarked on a two-pronged program: Increase productivity at home, and find other means—secure means—of procuring overseas supplies of food.

At home, the government has pushed forward with its "Danchi" plan, whose objective is to establish 10,000 farm units of 130 acres in ten years. The increased size of the unit would lead to more efficiency. But there is pressure against this plan, as the agricultural lobby in Japan—where 11 percent of the people are engaged in agriculture, as compared to 4 percent in the United States—wants to maintain the highly subsidized status quo. The lobby has succeeded in banning most beef imports, which has led to the high meat prices. There is a growing consensus that Japan must attain 75 percent food self-sufficiency by 1985.

The Japanese have also turned to other areas of the world for food supplies. Trade agreements were a primary motivation for Prime Minister Tanaka's trip to Brazil in 1974. Following this trip, the Japanese Foreign Ministry urged its Latin American ambassadors to work with Japan's large trading firms to set up consortiums to finance the development of agriculture in Latin America so as to increase exports of farm products to Japan. The Ministry of Agriculture requested an appropriation of $18 million to get this program under way not only in Latin America but in other parts of the world. One Japanese trading firm, for example, became a partner in a large farming enterprise in southwestern Iran.

The Japanese have by no means lost interest in the United States. The Marubeni firm, for example, bought the Western Grain Exchange in Portland, which in 1973 handled 1 million tons of grain. Of more importance, however, was that 1975 letter from Secretary Butz, stating that the United States would supply Japan with 14 million tons of grain for the next five years.

The "Costly Market"

When Britons were considering joining the European Common Market (EEC), one of the bigger issues was the increase in food costs that would result, due to the bewildering regulations and the subsidies that EEC farmers get. Fully 90 percent of the EEC's agricultural production is subsidized under the Common Agricultural Policy, which in 1974 cost European taxpayers $12.4 billion. The basic philosophy is to provide the EEC's farmers—who represent around 12 percent of the population—an incentive to produce. EEC farmers have obtained the subsidies because of their political power, which gets them high prices and causes consumers a rising food bill. The agricultural jargon of the EEC is a confusion of terms such as "green pound," "unit of account," "target price," "intervention level." One U.S. trader returning from Europe breathed a sigh of relief when he told me, "I'm glad we got out of that stuff."

To help the farmers keep prices high, the EEC established a variable levy system, which adjusts the usually lower world prices of imports to the higher domestic levels. The farmers are not the only ones who benefit from this system, and international grain traders have devised means to speculate and to profit from the levy system.

Import duties have an ebb and flow geared to world commodity markets: when the world price of grain increases, the levy decreases; and vice versa. Thus, if a grain trader feels that world prices will fall, the assumption is made that import levies will go up. Consequently, the trader will register to import grain at current levels. If he guesses right, then his cost of importing grain will be lower, giving him an extra margin.

Due to the time differential between Chicago, where world prices are determined, and Brussels, where the levies are posted, the international trader who never sleeps is a step ahead of the EEC bureaucrats who do. For example, up-or-down movements in grain occur after the European import levy has been set, allowing the grain trader to get a clear idea of market trends and whether the next duty posting will be higher or lower. One analysis of the duty guessing-game showed that an astute grain trader could make 20 cents a bushel on this type of deal; this comes to $14,000 on a 20,000-ton cargo.

The European consumer thus pays not only the farmer but also the speculator, leading one German I know to suggest that a more apt term for the Common Market would be the "Costly Market." The high prices persist in spite of the fact that the EEC is constantly burdened with surpluses—called beef, pork, or butter "mountains." Removed from the real marketplace of supply and demand, EEC farmers produce apart from the reality of how much the consumer needs; hence the surpluses.

Although the surpluses and the levy system discourage imports, the Netherlands and West Germany are still the second- and third-largest importers of U.S. agricultural commodities. Soybeans and soymeal enter free of duty, but grains are subject to tariffs. As a result, EEC grain prices are generally almost twice as high as world grain prices.

Even so, you can often find eager Italian buyers at Sam Kuhl's North Dakota mill, buying durum wheat with which to make pasta. However, the Italian Ministry of Agriculture is now proposing legislation that would allow the use of some soft wheat in pasta, as imported hard wheat is now costing inflation-racked Italy $500 million a year. And it is a chilling fact that half the 55 million dinners prepared in the United Kingdom each day depend on imported food.

Farms in the EEC are large by Japanese standards, but small compared to those in the Unites States (French farms average around twenty acres, while those in Great Britain average forty acres). The same technological changes that transformed American farms have come to Western Europe, particularly West Germany, where food output has increased by 430 percent since 1951.

In fact, the West Germans feel their agriculture is the most efficient, and they are tired of being the "milk cow" of Europe, as West Germany's finance minister put it. West Germany now contributes 28 percent of the EEC's budget, and wants to cut $384 million from the EEC budget for agriculture, most of which goes to the French.

The beneficiaries of the system have been not only the European farmers but also those great food shoppers, the Soviets. In 1973, 200,000 tons of subsidized surplus butter went to the Russians, costing the EEC $500 million—the difference between the price the farmer got and the price the Soviets paid. This was the type of deal Dwayne Andreas wanted to make in 1954, but couldn't. These subsidized exports have also hurt the United States, as the EEC will often lower the price to get the business.

Since 1974, 115,000 tons of meat—some of which was stored in refrigerator ships—have been shipped from Western Europe to the Soviet Union for a price that European shoppers could not dream of. This surplus situation seems likely to continue, to the chagrin not only of the European consumer but also of the American farmer, who could sell more grain to the EEC's 250 million consumers without the EEC's protectionist policies.

Secretary of Agriculture Butz has lashed out at the EEC farming system on a number of occasions. In one speech to the British National Farmers Union, Butz criticized those who turned toward protectionism in a period of world recession, and regretted that the fear of food shortages was leading to "new and sometimes questionable policies of self-sufficiency."

Butz has long maintained that the United States has a comparative advantage in agriculture and so should serve as the granary of the world. Butz's question to the Europeans is: Why do you support your uneconomic agriculture and introduce levies when you could import more cheaply from us?

The answer, of course, lies in nationalism, memories of the food shortages and notorious food black market of 1948, and, in particular, the 1973 soybean embargo. Europeans trust Dale Yahnke to grow his soybeans, but they are not so sure about the USDA's allowing their export. The embargo almost brought the European livestock industry to its knees, and since that time, according to a French agricultural publication, many soybean users have decided that this will not happen again.

Accordingly, the French have embarked on a number of projects to ensure a better supply of raw materials. They first tried raising their own soybeans, but came up short in that effort, as they do not have the right growing conditions.

They then followed the Japanese to Brazil and arranged a supply agreement with Brazilian cooperatives, independent of world commodity exchange prices. Furthermore, they agreed to build a large crushing plant in France. Joining this twosome in the project (Comptoir National Technique Agricole—CNTA) was the Algerian government, with a financial interest. Not only was the return on their investment attractive, but the Boumediene government saw this step as a means of further breaking down "international capitalist commerce" (meaning the big grain exporters) and of establishing new trade relationships.

About this plan, one French journal noted that it may be "a drop of water in the ocean," but "such drops of water can very well become grains of sand that might well lodge in the well-oiled wheels of the wild trade liberalism machinery."

To make further inroads in the European market, the United States will probably have to make some concessions, such as more dairy imports. These are strongly opposed by U.S. farmers, but they have a tough row to hoe in preventing imports. Switzerland, for example, subsidizes its cheese exports to the United States, and thus far has not faced any retaliation, even though the American Farm Bureau requested it. Perhaps the United States's lack of resistance stems from the Bern government's preference for an American fighter plane over the French Mirage, as one publication pointed out.

No Joke about Poland

Many people have their favorite "Polish joke," which invariably centers on a Pole's incompetence. Despite the jokes, it is the Polish consumer who is at least partially responsible for the greater ties between Eastern Europe and the United States, the Soviet wheat deal, and the later grain agreement.

In 1970, a severe winter, followed by a wet spring, topped off by floods, drought, and finally a wet harvest, brought havoc to Poland's grain supply. Poles eat a lot of rye, and production of this important grain was down by 26 percent that year.

Food was scarce, and the Polish government led by Wladyslaw Gomulka had the misfortune to raise food and clothing prices in a new economic program. Raising the prices was bad enough, but to do so twelve days before Christmas was the epitome of bad timing in a country where an estimated 60 percent of the adults still go to church.

The result was bloody food riots in a number of Polish cities, resulting in Gomulka's resignation on December 20. Edward Gierek succeeded Gomulka as first secretary of the party, and promised to get rid of the "ill-considered economic policies" of the past. However, responsibility for the food problem could not be placed entirely on the state, for 90 percent of the land in Poland is privately owned.

The significance of the riots was that people were getting more concerned about what they ate and how much they paid for it.

Austerity in the name of political revolution was no longer an accepted catchword. Good food at reasonable prices would have to be made available, and the message did not go unnoticed in other Eastern European politburos, nor in the Kremlin itself.

The Polish reaction produced a new food policy, but in the following five years, annual per-capita meat consumption jumped to thirty-seven pounds instead of the fifteen to twenty pounds that the government had "planned." Poles now consume around 80 percent of the meat that Americans take in, on the average.

To sustain this meat consumption, Poland has had to import feed grains. For many years, it got grain from the Soviets, but when the Russian crops suffered, Poland began looking elsewhere. Poland's Five-Year Plan (1976–80) calls for a sizable increase in livestock production and was one of the main reasons the Poles signed a five-year grain agreement with the United States. Upon hearing about this agreement, I immediately remembered the picture of a man harvesting by hand that I'd seen in Dale Yahnke's house.

Other Eastern European countries have similar growth plans under way. East Germany spent $100 million to buy a meat-processing plant that can handle 155,000 tons, reputed to be Europe's largest. The West Berlin firm that sold the plant is negotiating other sales with Hungary and Bulgaria. When I learned that Dale Yahnke had visited Poland, I thought it strange until I found out that soybean usage in Eastern Europe is up 100 percent from the 1969–71 average. Dale Yahnke wasn't just getting away from cold Minnesota winters; he was doing market research.

Most Eastern European countries had earlier chosen not to buy from the West so as not to reveal any embarrassing shortages. Most years, any shortfalls on their private and collective farms could be made up by grain from the Soviet Union. But when they couldn't, and the choice was Gordon MacClean's wheat or their pride, then Gilbey, North Dakota, didn't seem so bad after all.

With imports now an accepted fact, Communist leaders are worried that people may begin to take it easy. After the 1975 harvest was in, Gustav Husak, chairman of the Czech Communist Party, not only criticized the poor harvest as "a shambles," but also disparaged people who fed bread to animals and otherwise "had no conception of the value of grain." Referring to his country's imports, Husak stated that an educational campaign was needed to convince Czechs that grain is a precious commodity that has to be paid for in gold.

Eastern European countries are also buying American farm technology to help increase their own production. One particular problem has always been farm machinery. Once, on an agricultural project in Iran, I saw a Rumanian tractor that had a lot of horsepower—but only enough to power itself, with no thought given to any implements. Consequently, the Iranians preferred American tractors and used the Rumanian one only to thresh wheat.

Hungary is also intent on improving its agriculture and has resorted to airlifting dairy animals from the United States, some 6,500 in 1974. The animal airlift became quite well known and a humorous topic in Hungary after two American bulls escaped their air freighter in Budapest and ran loose on the runway, preventing the plane carrying the already late Hungarian symphony orchestra from landing. No bull.

The Kremlin in the Kitchen

If the rallying cry of the 1917 Russian Revolution that brought the Communists to power was "Peace, Bread, and Land," they now want to remain in power by offering "Poultry, Bacon, and Ham" to the 250 million Soviet citizens.

The famines are over in Russia, and there is enough food, but now consumers want a better variety and more meat. On the average, Russians consume 550 pounds of bread annually—the most in the world—compared to 70 pounds for the average American, but only half as much eggs and meat as in the United States. The emphasis on a better diet is evident, for an analysis of recent Soviet grain purchases shows that corn and soybeans are going to Russia in increasing quantities for animal, not human, consumption.

This demand was a long time coming, as Stalin sacrificed agricultural production in order to build up Soviet industry. Investment in agriculture was neglected, even though Stalin expected continually increasing production. Nikita Khrushchev remembered the quotas the state wanted out of the Ukraine in 1946: "The quota had been calculated not on the basis of how much we could really produce, but on the basis of how much the state thought it could beat out of us." He added, "The quota system was really a system of extortion."

Added to the lack of investment in agriculture in the first decades of the Revolution were the various new forms of organization that were placed upon farmers. Lenin advocated a slower pace, but Stalin sought to collectivize the land as quickly as possible. Stalin came to power in 1926, and by 1930 Russia was experiencing famine.

In those years, fear produced the grain that did grow. Very few new ideas about farming appeared. An attempt was made to introduce shallow tillage as a means of conserving topsoil, but the professor who introduced the idea was punished for his political beliefs and it became illegal to practice the method he advocated. Those who did were tried and condemned to death.

Political judgments were also made to plant winter wheat (sown in the fall) or spring wheat (sown in the spring). Stalin decreed spring wheat should be planted, even though winter wheat would have given better yields in some areas. Stalin told Khrushchev, "There should be a resolution to that effect."

When Khrushchev came to power in 1952, he inherited a torpid agricultural sector that produced the same amount in 1952 that it had in 1916, the last year of czarist rule. To try to bring it out of the doldrums, he sent 500,000 people to open up new lands to grain farming in the far-off regions of Kazakhstan. The pioneers opened up 90 million acres (the combined cultivated area of England, France, and Spain). Khrushchev was more flexible in rural organization; he placed more emphasis on the sovkhoz (state farm) than the kolkhoz (collective farm).

In spite of his efforts, Khrushchev came under criticism when, after the initial spurt, Kazakhstan's wheat production declined, necessitating imports. Poor weather was one reason for the decline; another was the difficulty in obtaining good farm management. The joke among Russians was that "Comrade Khrushchev has performed a miracle; he has sown wheat in Kazakhstan and reaped it in Canada." The decline in Kazakhstan's wheat production was one of the factors, if not the main one, that eventually brought about Khrushchev's fall from leadership.

Nevertheless, Khrushchev gave direction and goals to Soviet agriculture. In 1957, after Khrushchev took off his shoe to pound it on a table at the United Nations, he put it on again to tour an Iowa farm. He afterward proclaimed that in ten years the Soviets would surpass the United States in dairy and meat production. But ten years later, Khrushchev had resigned, and the Soviet Union was still far behind the United States in the production of most farm commodities. The total grain area of the Soviet Union is a tremendous

315 million acres, or about twice as much as that of the United States, yet the total U.S grain production is 20 percent larger. In fact, the year that Khrushchev resigned all his offices, 1964, was the year of the first large Soviet imports of grain and the first year U.S. exports to Russia reached $100 million. The 1964 imports of 9.3 million tons were second only to the 1972–73 imports of 40 million, which similarly came after a poor harvest.

Alexander Yanov, a writer and Russian émigré, feels that agriculture in the Soviet Union will continue to suffer until the kolkhozy are done away with. Stalin developed these gigantic estates that are manned by peasants who live in nearby villages. In addition to their duties on the kolkhoz, the peasants also tend their own little plots, which they use to feed themselves. This, according to Yanov, is the first contradiction of the kolkhoz: Whether there is a good harvest or not, the kolkhoznik still gets enough from his plot to live.

Responsible farm management is lacking under this system, as one kolkhoznik tills the soil, another plants, a third cultivates, while a fourth harvests. Furthermore, Yanov states, this system is comparable to one in which a hunter in the forest is paid not by the pelts he bags but by the shots he fires.

With Stalin at the helm, the Soviet Union, states Yanov, did not buy grain, for if the kolkhoz did not produce enough, half the population simply did not eat bread. Since the Polish riots, this approach is no longer politically possible.

State farms, where workers get a fixed salary regardless of the harvest, don't do much better. Workers are paid on the quantity of work they do, which leads to some bizarre farming practices. For example, a tractor driver is paid in accordance with the size of the area he covers, which gives him the incentive to go as fast and as carelessly as possible. Other tasks are approached in similar fashion. Under this sort of incentive system, I doubt that anyone would take the time to add a half pound of boron per acre to solve a trace-mineral deficiency, as Dale Yahnke did.

Unsuccessful attempts have been made to change the agricultural structure. Some liberal planners came up with a plan to turn state or collective land over to farm "links," or units, which, in turn, would be managed by ten or so specialists whose income would be entirely dependent on the income from the tract. The link would also be responsible for land cultivation and machinery repair. In other words, the link would be a capitalist farm in Socialist clothing.

One Soviet planner, Ivan Khudenko, experimented with this

structure and found that labor productivity on his link was twenty times higher than on neighboring state farms. But instead of receiving an award, Khudenko was sentenced to six years in prison, for higher-ups realized that if Khudenko was right, the entire foundation of Soviet agriculture was wrong.

Farm workers are also frustrated, particularly by the sterile life on the collective and state farms, which have none of the amenities that even Gilbey, North Dakota (population 700), provides. Despite the fact that, from 1959 to 1970, collective workers were not given domestic passports permitting free internal movement, 21 million Russians left the land and headed for the cities during that period. Of particular concern is the flight of the young, who see only boredom awaiting them on the farm.

But politics and rural organization are not the only factors holding back Soviet agriculture. Although the Soviet Union is an immense country—two and a half times the size of the United States—90 percent of it lies north of Minneapolis, and, more importantly, only 10 percent receives more than 20 inches of rain a year. These two inexorable physical facts are hard to overcome, even by 40 million farm workers—about ten times the U.S. number—and investments in the billions. Perhaps predictably, a third of Russia's meat, milk, and vegetables comes from the private plots of individual peasants. These plots receive little, if any, government investment, average half an acre in size, and represent a mere 3 percent of the agricultural land. The rest of the production comes from 50,000 state farms, which are as large as 10,000 acres each.

But while private initiative has been able to contend with the elements somewhat better than the state has, it, too, is affected by howling winds and the piercing cold that often drives frost ten feet into the ground. One U.S. agricultural expert stated: "The best Russian land is comparable to North Dakota—it gets worse from then on." The best Soviet grain lands get little moisture, so the Soviets have tried every means possible to capture moisture, particularly from the snow: fences, tree belts, sunflowers, mounds of dirt against the wind. Winter scenes from the motion picture *Dr. Zhivago* notwithstanding, most of Russia's interior seldom gets more than a foot of snow cover—essential for protecting the first shoots of grain. A popular farm expression goes, "A winter without snow is a summer without bread."

In spite of the ups and downs in Soviet agricultural production, retail prices of meat and milk have remained unchanged since 1962.

Soviet incomes have gone up during that period, hence the increased demand for better foods. Recalling the Polish food riots, the Soviet leaders have been trying to keep pace with the demand, and beef production has gone up 100 percent since 1960.

Bread is now taken so much for granted that an editorial in *Izvestia* in September 1975 urged Soviet citizens to be more frugal with bread. "The fact that bread in our shops is cheap creates for some people an erroneous idea of our wealth." The editorial went on to urge housewives to cut loaves into thin slices and wrap them in napkins to prevent them from going stale. The suggestion was also made that consumers buy the new mini-loaves, which cost 3 kopecks (4 cents), instead of the larger loaves, which might go to waste. Bread is so cheap that it is often fed to cattle, which is illegal.

Increased imports represented one stop-gap measure in the effort to keep consumers happy. In 1962, grain imports totaled only 600,000 tons, but by 1972–73 they were up to 40 million. The latter figure is equal to the combined total imports for the previous twelve years. In considering Soviet imports, it is important to remember that 20 percent of Soviet grain production comes from distant Kazakhstan, and transporting that grain to the European Soviet Union is often more expensive than bringing it from Canada or Pretty Prairie, Kansas. Although most of the imports have come from the United States, the Soviets are also trying to diversify their suppliers, fearing more U.S. embargoes. In 1975, for example, the Soviets bought 1.5 million tons of soybeans from Brazil.

At the same time, the Soviets are exporting less. In 1960, 5.5 percent of the total grain supply was exported, but by 1973 this figure had fallen to 2.5 percent. Khrushchev remembered Poland's Gomulka coming to Moscow pleading for grain—not to feed humans, but for hogs. Polish bacon had a good market in the United States, and Gomulka wanted to keep it through Soviet grain, even though direct trade between the United States and Russia was nil during the height of the Cold War.

All these circumstances led to the Soviet purchases of 1972, sometimes referred to as the "Great Grain Robbery." Hindsight shows that the "robbery" was inevitable, but what made the United States look so bad was the Soviets' timing. They had "cased" us for quite some time, so when they made their move, it was the right one. The Soviet–United States grain agreement made them change their style.

The USSR does not keep from its citizens the fact that it buys grain from abroad, and far from regarding such purchases as an embarrassment, the Soviets tell the world that they are a sign of strength. A dispatch released in January 1976 by the Novosti Press Agency stated: "Today, the USSR is able to purchase grain, not because it is having a hard time, but because it is getting along very well and is rich enough to provide bread for 250 million Soviet people even during years of poor harvests." This is consistent with other Soviet setbacks that, through their media skill, have been made into victories.

The Novosti dispatch reminded me of a similar defeat-into-victory situation that I learned of when I was studying political science in Washington. The Soviet news agency, Tass, was reporting an automobile race between an American and a Russian that the American press had announced was won by the American. The Soviet version of this two-car race was somewhat different, as there was no mention of how many cars had competed, and the results showed that the "Soviet car came in second while the American finished next to last."

A similar coyness faced a group of U.S. agricultural experts who visited the Soviet Union's "New Lands" in the summer of 1975. (The "New Lands" is the area in and around Kazakhstan, which was not intensively farmed until 1956 when Khrushchev began to try to exploit it.) In response to a question one of the group asked a Soviet official as to why his government didn't reveal statistics, the official replied: "You are a government; we are both a government and a business. You shouldn't expect us to tell you and your farmers what we're going to buy ahead of time any more than you would expect it of Continental Grain."

Then later, in December, Soviet planning chief Nikolai Baibakov failed to give the figures for the 1975 grain harvest at the winter session of the Supreme Soviet. The last time that Baibakov had failed to give the harvest figures was in 1972, immediately preceding the large purchases of U.S. grain. This omission produced some displeasure at the USDA, for it goes against the Soviet-American agriculture agreement of July 1973, which requires both countries to exchange "forward estimates on production, consumption, demand and trade of major agricultural commodities." This market information is essential, since many top USDA officials feel the Soviets will continue to need grain in excess of what the agreement calls for. How much? Only the Kremlin knows, and it's not saying.

Perhaps the most mysterious aspect of the Soviet grain trade with the United States involved a series of phone calls in 1972 that revealed the Soviet grain-purchase plans in advance. In June and July, Morton Sosland, publisher of *Milling and Baking News*, began to receive overseas calls from a man in London who had an English accent and stated he was with the London *Financial Times*, which was doing a story on the Soviet grain purchases. Identifying himself as "John Smith," he queried Sosland as to how the American public might react to the sales, and gave information on Soviet purchase plans and the status of the Russian crops. He accurately predicted how futures prices would rise, and gave insights on the progress of the Soviet buying mission. What the mysterious, but informative, "Deep Throat" was to Bob Woodward and Carl Bernstein in their Watergate investigation, "John Smith" was to Sosland and the Russian grain deal. It is now thought that the man was a Russian whose motive was to learn what people in the trade were thinking and perhaps to prime everyone for the large purchases then being negotiated.

Most U.S. experts feel that the Soviets will continue to buy grain, for they are committed to their 1976–80 Five-Year Plan, which calls for rapid increases in meat, egg, and dairy production. In egg production alone, they are seeking an 87 percent increase. They also plan the construction of feedlots capable of handling 54,000 to 108,000 hogs and 20,000 cattle. To develop the cattle feedlots, the Russians have brought in some Texas cowmen as consultants, though none has yet been heard to yell, "Ride 'em, Comrade." Poultry will come from complexes of 100,000 to 200,000 chickens; it is still somewhat of an embarrassment that 50 percent of the poultry meat comes from little private chicken coops out back.

These plans are all part of a modernization process that the *Soviet Federation of Writers Union Monthly* has stated is the crucial item in self-sufficiency—not the adverse weather. "The pivotal point is that we as farmers do not come up to the level of our own achievements in the scientific-technical revolution." But the modernization process is founded on even larger production units, which become very bureaucratic in their operation, leading Leonid Brezhnev to complain that farm managers avoid "innovation the way the devil shies away from incense."

Russia's lack of innovation in many crop areas is ironic, since in the past she provided a great deal of innovation to the United States.

A Mennonite colony suffering persecution under the czars looked around for a new home in the 1880s at the same time the U.S. railroads were opening up the West to settlers. The Mennonites heard about the opportunity and came to the Midwest, settling in Kansas. They brought along Turkey Red Wheat seed, which produced excellent crops on land that no one had thought was worth a lick. Thus, when the Soviets came buying in 1972, they probably bought wheat that was related to the original seeds brought over from Russia by the Mennonites.

An equally significant transfer occurred when N. E. Hanson of the South Dakota Agricultural Experiment Station visited Russia at the turn of the century. He observed something called "crested wheat grass" and brought it home with him. When the Dust Bowl descended upon the Midwest in the 1930s, it was crested wheat grass that was used for revegetation and for cattle forage, leading one USDA official to say that without the grass research, "beef steak might be as rare in the United States as it is in many other countries of the world today."

12

One in a Million

Of no small importance to Dale Yahnke or any other farmer is the fact that most of the developing countries of the world—those with $500-per-capita annual income or less—have a hard time producing the food they need. With little enough food to go around now, the problem will worsen, as the 2.5 percent annual increase in births—centered primarily in the poorer countries—promises to double the world's population in about thirty years. Each day sees the addition of 200,000 more people.

The United States has responded to food shortages by being the largest food-aid donor. During 1965–72, the United States provided 85 percent of the food-aid contributions of the developed countries, and since 1954 has sent 143 million tons of wheat, rice, and other grains overseas in aid programs. Since World War II, the United States has given away $80 billion worth of food and development aid.

Most politicians and statesmen credit these donations to our humanity, while others less nobly point out that they were the result of our surpluses. And the reasons given as to why we should continue the effort range from showing the world that we care, to strategic considerations. Robert McNamara, former Secretary of Defense and now president of the World Bank, has stated that everyone should consider that misery in poor countries may boil over. This reasoning brings to mind the oft-quoted statement that "a man who goes without food for twenty-four hours will quarrel, one who is denied food for forty-eight hours will steal, and one who is without food for seventy-two hours will fight."

To date, food wars have been avoided, but no one knows whether this will continue to be the case. Landowners in the Mexican states of Sonora and Sinaloa were threatening to grow no crops in 1976 if the government refused to protect them from invading landless farmers. Of particular significance to Mexico—and to Gilbey, North Dakota—is that Sonora produces most of Mexico's wheat.

Most of the solutions offered to solve the world's food problems center on increasing agricultural production and establishing the proper political structure to accomplish same. One radical student I knew in Colombia told me that his country needed a "red and then a green revolution."

Solutions abound. The FMC Corporation feels the problem is that there is enough fertile land but too little under the plow. UNICEF feels it can solve the problem by giving more aid, and implores us to "spare a bite to save a life." And Vicki Jones, a Saint Paul, Minnesota, nice person and erstwhile health-food faddist, suggests we give up meat so that more grain can be given to starving Africans. She really believes that if we give up Saturday night's chili, Africans will eat better.

An opposite view is held by groups such as the Environmental Fund, which claims talk of a food shortage avoids the real issue of too many people. The fund contends, as did Thomas Malthus and other "Limits to Growth" advocates, that world food production cannot keep pace with the galloping growth in population and that "family planning" cannot, and will not, in the foreseeable future, check this growth. The fund is quite insistent that "no amount of scientific wizardry or improved weather will change this situation."

Perhaps the best example of this is the construction of Egypt's Aswan High Dam, which cost billions, but has added 25 percent to Egypt's arable land area. Yet, between 1955, when the plans were conceived, and 1970, when the dam was completed, the population of the country grew by 50 percent!

With some justification, the fund points out that, for all the efforts and food aid, the developing world is worse off now than it was before all the aid began. Food reserves are at an all-time low, and whereas a generation ago the population of the developing countries was increasing by 16 million births a year, it now increases by 67 million.

The Population Conference in Bucharest in 1974 recognized only part of these problems and came out with several policy statements many people in the developed countries found difficult to accept—for example, that hungry nations have the right to produce as many children as they please, and others have the responsibility of feeding them. The representative of the People's Republic of China, Huang Shu-tse, was forceful in his denunciation of population control, stating: "The large population of the Third World is an important condition for the fight against imperialism."

In nearby, friendly Mexico, a newspaper cartoon recently showed the arms of Uncle Sam spraying "baby kill" at a Mexican baby. The United States had advocated a birth-control program for Mexico to stem the tide of illegal immigration to the United States. Marshall Green, coordinator of the State Department's Population Affairs Bureau, said that Mexico's population has "serious implications for the United States," adding that nations made economically desperate by excessive population could obtain atomic weapons and make irrational decisions endangering the entire world. The director of Mexico's population council responded that he did not like U.S. "interventionism, open or veiled," in their population problems.

A peasant with ten kids doesn't understand the foreign-policy implications of his family, but he does know that they will serve as his old-age insurance. They are also a sign of his manhood. Given this attitude, the Environmental Fund feels, there is little hope of solving the population problem. Some believe that the hopeless countries might just as well be written off, and efforts be directed at saving "the walking wounded," as one author put it.

In this triage approach, India emerges as the most hopeless; 70 percent of India works on the farm, but their production still can't keep up with the population growth. Today, the average Indian subsists on an intake of 990 calories, nearly one-third less than the safe minimum set by U.S. experts. Some estimates put deaths from malnutrition in India at between 3 and 4 million annually.

Attempts at increasing productivity, even with miracle seeds, have not been successful. Chemical fertilizer is lacking, and organic fertilizer, such as cow manure, is burned for fuel; one research organization stated that the contribution of cow dung to total energy consumption in India has been variously estimated at between 32 and 77 percent.

Family planning, despite public-education programs, has accomplished little. India's population in 1951, when birth-control programs began, grew by 3.6 million, but now grows by 16.2 million each year. However, some observers feel that even with half its people, India would be poor, since its institutions—the castes, the taboos, inefficient government—exacerbate the problems and are unable to cope with them.

In the western hemisphere, countries such as Honduras, Bolivia, and Haiti have, and will continue to have, increasing difficulties in coming to grips with their population problems. With excess population comes the concomitant problem of little or no education. A well-quoted story went around Port-au-Prince in 1975, when a player on Haiti's national soccer team was suspended from the team for refusing to eat lettuce, which the coach had ordered to balance player diets. "What does he think we are—rabbits?" queried the player. It was also in Haiti where poverty struck me the most on one particular day. My wife and I had driven to the beach, and on our way back to Port-au-Prince our battered and aged Peugeot got a flat tire. People—lots of people—suddenly appeared from the bush and watched as we changed the tire. One little kid, intent on getting some money for his services, found the nail that had caused the flat and began pulling it out—with his teeth.

Population pressure will also begin to put a strain on other Latin American countries—where the world's fastest population growth is centered. By the year 2000, Mexico City alone will have a whopping 32 million people, nearly three times more than Australia's present population. In all, by the year 2000, Latin America will have 645 million inhabitants, thus outstripping the combined populations of the United States, Western Europe, and Canada.

Things are not much better in the Sahel region of Africa, which has suffered from drought in the past few years, but whose real problem is too many people and animals. The most telling picture I saw of the hopeless situation was a family sitting in a dusty, wind-buffeted tent while their goats munched at the sparse grass shoots in the advancing sand dunes. What a conventional analysis of the scene would miss is that those grass shoots were keeping the desert away. But the goats needed the grass to live, and the family needed the goat's milk to survive. However, once the grass shoots were gone, the desert would advance, and the family would have to pack up and move. Which part of the vicious circle do you attack first?

Hearts and Minds

The People's Republic of China is by no means a rich agricultural country, yet, in spite of its huge population, it has been able to feed itself. Although agricultural technology has taken some credit for China's agricultural development, the political changes that have captured the hearts and minds of the people have been the chief reason. China has never used gimmicks to feed itself, but rather the practical hard work of its 900 million people, 780 million of whom work on communes. A recent visitor to some communes in China found the use of manpower overwhelming. On one 50,000-acre commune, there were 18,000 people working the land and 2,000 holding administrative jobs. This led the visitor to remark, "They could almost dust the crops by hand."

The national model for communal farming is found at Ta Chai, in Shansi Province, to the southwest of Peking. Twenty-five years of hard labor were spent in leveling hills and building stone retaining walls for reservoirs. Until recently, the aged peasant chairman toiled in the fields with everyone else. The result was a good yield of 8 metric tons of grain per hectare. Mao Tse-Tung is always telling his people, "Learn from Ta Chai." The human cost is high in developing such a work mentality, but as the late Chou En-Lai told a journalist in 1972, "We can still say that what we gained was far, far more than we lost."

The statistics bear Chou out, as the 1970 grain crop showed a net gain of 200 percent over the 1950 output, or a growth rate of 5 percent a year over the twenty-year period. China came out with a little surplus, as its population had grown at a rate of about 2 percent a year.

However, China has come into the world market with and for its grains in recent years. For a time in the early 1970s, it was China's strategy to import wheat for domestic use and export rice in exchange for sugar from Cuba and rubber from Sri Lanka. The rice also served to feed North Vietnam's armies. Richard Nixon's 1972 trip to the People's Republic opened up a good trade in grain between the United States and the PRC. During 1973 and 1974, the PRC bought U.S. wheat, corn, and, oddly, soybeans, even though it is the world's third-largest soybean producer.

Since then, trade has fallen off, for several reasons. One mentioned openly by the Chinese is that U.S. quality has not met Chinese standards. Some speculate that this is related to the grain-inspection scandals already mentioned. Another factor is undoubtedly a lack of foreign exchange, since the trade balance between the United States and the PRC is 11 to 1 in America's favor. Finally, and perhaps most important, the United States has been only a residual supplier, as China has long-term purchase contracts with Canada and Australia.

This might change, however, as American firms court the Chinese. Cargill and Continental are regular visitors to the Canton Trade Fair, while presidents and top executives of Pillsbury, Multifoods, Archer Daniels Midland, and the I. S. Joseph Company were invited to visit the PRC in September 1975 as part of a trip arranged for Governor Wendell Anderson of Minnesota. The Chinese invited Anderson because their political analysts concluded he would be going someplace in American national politics.

Perhaps in anticipation of greater U.S.-Chinese trade, the PRC in 1974 invited Warren Lebeck, president of the Chicago Board of Trade, to visit China and explain the workings of the American and international commodity markets. After his trip, Lebeck stated that the Chinese did not fully understand the futures market because "it was alien to their way of pricing in which the government maintains lower than world prices domestically." Lebeck, however, thought that the Chinese might soon begin to use the futures market on the Chicago Board of Trade.

The Chinese feel their approach to agriculture is the best and do not hesitate to criticize Soviet efforts in developing agriculture. In January 1976, China faulted Brezhnev for the poor Soviet harvest. "In his 11 years in power, as the array of shining medals grew on Brezhnev's chest, the country's grain production shrank significantly and bread available to the Soviet people became less, in a sort of inverse proportion." In addition, the Chinese try harder and seem almost mesmerized in their dedication to have their revolution succeed. It is hard to find the same enthusiasm in the Soviet Union.

The progress of the Cubans in agriculture could also be attributed to their regimentation, if not the devotion many show to the revolution. When I was in Cuba, the most prevalent sign I saw was one depicting two Cuban heroes, Camilo Cienfuegos and Ché Guevara, bearing the inscription "The best way to honor them is through daily work."

Castro took a poor, rural country (notwithstanding the urban opulence, if not corruption, of Havana) and turned it into an efficient agricultural producer. Agriculture has become the preoccupation of the Cuban people. Traditional Christmas holidays have been eliminated, not so much because of Castro's views on religion, but because they conflicted with the peak period of the sugarcane harvest.

The centerpiece of Cuba's agriculture has been the *granja,* or people's farm. These farms are large units of land that are administered professionally and on which the workers receive a wage. Sugarcane and cattle raising are handled on this basis.

Castro did one interesting thing when he took power: He did not redistribute the land to the peasants, but kept the large units with their economies of scale intact. Large private sugar plantations became large public plantations. This avoided the problem that China's land reform ran into, as land confiscation provided land for the landless, as well as the "spontaneous desire to become a capitalist," as Chou En-lai put it.

After the initial land distribution that parceled out individual plots to farmers, the Chinese government had second thoughts about allowing private farming, and had farmers pool their individual plots to form communes. To demonstrate their solidarity with the common, rather than private, ownership of land, peasants burned their individual deeds. Cuba avoided the individual plot by going to the *granja* directly, which, according to Castro, saved time.

The Castro family is particularly interested in cattle, and Fidel's brother Ramón runs a ranch that is often shown to foreign visitors. When I went through it, I knew I was not the first, as signs posted throughout the ranch were written in French, Chinese, German, Russian, and English.

Cuban results are undeniable and abound with statistics that economic planners love to rattle off. Egg production, for example, has increased tenfold in the past ten years, making this nation of 8 million self-sufficient. Insofar as chickens for meat are concerned, the next Five-Year Plan calls for broiler production to increase 230 percent.

In cattle production, the Cubans have made headway in breeding their native cattle to Holsteins. Native Brahman cattle that the Spanish first brought over to Cuba are hardy and well adapted to the heat of the tropics. Purebred Holsteins, however, don't do so well; some even get sunburned on their eyelids. The Cubans, by combining the hardy Brahman with the high-milk-producing Holstein, have bred a superior animal.

Looking for a Better Mousetrap

Not all countries, or at least their ruling powers, are willing to follow a Socialist path to solve their agricultural problems. For these countries, any number of different methods, sometimes appearing to be incompatible, may be at work at the same time. Many developing countries take the view that with slight improvements in their agricultural structure, plus the addition of modern technology, their food problems could be solved.

The structural question relates not only to land reform but to overall strategy as well. In late 1975, for example, the U.S. General Accounting Office (GAO) found that such food-poor countries as India, Pakistan, and Indonesia have agricultural policies that discourage food output. The chief constraint, according to the GAO, was that farm prices are kept low, giving farmers little incentive to produce. The GAO went so far as to propose that Food for Peace shipments be banned to countries that do not adopt satisfactory production-boosting policies. But even if reforms were instituted, developing countries would have to figure out how to stimulate peasants to produce more.

Miguel Garavito, with his half-acre plot of corn high in the Colombian Andes, is wealthy by most peasant standards, since in his area many farmers have less. Generations have eroded farm sizes as fathers have passed their lands on to many sons, the sons in turn passing them on to their sons. "Minifundia" develops and the countryside viewed from a plane looks like a patchwork of postage stamps. There are no economies of scale in this system. Worse yet, there is not even enough land to produce sufficient food to feed everyone. Miguel has five children and a pregnant wife to feed from his half acre. When his two sons grow up, the half acre will become two quarter-acre plots.

In spite of the hopelessness in dealing with this system, many governments, foreign assistance agencies, and idealistic Peace Corps volunteers like my wife and I have tried to improve traditional agriculture within the existing structure. When I was a volunteer in Panama and Colombia, I calculated the odds of success at one in a million, and nothing has happened to change my mind. A lot of people keep trying, particularly American aid officials acting out what George F. Kennan once called "the great American capacity for enthusiasm and self-hypnosis."

Small landholdings have proven to be successful in Japan and Taiwan. In Taiwan, for example, between 1911 and 1965, total agricultural production quadrupled, despite the fact that population pressure halved the average farm size from about five acres to a mere two and one-half. And the Japanese can produce food grain yields of 4,500 pounds per acre, compared to 3,050 for the United States.

The Japanese and Taiwanese have been able to get such phenomenal yields because of the no-nonsense attitudes of their small farmers and heavy dosages of fertilizer. Many developing countries hope they can instill their farmers with equal determination and provide the needed fertilizer to obtain equal yields.

Due to the large populations in most developing countries, many development planners favor small, labor-intensive farms instead of large, mechanized ones in order to make better use of capital and labor. It doesn't make much sense to introduce large-scale mechanized farming if all you end up doing is causing unemployment and spending foreign exchange to import tractors.

In the late 1960s, new technology, particularly in the form of improved seeds, gave hopes that the "green revolution" would provide the uplift peasant agriculture needed. The revolution began with a bang, for the acreage in high-yielding grain varieties rose by 100,000 times from 1964 to 1967. Pakistan and the Philippines became food exporters as a result.

But after some dramatic initial gains, the revolution slowed down. The reason, of course, was that seeds alone do not a revolution make. The new seeds required irrigation, fertilizer, insecticides, and management skills the small holders did not have. In the Philippines, the new rice seeds with all the modern inputs cost around $220 a hectare (1 hectare equals 2.47 acres) to grow in 1970, compared to $20 a hectare using traditional seeds and methods. The initial gains of the green revolution thus went to the larger commercial farmers, for they alone were able to afford the new seeds and fertilizer to go with them as well as to understand how to use the new growing techniques that the seeds required.

I remember the frustration of my Peace Corps colleague, Walter Price, when we worked together in a poor valley sixty miles from Bogotá, Colombia. Walter, a farm boy from Malta, Ohio, had gotten thirty new corn varieties from a Rockefeller Foundation–supported research station and wanted to experiment to find out which ones would do best in our misty valley. He got a farmer to grow some, and, as we predicted, three-quarters did not do well at all. One-quarter of those planted came out fine, and we looked forward to getting more of those varieties. Then we learned that the word in the valley was that farmers should stay away from our farming techniques, for three-quarters of our corn crop had failed.

Walter and I had a similar lack of success in getting farmers to plant a new potato variety that outyielded the standard by five to one. Yet farmers clung to the old one because of its "comforting" yellowish color and pungent taste, compared to our large but watery and "tasteless" hybrid.

Results were not much better for an ill-fated attempt to provide more fertilizer to go with the better seeds in India. The Indian people commonly use dried manure as fuel for cooking food. A solar-powered cooker was introduced to India for the purpose of conserving this dried manure, thus allowing it to be used as fertilizer. The cooker was important, for, translated into grain, one ton of fertilizer is worth as much as *ten* extra tons of grain. However, Indian villagers work in their fields during the day and eat their meals at night. Villagers would therefore have had to change their entire daily pattern in order to utilize the solar cooker. Scratch several thousand solar cookers.

National extension people also had their problems in getting through. In another project that I worked on in Colombia, some dedicated young Colombians administered the local branch of the Colombian Land Reform Agency (INCORA) to which I was assigned. INCORA received lots of government money, which my office lent to farmers. Trouble was, no one really knew what the farmer needed; little thought was given as to whether this fertilizer was better than that one, or whether the farmer should buy a two- or three-horsepower pump.

A chart in the cool, tiled office where I worked showed that each successive year of operation had seen an increase in loans given out. However, the amount paid back had stayed the same, and no one had bothered to calculate it for the last year. The end result of the project seemed to be that most of the farmers who had gotten loans had found themselves at the same production level as before, but now deeper in debt.

INCORA, similar to agrarian-reform agencies in other countries, had trouble assembling all the necessary people and skills to help improve the peasants' lot. More people are needed to work in all aspects of agricultural development; but in Latin American countries, where 50 percent of the people earn their living from agriculture, only 1 percent of the college graduates earn degrees in agriculture. It is more fashionable—and remunerative—to earn a degree in law, philosophy, or medicine. Agriculture is expected to take care of itself.

This fatalism makes itself most conspicuous in the driving patterns in many developing countries: Drivers pass on curves and do other interesting things that have made my heart throb on overseas trips. Muslims express the feeling that they are helpless to determine their fate by chanting *"Enshallah"* ("Allah willing"). Reflecting the Arabs' seven-hundred-year stay on the Iberian peninsula, Spanish speakers say *"Ojalá,"* and the Portuguese cry *"Oshalla,"* which are derived from and parallel the Muslim word and meaning. Thus, when someone says *"Mañana,"* it is not so much an expression of laziness as of What damn difference does it make, anyway?

In many Latin American countries, the Church reinforces this mentality, and in so doing, acts as a break to development. There are exceptions. In the valley where I worked in Colombia, Padre Varela, the parish priest of the remote and poor town of Gama, refused to buy pews for his church because they cost too much. He also announced one Sunday that people would go to Hell if they didn't use fertilizer. Other priests were not so progressive and decreed that they considered coins an insult in the collection plate—bills were much better. Worse yet, many parishes in Colombia that were supposed to give out U.S. grains for free made a practice of selling them. The bags carried a prohibition against their sale written in Spanish, but then how many of the people could read? Added to this was the dictum that the afterlife will be better, so be patient with your present situation.

People living close to starvation are in no position to experiment. If they try your new seeds and they fail, they have no reserve to turn to. This proved to be part of Ché Guevara's problem in starting a revolution in Bolivia. True, the peasants Guevara talked to were poor and exploited, but they were so close to starvation that they didn't have time to devote to revolution.

When Guevara first arrived in Bolivia, his disillusionment with his reception led him to write in his diary: "The inhabitants are as impenetrable as stones. When you speak to them, it seems as if they are making fun of you deep down in their eyes."

The resignation of the poor to their plight came across to me best in a story told to me by an ex-classmate of mine whom I met in Iran. The story dealt with a four-person family living in a mud hut under three date palms on the scorching shore of the Persian Gulf, where temperatures reach 125°F. in the summer. The man of the family spent half a day walking to the nearest nonbrackish well to bring back water for his wife and two small children. After observing this daily trek for a number of days, my classmate, now a Peace Corps volunteer, approached him as he left his hut and asked, "Why don't you move closer to the well?" Looking first at the date palms and then at his mud hut, he responded, "What, and leave all this?"

Distrust also inhibits any change from getting under way. The peasants I have worked with in Panama, Colombia, and Iran all began with the premise that you are guilty until you prove yourself innocent. And the proof may take years to develop. When I worked in Colombia, I tried to get two small cooperatives to buy their farm supplies together, but couldn't pull it off; one cooperative insisted that the truck delivering the supplies come to it first, while the other refused to cooperate unless it got preferential shipments. Each suspected the other would steal from the joint purchase. In addition, the town where one cooperative was located—and where Padre Varela gave his Hell-and-fertilizer sermon—was so distrustful of everyone that it had declared its independence from Colombia during the 1948 civil war.

Suspicion of anything new is not unique to rural societies in developing countries. Once when I was doing a seed-marketing study in Alabama, I met a seed salesman in Albertville, a prosperous farm community in the northern Alabama hills. The salesman told me that even though he was from neighboring Mississippi and had lived in Albertville for nineteen years, local folks still regarded him as a "drifter."

Getting agriculture moving in a traditional society also involves education, which is woefully lacking in most developing countries. To get anything across, you have to take your time. When I began working with one farm cooperative in Gacheta, Colombia, I guess I expected too much of the co-op's peasant manager, Luis Garavito.

Prior to his coming to work as manager, he had run his own little store, selling farm needs, seeds, fertilizer, and the like to other peasants. Don Luis also had a little carpentry business, specializing in baby coffins, as infant mortality was high.

So when I asked Luis Garavito to accompany me on an inspection trip to a neighboring valley where some really successful cooperatives were operating, I thought he could soak it all in. We set out enthused and spent two full days looking at cooperative operations: purchasing, bookkeeping, transport, farm storage—we covered it all. I returned from the valley feeling that the Gacheta co-op could really take off. About a week after our return, the co-op had a board of directors meeting and Garavito was asked to tell about what he had learned in the other valley. At the meeting, he got up and thanked me effusively and publicly for arranging the trip. He then turned to the board members and stated: "It was very interesting. And I saw an ingenious mousetrap that we shall use in the co-op store here." That was all. He sat down. I was crushed, but better aware that it was going to take more than a two-day trip to undo decades of illiteracy, ignorance, and suspicion.

Combine this peasant mentality with structural problems like unequal land distribution, lack of incentives to produce, and you have an agricultural sector that is not going to go anywhere. I talked about these problems in Cuba, and someone asked, "How are you going to do anything without changing the system?"

These rural sociology problems came closest to Americans in recent years during our "Vietnamization" program in South Vietnam. Where the United States and the Thieu government failed was in sending more bombs and troops instead of people who understood the culture of poverty. Urban military people with no experience sought to change the thinking in the countryside overnight, a goal anyone familiar with development would have known was doomed to failure.

But cultural constraints are not the only barriers to getting new technology and opportunities to farmers. When I worked in the beautiful, fertile, but remote part of Panama hard on the border with Costa Rica, I tried to encourage farmers to grow grain. They responded, "We need a road first, then we can move the grain to market." Panama continues to import a major part of its food. But my efforts in that part of Panama yielded one interesting sidelight.

Since the government was unmoved by that area's agricultural potential, I half-seriously told several farmers that the only way they could ever get a road would be if the government thought revolutionaries prowled those verdant uplands. Sure enough, soon after Panama's present government under Omar Torrijos seized power on October 11, 1968, a countercoup began in the hills, and not so long thereafter, a road was put in to make the area more accessible—for the military. I have a deep desire to go back and see if any grain is being grown now.

One further problem with Panama's road system—which consists mainly of the well-constructed concrete ribbon they call the Inter-American Highway—is that they shot their entire wad on that big effort. The problem then becomes how to reach the Inter-American, for the access roads are just not there. By contrast, in neighboring Costa Rica, their portion of the Inter-American is not paved, yet they have far more access roads. I have to believe that because the Costa Rican government spent less on the big road, money was left for the important little ones.

Similar barriers face farmers in the rugged Andes in Peru. The government spent a long time telling farmers about the wonders of fertilizer; however, as one Peace Corps volunteer told it, the fertilizer could be helpful only to farmers along the precious few roads and railroads. Many farmers had the money and interest to use fertilizer, but were not overly enthusiastic about carrying a hundred pounds of it on their backs, as walking was the only way to get to their farms.

Having learned from others' mistakes, many developing countries are trying to change their mentality and structure, but have a long way to go. In the late 1960s, Guatemala had 516 farms, representing 40 percent of the agricultural land, while in Brazil, half the land was in the hands of 2 percent of the owners. Both countries now are trying to change this.

But rather than face the delicate question of land reform, a number of countries have embarked on colonization schemes in an attempt to increase agricultural production and to divert attention from the more insoluble problems. Probably the best-known effort is the construction of the Trans-Amazon Highway and its related farm settlements by the Brazilian government.

At first glance, this seemed like a good move. Peasants who farmed small plots in the drought-ridden northeast of Brazil would be brought in to farm larger lands amid lush vegetation. The allure was the provision of 217 acres of land, priced from $1.75 to $17 per acre, and easy credit for tools and seed, with repayment to begin only when the settler got on his feet.

The problem was that lush vegetation does not mean good farming. Jungles are closed and very delicate ecosystems, which have fed on themselves for centuries. Break the ecological chain and the whole system breaks down, which is what happened when hundreds of settlers began to move in. Trees came down and the underbrush was burned. Some crops were planted, but the poor soil, "leached" or drained of nutrients by centuries of tropical rains, yielded only one or two harvests. The next year, the farmer slashed and burned some more forest. Meanwhile, ecologists looked on in dismay as the western hemisphere's main oxygen source—the verdant green jungle—literally went up in smoke. Knowledgeable agricultural development experts had anticipated these problems long before the Trans-Amazon experiment began, and had asked, "If the jungle was so good for agriculture, why wasn't it settled and farmed before?"

The reality of Brazil is neither the Trans-Amazon Highway nor the beaches of Rio de Janeiro, but the drought-stricken Northeast— the hump of Brazil. The plight of the 32 million people living there led Brazil's former president Emilio Medici to say, "The economy is getting along fine, but the majority of people are still getting along badly."

Traveling through the almost desert-like region, as I did in 1972, is almost as grim as going over the statistics: Parasites are responsible for 23 percent of all deaths, 70 percent of the children are seriously underweight, and the average life span is only fifty years, compared to sixty-eight in the United States. Forty percent of the homes are inadequate, and the average per-capita income is $190 per year. It was this almost hopeless situation that contributed to the Trans-Amazon Highway and colonization program.

Big projects like the Aswan High Dam or the Trans-Amazon colonization program and big publicized cures like the "green revolution" are not really the solution. One wizened but dedicated United Nations worker I met in the Iranian desert told me, "The solution to poverty lies in the trenches right here, not in any fancy irrigation project. You got to deal with the people."

But even if you deal with the people and push land reform in a settled area, it still does not follow that agricultural development will result. In 1910, Mexico had the first peasant revolution in Latin

America, which brought about the *ejido,* a form of communal village ownership under which land may be worked collectively or individually, though in neither case may it be sold, leased, or mortgaged. And although land redistribution did occur, only 35 percent of the annual farm production is reaped from this 70 percent of the total cultivated land. Big commercial farms—agribusiness again—produce most of Mexico's food, creating a problem for Mexico's planners: Do you stimulate the *ejido*s, which is the politically desirable thing to do, or do you give further help to the commercial farms, which you know will produce the food you need?

President Abdul Gamal Nasser faced a similar problem in Egypt after the construction of the Aswan High Dam. Nikita Khrushchev and Nasser went on a tour of the dam and its irrigation works, which prompted Khrushchev to ask Nasser how he intended to structure the farming. Nasser told Khrushchev that he intended to go through a land-reform program and give each farmer his own little plot of land. This prompted Khrushchev to tell Nasser that he would not divide up the land and portion it out to individual peasants, but rather, he would set up state farms. Khrushchev went on to explain that only on large farm units can you expect to use modern farm machinery and technology. He then emphasized to Nasser, "Believe me, if you share out small pieces of land to individual farmers, the Egyptian peasant will remain just as much a slave to his own land as he has been for centuries."

Nasser listened, agreed, but had to point out that he didn't have the talent to set up a state farm system, and was concerned over the corruption of state farm managers. He also pointed out to Khrushchev that he was politically better off giving every farmer his own plot of land, instead of creating large state farms.

Lock, Stock, and Barrel

The slowness many developing countries have experienced in increasing agricultural production—given the peasant mentality and their structural problems, not to mention lack of funds and technicians—has created an interest in bringing in American agribusiness "lock, stock, and barrel," as one transplanted California farmer told me in Iran.

I went to Iran for the first time in 1970 as an economist assigned to the Dez Irrigation Project in torrid Khuzistan Province. As the various ruins attest, the project area was once the headquarters of Darius the Great and the breadbasket of the ancient Persian empire. But centuries of neglect had turned the region into a barren wasteland.

The Shah of Iran had read of the transformation brought about by the Tennessee Valley Authority and had sought out David Lilienthal, its first chairman, who had since begun his own consulting firm with the expressed desire of creating little TVAs around the world. Lilienthal's firm, the Development and Resources Corporation, began planning and then constructing a dam and an irrigation network in the Dez area. A research station was constructed, as was a sugarcane mill. Rural sociologists and farm managers were brought in to help develop the 250,000 acres that the irrigation project would encompass. The water began to flow to the farms of traditional farmers, but agricultural production did not increase as fast as the government had hoped—it rarely does.

Finally, the government decided to wait no longer and granted long-term leases to foreign and domestic agribusiness companies. The World Bank, which had extended $30 million to the Iranian government for this project, was upset that the traditional farmer was being phased out. A development economist lamented that the project had "lost its soul."

Nevertheless, private companies from California and Great Britain, with financial and technical backing from some of the world's largest banks and farm-equipment manufacturers, were ready to spend the $2,500 necessary to properly capitalize each acre for intensive mechanized farming. One of the first U.S. farmers to arrive was George Wilson, who began his Iranian operation in 1970. Seventy-eight at the time, the no-nonsense Wilson, who once headed the California Farm Bureau, first saw the Dez area in 1949. "I saw those big rivers and all that land laying there," he reflects, "and it looked goldurned good to a farmer like me. I thought then I'd like to have a piece of it someday."

The Iranian government welcomed the interest and the investment; barley yields would increase by 50 percent, wheat by 60 percent, and alfalfa by 25 percent. Furthermore, the new firms, with names like Iran-America and Iran-California, would give employment to displaced farmers, some of whom had had their homes bulldozed to offer greater farming efficiencies. To emphasize the transformation, one of the firms paraded all its agricultural ma-

chinery three hundred miles from the port to the irrigation project.
Green John Deere tractors became as common a sight as the donkey.

Not dissimilar efforts are under way in other parts of the world.
Recognizing the interest many developing countries have in the total
transfer of our agriculture, an organization called the Agribusiness
Council was created in 1967 "to aid in relieving the problems of
world food supply through using the skill and resources of private
business." Through the use of money from the U.S. Agency for
International Development (AID) and subscriptions from its members (for example, Cargill, Del Monte, and Ralston Purina), the
council would finance studies of agribusiness opportunities in
developing countries. If the study led to an investment, you would
pay back the cost; if it didn't, the council would pay, of course. The
companies going into developing countries did so primarily for
profit, rather than to "do good."

The council now gets much of its funding from the Overseas
Private Investment Corporation (OPIC), which has granted loans to
U.S. firms to raise corn in Yugoslavia, cattle in Korea, and poultry in
Thailand, as well as for farming in the Dez Irrigation Project in Iran
and the controversial support of Cargill's soybean-processing venture
in Brazil. This was the investment that infuriated the American
Soybean Association because the soybeans processed will compete
for markets with U.S. exports with the assistance of U.S. tax dollars.
U.S. farmers have also complained about World Bank loans to the
Malaysian Palm Oil industry, which competes with U.S. soybean oil.
In testimony before the Senate Agriculture Committee, a spokesman
for the American Soybean Association said that giving this type of
foreign aid would "be a little bit like the New York Yankees loaning
Catfish Hunter to the Oakland A's."

The Agribusiness Accountability Project has also attacked the
spread of U.S. agribusiness abroad, but for different reasons. The
project contends that U.S. agribusiness is a "destructive alternative
for developing countries" because U.S. agribusiness multinationals
want to instill the same control over the foreign consumer that they
have in the United States. The project contends that people in
developing countries are to be "serfs to the processing and marketing
systems and captive buyers of inputs."

André Gillette, vice-president of the International Division of
Multifoods, doesn't feel that way. In 1957, Multifoods built the first

flour mill in Venezuela, and Gillette feels it has made solid contributions to that oil-rich, but agriculturally poor, country's development. Gillette recalls with a gleam in his French eye that when the plant was first built the employees came to work barefoot; then, through his ten years in Venezuela, he saw them wear shoes, buy bicycles, and finally come in cars. Gillette insisted that a union be formed at the mill and that all the Americans working at the plant speak Spanish. While he admits Multifoods found its Venezuelan operation profitable, he adds that Venezuela saved money by importing wheat in bulk for milling, instead of importing cumbersome sacks of flour. Shipping in sacks may cost as much as four times as shipping in bulk, due to the extra handling involved.

Multifoods' operations grew and sought to develop local sources of feed grains by beginning a 25,000-acre farming operation. It failed, but Gillette feels it served to give the government a better insight into what could be grown. One of the reasons the farming venture failed was that large flocks of birds arrived at a time when the grain was most susceptible, although statistical averages showed that they should not have come during that time of year.

Multifoods became somewhat of an agribusiness pioneer in Venezuela, and Pillsbury may become one in Saudi Arabia. In 1974, Pillsbury signed an agreement with that petroleum-rich country for the construction of three flour mills, valued at $90 million. Six months later, the Saudis went after more U.S. grain technology, with a contract for the construction of a $30-million rice mill to be built by a Houston engineering firm and supplied with rice by a Texas rice mill.

Not only are Middle East countries pursuing U.S. agribusiness, but the U.S. firms are courting them as well, in the face of U.S. energy problems. In 1975, a two-man team representing eighteen of the largest farm cooperatives in the United States visited Saudi Arabia. They proposed to trade the cooperatives' collective agricultural wisdom and technology for crude oil. The Saudis turned the proposal down, wanting to keep the two items separate.

American agribusiness firms can always depend on farmers like Dale Yahnke to produce the raw materials they need to run their food-manufacturing operations. But in a developing country they have no one like Dale to depend on, and as a result can't operate their plants at maximum efficiency. Commodities simply cannot be produced locally in sufficient quantity, and if they have to be imported, arrive late. This causes havoc with production schedules and the shortened incumbency of American plant managers.

In Panama, one dairy products plant in David, the third-largest city, depends on farmers to make daily deliveries of milk. A lot of the milk comes from the high plateau area where the roads become impassable during the rainy season. I remember several occasions when I went on the proverbial milk run, which sometimes took fourteen hours to cover forty miles because of the mud-clogged roads. And whenever it took this long (instead of the usual four hours), the milk would arrive spoiled.

Multifoods in Venezuela was well off by comparison because all the wheat they used was imported. Nevertheless, they lost eighty-one days' milling time in 1975 because the government buying agency, through which Multifoods has to buy its imported wheat, proved less than dependable in securing on-time shipments.

As a consequence, many U.S. agribusiness firms have had to get into food production in order to be able to do their processing overseas. At one time, CPC International in Pakistan had to buy a twelve months' supply of corn at a time to be assured of enough inventory to make various corn products. It then decided to provide technical assistance to farmers and set up farm service centers to give corn farmers credit, seeds, and agricultural chemicals. It seems to have worked, as CPC could process four times as much after it got into farming than before, when it relied on the farmers alone.

Foremost Foods Company's Pak Dairy Company in Tehran underwent the same transformation to the point where it now has nine hundred of its own cows, and plans to buy land and grow its own feed, as well.

The administrative disarray and corruption in many developing countries also hinder their agricultural development and inhibit, if not eliminate, the interest of agribusiness firms in transferring their technology. Haiti is perhaps the poorest country in the western hemisphere and is run by Jean Claude Duvalier, whose official title is "President for Life," but who has become known affectionately to the world's press as "Baby Doc." Not imbued with the ruthlessness of his father ("Papa Doc"), young Jean Claude is content to ride his motorcycle and his 240-Z on the few stretches of good road in his poor country. Corruption has been rife over the years, while agricultural development has floundered. Consequently, Haiti's five million people have a very lean look to them. It is no wonder that when ships arrive to unload vegetable oil, people set off in rowboats to gather any that might spill in the unloading.

Into this setting stepped one U.S. commodities firm, which in 1972 began shipping vegetable oil to Haiti. Sensing an opportunity to do something different, the company's president decided to build a soybean-crushing factory in Haiti. Not only would Haiti gain from having Dale Yahnke's soybeans crushed there, instead of in Minnesota, but the project would act as a stimulus to develop a local oilseeds industry. Called St. Pierre Industries, the proposed factory picked up support with the government, strongly influenced by the mysterious, if not sinister, cabinet minister Lucknor Cambronne.

The U.S. government was also pleased, as this project had more social redemption connected with it than other American enterprises in Haiti such as those that bought and exported human blood, or a number of gambling casinos with reputed Mafia connections.

In 1973, the Haitian government accepted the company's proposal, signed and published a contract, but inexplicably disavowed it a week later. The government then said the project would have exploited the Haitian people. Some American observers felt that some of the importers of vegetable oil must have bought the government off.

Whatever the case, the project was dead until "Baby Doc" got rid of Cambronne and his minister of commerce. A bright new minister of commerce by the name of Serge Fourcand came in. He liked the project and asked the U.S. company to make a new proposal, which it enthusiastically did. Fourcand also asked the company's president to come to Haiti to present it. Even the oil importers seemed more cooperative.

The American executive had hoped for an attentive, all-day discussion with Fourcand, but, instead, received a rather cold, nervous interview. Soldiers with guns sat in the next office. The next day's news gave a deeper insight into Fourcand's attitude: He had been arrested the night before and charged with a $1-million scheme to counterfeit postage stamps and sell them to collectors. The project was shelved again, where it remains.

Since World War II, the most interesting, if not the most controversial, U.S. agribusiness abroad has been the International Basic Economy Corporation (IBEC). While most U.S. agribusiness overseas springs from domestic U.S. operations, IBEC began overseas and had as its goal "to initiate and operate ventures that are responsive to basic human needs." Nelson Rockefeller spurred the development of IBEC, which is now headed by his son Rodman. Some officials in developing countries were wary of this effort, recalling Henry David Thoreau's famous comment; "If I knew for a certainty that a man was coming to my house with a conscious design of doing me good, I should run for my life."

In the few decades IBEC has operated, it has become the largest single food retailer in Latin America through its operation of supermarkets in Argentina, Brazil, Venezuela, Puerto Rico, and Peru. In addition, its Sementes Agroceres hybrid-seed operation in Brazil is the world's largest hybrid-seed producer outside the United States. Apart from these operations, IBEC engages in poultry breeding, oilseed crushing, and milk production. It has become both an example of the "good" American agribusiness can do and a rallying point against too much American influence in food production in developing countries.

IBEC came under considerable attack in 1969 when President Richard Nixon chose Nelson Rockefeller to make a goodwill tour of Latin America. While it may be true that Rockefeller knows Latin America and speaks Spanish, he was the worst possible choice Nixon could have made, for to many Latins "Rocky" represented U.S. imperialism and exploitation. I was in Colombia at the time, and Colombians saw the worst of the United States in Rockefeller and would even get violent when a movie newsreel of his trip was shown; garbage was actually thrown at the screen.

Worse for Rockefeller, bombs were thrown at IBEC supermarkets, leveling just about every one in Argentina as a protest against his Latin American trip. But an IBEC vice-president later told me it was not all bad, for the Argentina markets were in bad locations, anyway. The rebuilt stores really picked up business in better locations.

Recently, Venezuela became concerned that a foreign company controlled the largest supermarket, so it forced IBEC to sell an 80 percent interest to Venezuelans. The Venezuelans also moved against flour millers like Multifoods by requiring them to buy their grain through the government food-import agency. While this satisfied nationalist fervor, it did not stop American food firms from growing in Venezuela. Once when I was in Caracas, a local Venezuelan pointed out, with pride, the building housing the food agency, but said nothing about the Kentucky Fried Chicken take-out across the street, where many of the import agency's personnel ate.

Cook Industries, the large grain exporter, has embarked on a program similar to IBEC's to bring its management skills to food distribution. In 1975, Cook bought a controlling interest in World Food Systems, whose goal is to eliminate the waste in the food-marketing systems of developing countries. This waste became apparent to many Americans during our relief food shipments at the time of the West African drought. The food arrived in Africa, but a lot of it rotted on the docks, as there was no means of delivering it inland. Eventually, the food was airlifted in, but the United States paid the bill. None of the West African countries could have done this on their own. Grain shipments to Afghanistan faced the same distribution problems, and eventually Peace Corps volunteers played a large role in that spectacular, but landlocked, country's food distribution.

World Food Systems contends that sufficient food is already produced; it just doesn't get distributed. In its presentation, World Food points out that in some areas of the world, 30 percent of the food produced is wasted or lost between farm and market. One specific way World Food figures it can help developing countries is through the creation of better institutional feeding programs, such as school lunches. Accordingly, it has set up a school lunch program for 70,000 children in Jamaica. The acquisition of World Food puts Cook Industries in the unique position of distributing food from the field to the table. While this prospect frightens some nationalists, it does bring some good ideas to food distribution.

Seizing on the examples of foreign agribusiness firms, the governments of developing countries are creating their own institutions to deal with food problems on a more modern business basis. One such effort is Jamaica Nutrition Holdings Limited (JNH), which was set up in 1974 to take over all foreign commodity buying previously done by local firms and to develop local food industries. JNH was seen as one way Jamaica could lower its food-import bill and develop high-nutrition food industries that private industry would not undertake. Mexico's CONASUPO (an acronym for National Basic Foods Company) performs basically the same function and has put increased emphasis on introducing soy protein into tortillas and meat products.

To support similar programs in other countries, AID has financed qualified food processors in the development of protein-enriched foods. A commercial approach was needed because low-income consumers in developing countries simply wouldn't buy food that upper-income consumers rejected. "Why should I eat something that the rich won't?" was the common complaint. The new foods are now marketed similarly to Pepsi-Cola or any other consumer item.

But while all these indigenous food programs may develop local food industries and improve local distribution, many of the raw materials will still have to come from Dale Yahnke's or Gordon MacClean's farm. The frustrating thing to consider is that we find ourselves in the position of having discussed the cure for hunger, yet are restrained, due to political and social problems in developing countries, from making the cure available to the rest of the world.

13

FOOD IN THE FUTURE

Steak in a capsule. A return to hunting. Push-button farming. Fish farms. A global food war caused when a secret chemical devastates American agriculture, leading to a takeover of Brazil by the United States, which the Soviets oppose. Or perhaps just a progression of our food habits as they are. All of the above have been put forth as possibilities for the way we will sustain ourselves in the future.

Few foresee push-button farming, although enclosed hydroponic greenhouses (soilless agriculture) come close—but it can't be used on a large scale. The questions facing agricultural planners today are how large farms should be and whether the government should have anything to do with farming at all.

These questions were examined by the USDA in the latter part of 1975 at a symposium on alternative futures for U.S. agriculture. Department of Agriculture planners looked into their crystal balls and tried to envision the American farm in 2010 under three separate circumstances, or "scenarios."

By 2010, Americans should number 300 million people, who, regardless of which scenario you look at, will spend only about 8 percent of their disposable income on food. A Chicago consulting firm has indicated that this percentage may hold, but that prices by the year 2000—based on current rates of inflation—may be staggering, citing $130 for a dozen grade A eggs and $230 for a pound of ground beef.

The type of farming we end up with will depend more on politics than on economics, as the three scenarios examined by the USDA—supply-management future, maximum-efficiency future, and small-farm future—can all produce enough food for all Americans at reasonable costs.

The supply-management future would basically be a repeat of the farm policies the United States pursued from 1930 to 1970, with the government's jumping in to restrict production and to manage exports and prices. The number of farms would be reduced by half the present total, and the risk of water pollution would rise as chemical-fertilizer use was increased in attempts to overcome acreage restrictions and maintain production. Farm size would be around 50 percent larger than present.

The biggest farms would result from leaving agriculture alone and letting the most efficient farmers continue expanding. USDA planners feel that if this type of farming were allowed to flourish, the present number of farms would be decreased by two-thirds while the "average" farm would increase to 1,000 acres. The planners feel that this scenario would produce superior benefits to consumers in terms of lower food costs, and to taxpayers, as no subsidy payments would be necessary. However, medium-size farmers like Lester Wolverton wonder what would happen to the fiber of the country if his grandchildren were forced to leave the farm. "The family tree grows best in Pretty Prairie."

Whatever the farm scenario will be, it is a sure bet that we will still have the same crops, although we will utilize them differently.

Soybean-based foods will continue to grow in importance: One food analyst anticipates a growth of 25 percent per annum to 1985. Part of the boom is due to a Federal Drug Administration ruling that the word *imitation* no longer has to be used on labels as long as soy products—bacon strips to coffee whiteners—are nutritionally equivalent to the real thing. Some companies in the meat industry are upset by these developments, while others, like Swift, are hedging their bets and getting involved in soy foods as well. And Ralston Purina, which has made billions by feeding the animals that we, in turn, eat, has also gone into soy proteins. In fact, all the big agribusiness firms—Cargill, Carnation, Central Soya, and General Mills, for example—have invested millions in soy-protein development. The reason is obvious, as some researchers predict that 20 percent of the "meat" we eat in 1980 will be made from soy proteins.

This trend would no doubt please George Bernard Shaw's vegetarian soul; he once stated that eating meat "involves a prodigious slavery of men to animals ... graziers, shepherds, slaughtermen, butchers, milkmaids and so forth absorb a mass of human labor that should be devoted to the breeding and care of human beings."

However, soybeans are not the only new protein source of the future. Scientists have come up with something called "single-cell protein," made from petroleum. Accordingly, some folks in Hutchinson, Minnesota, a soybean-growing area, were shocked when they saw a new food firm named Amoco Foods begin operations there in 1975. Amoco is producing yeast from ethyl alcohol refined from petroleum. The yeast serves as a nutritional flavor-enhancer for meat and bread. One low-calorie Thousand Island dressing also uses Amoco's "food oil" to liven up its products, and Morton Frozen Foods and ITT-Continental baking use the yeast to make high-protein macaroni for a federally funded school lunch program in New York. Amoco Foods' marketing director says that by the end of 1976 supermarket shoppers will find twenty-five to thirty meat and bakery products containing yeast produced from petroleum.

The value of using petroleum for protein is that it shortens the food chain. You get the protein direct instead of having to raise plants or animals, both of which require large amounts of petroleum in the form of fertilizer, gasoline for tractors and trucks, not to mention the energy used to process them into an edible form.

These new types of proteins are potent, but Dr. Alvan Pyne, International Multifoods' chief food technologist, warns not to expect a steak in a pill, as the technology doesn't exist to pack that much power into such a small space. As he put it, the "caloric density is lacking."

The year 1974 was an important one for food from petroleum, which a research firm highlighted by stating, "This breakthrough has introduced the oil majors to the supply chain of the food industry, and manufacturers are now able to establish a new industry, the industry of plastic foods, which will not depend on agriculture."

Iran's National Oil Company promises to make artificial meat from oil available by 1979, while other foreign oil companies are already making animal feeds from oil. British Petroleum has factories making petroleum-based animal feeds in Scotland and France and has plans for similar projects in Venezuela and Indonesia.

Not everyone is willing to go along with this new technology. A countermovement directed against junk-food addicts as well as against chemically made-up foods has sprung up in many parts of the world. Jewel Foods in Chicago reported that its 1975 flour sales were up 10 percent from the previous year, while its sales of frozen foods and canned products were down. Some consumers are going a step further and are home-milling their wheat. This is not only from a desire to get back to basics, but, as one health-food proponent stated, "Eating natural food is a way of subverting Safeway."

How strong an urge there will be to get back to basics remains to be seen. It is ironic that Kellogg's Corn Flakes, which today is nowhere to be found in health-food stores, was once considered a "health food." Dr. John Harvey Kellogg believed that "it was God's law that man eat only plants and fruits," and accordingly Dr. Kellogg's sanitarium began to offer granola—that is, the original cornflakes.

One naturalist, Paul Shephard of Dartmouth College, feels that man's diet should go back even farther than granola. Shephard thinks that because man arose in the Pleistocene ice ages, he should seek to recreate that original life-style. "The past is the formula for our being." The Dartmouth philosopher has no kind words to say about farming or eating grains, and feels we will not get anywhere by "backtracking to the barnyard"; he wants man to "embrace the hunter as part of ourselves as a step towards repairing the injury to our planet." To Shephard's way of thinking, Dale Yahnke despoils the planet as much as the Los Angeles freeway.

Most food company executives I talked to didn't want to reveal their thoughts concerning what direction man's eating habits would —or, for that matter, should—take. Dwight Stuart, Carnation's president, replied quite bluntly to my questions on food and the future: "Any ideas generated here on the types of food to be consumed, the packaging of this food, and where it might be eaten would be of consideration in our plans for the future and consequently confidential."

Dr. Pyne of Multifoods, despite his lack of optimism about steak in a pill, feels food technology has almost limitless possibilities. But the technology involved in making new foods out of grain or meat is not the problem, states Dr. Pyne; marketing is. Implicit in Dr. Pyne's look at the future is a confidence in America's present food-producing system, which gives him and the American food shopper the luxury of worrying about what kind of food we should have, while most of the rest of the world ponders: Will we have enough?

BIBLIOGRAPHY

CHAPTER 2. GETTING THE CROP IN

A great deal of the background for this chapter came from trips to North Dakota, Iowa and Kansas, where farmers and other agribusiness persons were interested in discussing their plans and prospects. Considerable secondary information was obtained from the following sources:

BOOKS.
Hightower, Jim. *Eat Your Heart Out.* New York: Crown, 1975.
Prestbo, John A. *This Abundant Land.* Princeton: Dow Jones Books, 1975.
Robbins, William. *The American Food Scandal.* New York: Morrow, 1974.
Trager, James. *Amber Waves of Grain.* New York: Arthur Fields, 1973.
Willford, Harrison. *Sowing the Wind.* New York: Grossman, 1972.

MAGAZINES AND NEWSPAPERS.
"Families to Continue Most Farming," *Madison Wisconsin State Journal,* October 7, 1975.
"Farmers Continue Upward Equipment Buying Trend," *Feedstuffs,* January 27, 1975.
"Farmfest '76 Planners Hope to Attract City Folk," *Minneapolis Tribune,* September 21, 1975.
"Farm-Managing Firms Find Demand Rising for Their Assistance," *Wall Street Journal,* August 25, 1975.
"Farm Production Expenses Hit $73 Billion in '74," *Feedstuffs,* August 18, 1975.
"Farm Supershow Draws 75,000 to Malta," *Chicago Tribune,* October 1, 1975.
"Food and Feud . . . And The Future of Animal Agriculture," *Feedstuffs,* June 9, 1975.
"Gleaners Gather After Reaper to Feed World's Poor," *The New York Times,* October 9, 1975.
"Increased Use of Irrigation Boosts Yields of Corn, Sugar Beets, Beans in Nebraska," *Wall Street Journal,* November 17, 1975.
"Issues, Food and Fiber 1974," *St. Paul Dispatch-Pioneer Press,* April 26, 1974.
"Management Decisions by Computer," *Soybean Digest,* October, 1975.
"Minnesota's Changing Farms," *Minneapolis Tribune,* February 2, 1975.
"New Farm Equipment Needs," *Minneapolis Tribune,* September 7, 1975.
Putney, Michael. "Harvest Tool: The Hammer and Sickle," *The National Observer,* August 16, 1975.
"Redefined 'Farm' Will Drop Small Farmers From Census," *Feedstuffs,* September 1, 1975.

"Suddenly, An Alarm Over Vanishing Farms," *U.S. News & World Report,* September 15, 1975.

"Super Technician Seen Replacing Super Salesman," *Feedstuffs,* September 29, 1975.

GOVERNMENT PUBLICATIONS.

Cropland For Today and Tomorrow. Economic Research Service, USDA Agricultural Economic Report 291, July 1975.

"The Farmer and His Farm," *The Farm Index.* USDA, April 1975.

Number of Farms and Land in Farms. USDA Statistical Reporting Service, December 30, 1974.

The Yearbook of Agriculture 1975. USDA, 1975.

PAMPHLETS, REPORTS, STUDIES.

"Agricultural Production Efficiency," National Academy of Sciences, 1975.

"Continental Grain Company—Export Controls," Case Study prepared by Harvard Business School, 1974.

Lockeretz, William, *et al. A Comparison of the Production, Economic Returns, and Energy Intensiveness of Corn Belt Farms That Do and Do Not Use Inorganic Fertilizers and Pesticides.* Center for the Biology of Natural Systems, Washington University, July 1975.

Professional Farmers of America Membership Brochure, 1976.

Rural America. "Energy and Rural People and Agriculture," Proceedings of the First National Conference on Rural America, April 14-17, 1975.

INTERVIEWS.

Hovland, Harvey. Northwood, North Dakota, November 1975.

MacClean, George. Gilbey, North Dakota, November 1975.

Wolverton, Lester. Pretty Prairie, Kansas, November 1975.

Yahnke, Dale. Lake Crystal, Minnesota, October 4, 1975.

CHAPTER 3. HOME COOKING

Domestic food policy is always changing and direct contacts with the Secretary of Agriculture, other public officials, and interest groups enabled a great deal of information to be assembled firsthand. Secondary data was gleaned from the following sources:

MAGAZINES AND NEWSPAPERS.

Ag World, November 1975.

Brown, Robert H. "Egg Industry's Future Depends on Ability to Overcome Cholesterol Misconceptions," *Feedstuffs,* August 25, 1975.

"Cookie-Cracker Industry Shipments Up," *Milling and Baking News,* March 4, 1975.

"Court Action Paves Way for New Meat Rules," *Minneapolis Tribune,* October 14, 1975.

Emerson, Gail. "Egg Substitute Market Hits $20 Million, But Value to Egg Industry Questioned," *Feedstuffs*, June 23, 1975.

"Federal Domination Must be Avoided," *Milling and Baking News*, March 25, 1975.

"Food Stamp Program Reform Urged," *Journal of Commerce*, October 9, 1975.

Foreman, Carol Tucker. "Hang Together or Separately," *Farm Journal*, December 1975.

Girres, Fred. "Administration Tries to Soothe Producers, Public," *Feedstuffs*, November 4, 1974.

———. "94th Congress: More Liberal and Reform-Minded," *ibid.*, December 30, 1974.

Gottschalk, Earl C. "In Tucson, Students are Down in Dumps But Most Are Happy," *Wall Street Journal*, December 5, 1975.

Hannifin, Jerry, and Witt, Linda. "Earl Butz of Agriculture Is Its Fastest Tongue," *Ag World*, November 1975.

Humphrey, Hubert H. "The Case for Stability in Commodity Prices," *Ag World*, July 1975.

"Industrial Flour Rise Offsets Family Drop," *Milling and Baking News*, July 8, 1975.

Jacqueney, Theodore. "Washington Pressures/Public Interest Groups Challenge Government Industry," *National Journal Reports*, February 23, 1974.

"Keep 'Em on the Farm," *St. Paul Pioneer Press*, October 3, 1975.

Kopperud, Steve. "Pet Food Consumption by Poor Debated," *Feedstuffs*, December 9, 1974.

"A Landmark Study," *Milling and Baking News*, October 7, 1975.

Lukes, Thomas H. "Feed Production and Acceptance: Consumer Attitudes and Problems," *Feedstuffs*, December 23, 1974.

"Many New Flour Consumption Insights," *Milling and Baking News*, August 26, 1975.

McClung, John. "Senate Passes Compromise Bill Banning DES Use," *Feedstuffs*, September 15, 1975.

"Millers Pleased with D.C. Offices," *Milling and Baking News*, February 18, 1975.

"Modest Increase in Farm Fuel Use Seen by 1080," *Feedstuffs*, November 4, 1974.

"Needed: Some New Colonists to Oppose Stamp Act," *Beef*, October 1975.

"New Control of Farm Policy Described," *Milling and Baking News*, September 23, 1975.

News From the AFL-CIO, September 3, 1975.

"Of PEC and PAC," *Milling and Baking News*, September 2, 1975.

"Rapport Urged Between Miller and Baker," *Milling and Baking News*, September 16, 1975.

"Rescue a Rail Line," *Farm Journal*, October 1975.

Robbins, William. "New Shepherd For Farm Legislation," *Ag World*, July 1975.

"The Saga of the Farm Bill," *Ag World*, August 1975.

"$78 Million Food Stamp Scandal Bared," *Miami Herald*, October 29, 1975.

"Storage Space Used by CCC Too Low," *Milling and Baking News*, May 13, 1975.

"Target Price Debate," *Milling and Baking News*, February 18, 1975.

"Urges Ending of Rice Controls to End World Hunger," *Milling and Baking News*, April 29, 1975.

Wall Street Journal: June 30, 1975, p. 14; October 8, 1975, p. 3; November 13, 1975, p. 16.

Weaver, Warren. "Ruling Strengthens Co-ops' Political Arm," *Minneapolis Tribune,* September 29, 1975.
"Wheat Allotment Raised for '76 Crop," *Milling and Baking News,* April 15, 1975.
"Wheat Institute Reviews Research and Promotion," *Milling and Baking News,* April 22, 1975.

GOVERNMENT PUBLICATIONS.
Congressional Record: February 18, April 17, April 22, April 29, May 13, August 1, September 8, September 19 and September 23, 1975.
Food, Consumption, Prices, Expenditures. Supplement for 1973 to Agricultural Economic Report No. 138, USDA, December 1974.
The Mid-Year Review Hearings: A Summary. U.S. Congress, Joint Economic Committee, August 25, 1975.
Sebelius, Keith. "Big First Farm Report," *Sebelius Congressional Newsletter:* March 11, April 22, May 20, September 23 and November 11, 1975.

SPEECHES AND STATEMENTS.
Butz, Earl. Twenty speeches presented to various organizations during 1975 made available by the Secretary to the author.
Gorman, Aileen. "The Agricultural Outlook for 1976: A Consumer Response." Talk at the National Agricultural Outlook Conference, Washington, D.C., November 17, 1975.
"Statement by the AFL-CIO Executive Council on Russian Grain Purchases," Chicago, Illinois, July 31, 1975.
West, Quentin. "A New Context for Agriculture," Speech presented to Great Plains Agricultural Council Meeting, Bismarck, North Dakota, July 31, 1975.

LETTERS.
Hughes, Thomas R. Letter to the author, September 29, 1975.
Humphrey, Hubert H. Letter to the author, October 20, 1975.
Paarlberg, Director of Agricultural Economics, USDA. Letter to the author, September 30, 1975.
Sebelius, Keith, U.S. Representative from Kansas. Letter to the author, November 6, 1976.
Talmadge, Herman E., Chairman, Senate Committee on Agriculture and Forestry. Letter to the author, October 8, 1975.

CHAPTER 4. GAMBLING IN GRAIN

I relied heavily on my experience in the grain trade to write this chapter and was helped considerably by several active commodity traders. Other information was derived from the following:

BOOKS.
Teweles, Richard J., Harlow, Charles V., and Stone, Herbert L. *The Commodity Futures Game.* New York: McGraw-Hill, 1974.

MAGAZINES AND NEWSPAPERS.
"Bagley Worries About Insider Trade," *Milling and Baking News,* July 22, 1975.
"Brazil Looks Toward the Future(s)," *Brazilian Business,* July 1975.
Commodities, September 1975.
"Commodity Traders Rig More Computers to Forecast Prices," *Wall Street Journal,* October 8, 1975.
"Estimating U.S. Crop is a Painstaking Job and an Important One," *Wall Street Journal,* August 11, 1975.
"Faisal Death Has Minimal Impact on Grain Exports," *Reuters News Service,* March 25, 1975.
Feedstuffs, December 8, 1975.
"Foreign Trading in Futures Markets," *Feedstuffs,* March 1975.
"Futures Markets," *African Development,* September 1975.
"Information Key to Grain Profits," *Washington Post,* January 3, 1976.
"Minneapolis: Hub of Grain Trading," *Washington Post,* September 16, 1975.
"Technical Analysis Refuses to Die," *Fortune,* August 1975.
"USDA Down—CIA Up on Soviet Estimates," *Reuters News Service,* August 29, 1975.
"Why All the Fuss? U.S. Grows Enough Grain for Selves and Russ," *Chicago Tribune,* September 29, 1975.

INTERVIEWS, LETTERS, AND PAMPHLETS.
Athena Futuronics, Panama City, Panama. Letter to the author, September 1975.
Beeson, Monte, Vice President, Grain Operations, International Multifoods, Minneapolis, Minnesota. Interviewed by the author, November 14, 1975.
Global Weather Forecasting prospectus, Agromet, Palo Alto, California.

CHAPTER 5. FOLLOWING THE HARVEST MOON

Most of the observations in this chapter have come from my direct association with the grain trade. Useful additional information was gathered from the following sources:

BOOKS.
Steen, Herman. *Flour Milling in America.* Minneapolis: T.S. Denison and Co., 1963.

MAGAZINES AND NEWSPAPERS.
Meyers, Gene. "More Farmers Are Trading Futures to Smooth Peaks, Valleys in Profit," *Wall Street Journal,* November 5, 1975.
Pro Farmer, November 15, 1975.
"Storage Becomes a Marketing Alternative," *Soybean Digest,* October 1975.
Thompson, Morris. "On Farm Storage of Grains is Increasing As Farmers Hold Crops for Better Prices," *Wall Street Journal,* September 15, 1975.

CHAPTER 6. FARMING FOR FOREIGNERS

Much of the background for this chapter came from my direct involvement with grain exports. Other useful material came from the following sources:

MAGAZINES AND NEWSPAPERS.
"Contract Validity," *Milling and Baking News,* May 20, 1975.
"Federal Grain Inspection Voted," *Journal of Commerce,* November 19, 1975.
Freivalds, John. "Foreign Trading in Futures Markets," *Feedstuffs,* March 10, 1975.
Morgan, Dan. "Grain Probers Find Corruption," *Miami Herald,* December 2, 1975.
"Resellers' Market Reduces Price Risks," *Milling and Baking News,* January 21, 1975.
Robbins, William. "Bunge Guilty in Theft of Grain," *The New York Times,* October 9, 1975.

GOVERNMENT PUBLICATIONS.
Congressional Record, October 6, 1972.
Grain Inspection. U.S. Senate Subcommittee on Foreign Agricultural Policy, June 18-19, 1975.

CHAPTER 7. LET'S MAKE A DEAL

Personal experiences served as the basis for this chapter.

CHAPTER 8. OMNIVORE

A great deal of information on the growth of the grain and food industries was made available by executives within the industries themselves. Other data was from the following sources:

BOOKS.
Grigg, D. B. *The Agricultural Systems of the World.* London: Cambridge University Press, 1974.
Hamilton, Martha M. *The Great American Grain Robbery and Other Stories.* Washington: Agribusiness Accountability Project, 1972.
Kravitz, Linda. *Who's Minding the Co-op.* Washington: Agribusiness Accountability Project, April 1974.
Meat Facts '75 edition. Washington: American Meat Institute, June 1975.

MAGAZINES AND NEWSPAPERS.
"Antitrust Attack on Agriculture Co-ops May be Triggered by FTC Investigations," *Wall Street Journal,* October 1, 1975.
"Anti-Trusters in Beef Biz Facing 2 Inquiries," *The NFO Reporter,* June 1975.
"Baking Companies and Officers Fined $276,000 at Baton Rouge," *Milling and Baking News,* September 30, 1975.

"Bid to Have U.S. Inspect Grain Fails," *Des Moines Register*, November 14, 1975.

"Bunge Fined $10,000 in Grain Theft," *Minneapolis Tribune*, October 9, 1975.

"Can We Afford to Eat?" *Skeptic*, December 1975.

"Cargill Inc., a Giant in Troubled Industry, Keeps Reaping Riches," *Wall Street Journal*, November 7, 1975.

"Cattle Feeders Sue Store Chains, Others in Anti-Trust Action," *Wall Street Journal*, December 3, 1975.

"Congress' Apathy on Grain Inspection is Likely to Stall New Rules Until Spring," *Wall Street Journal*, November 10, 1975.

"The Controversy at Iowa Beef: A Case of Misperception," *Wall Street Journal*, December 2, 1975.

"Co-op Export System Urged," *Journal of Commerce*, August 27, 1975.

"Cereal Executive Sees Wastes in FTC Study," *Milling and Baking News*, April 14, 1975.

"Consumer Group Gets Into Fight for Family Farms," *The NFO Reporter*, June 1975.

"Continental Building Unit Train Facility," *Feedstuffs*, December 23, 1974.

"Critic Defends Jim Hightower's 'Hell Raising'," *The NFO Reporter*, October 1974.

"Elevators Accuse Eight Grain Firms of Forcing Grain Discounts for Rail Cars," *Feedstuffs*, July 28, 1975.

"Exporters Reluctantly Gain Spotlight and Try to Polish Their Image," *Wall Street Journal*, November 5, 1975.

Feedstuffs, December 15, 1975.

"FTC Investigating Sales by Major Grain Traders for Possible Law Violations," *Feedstuffs*, January 13, 1975.

"GAO Asked to Investigate Grain Handling," *Feedstuffs*, June 30, 1975.

"Goodman to Join Continental Grain," *Reuters News Service*, September 29, 1975.

"Grain—The Big Five," *Newsweek*, August 4, 1975.

"Grain Theft Laid to Bunge Corp. by Federal Jury," *Wall Street Journal*, July 22, 1975.

"Higher Costs Cited in Bread Price Study," *Milling and Baking News*, September 16, 1975.

"How U.S. Promotes Brazilian Soybeans," *Des Moines Register*, November 19, 1975.

IBP Corveyor, July 1975.

"ICC Probers Say Big Grain Companies Hoard Freight Cars," *Minneapolis Tribune*, July 22, 1975.

"Inspection Scandals Widen, Adding to Woe of a Battered Industry," *Wall Street Journal*, November 10, 1975.

"Investigating the Grain Trade," *Minneapolis Tribune*, July 13, 1975.

"Iowa Beef Alleges *Journal* Distorted Reports Linked to Officials," *Wall Street Journal*, December 2, 1975.

"Iowa Beef and its Co-Chairman Convicted for Plotting to Bribe Union and Retailers," *Wall Street Journal*, October 8, 1974.

"Iowa Beef Names Steinman's Son-in-Law, Bodenstein, to Replace Operations Chief," *Wall Street Journal*, November 19, 1975.

"Local Boards of 127 Far-Mar-Co Elevators Accept Wheat Pool," *Milling and Baking News*, October 7, 1975.

"Let 'Em Eat Cake Too," *Wall Street Journal*, April 22, 1975.

"Meat Price Fixing," *The NFO Reporter*, August 1975.

"New Government Report Escalates Budding Controversy Over Co-ops," *Minneapolis Tribune*.

"A New Wheat Pool to Beat the Middleman," *Ag World*, November 1975.

"NFO Backs Ban on Packer or Chain Feedlots," *The NFO Reporter*, July 1975.

"Off its Feed," *Wall Street Journal*, October 1, 1975.

"Peyser Introduces Dairy Farmers Bill of Rights," *Ag World*, October 1975.

"Picking on Farmers," *Des Moines Register*, February 26, 1974.

"Pillsbury and Weight Watchers Break Off Merger Discussion," *Milling and Baking News*, June 3, 1975.

"Problems in Handling Grain for Overseas Sale," *Minneapolis Tribune*, July 13, 1975.

"Quick Response to Markets Cited," *Milling and Baking News*, March 18, 1975.

"Right Light for Census," *Milling and Baking News*, March 4, 1975.

Ryan, Ann K. "The Farmer, The Co-ops, The Critics," *Corporate Report*, March 1976.

"Sales Soar, Nearly Triple Cargill Profits," *Minneapolis Tribune*, December 2, 1973.

"Staley Is Still the NFO—Despite Its Woes," *Minneapolis Tribune*, October 19, 1975.

"Supermarket Chains Sued by Cattlemen," *Des Moines Register*, December 2, 1975.

"Texas Fails to Act on Corporate Farming," *Journal of Commerce*, October 10, 1975.

"USDA Agency Talks of Saving Family Farms; Now It's Abolished," *The NFO Reporter*, September 1975.

"USDA Report Predicts Domination by Handful of Huge Farms by 1990," *The NFO Reporter*, November 1974.

"U.S. Indicts Bunge, 13 Executives," *Minneapolis Tribune*, July 22, 1975.

"Wager Points to New Era in Marketing," *Milling and Baking News*, October 22, 1974.

Wennblom, Ralph D. "They're Blaming Co-ops for High Food Prices," *Farm Journal*, December 1975.

"World Food 'Facts and Myths' Explored," *Milling and Baking News*, April 22, 1975.

GOVERNMENT PUBLICATIONS.

Agricultural Outlook. USDA, March 1976.

Agriculture and Anti-Depression Act of 1975. U.S. Senate Committee on Agriculture and Forestry, February 3-21, 1975.

Engelman, Gerald. "Trends in Livestock Marketing Before and After the Consent Decree of 1920 and the Packers and Stockyards Act of 1921," USDA, June 23, 1975.

Food Chain Pricing Activities. U.S. Congress Joint Economic Committee, December 1974.

Food Retailing and Processing Practices. U.S. Congress Subcommittee on Consumer Economics of the Joint Economic Committee, May 21, 1974.

Grain Inspection Irregularities and Problems. U.S. Congress Subcommittee on

Foreign Agricultural Policy and the Subcommittee on Agricultural Production, Marketing and Stabilization of Prices, June 19, 1975.

Hearings before the House Judiciary Committee and Senate Select Committee, Volumes 20-24, Washington, D.C., 1974.

Kiplinger Washington Letter, June 20, 1975.

Russian Grain Sale. U.S. Senate Committee on Agriculture and Forestry, September 4, 1976.

U.S. Agricultural Exports Under Public Law 480. USDA, October 1974.

PAMPHLETS AND REPORTS.

"Feeding the World's Hungry: The Challenge to Business," Continental Bank, May 20, 1974.

Iowa Beef Processors, Inc., 1974 Annual Report.

Palmby, Clarence D. "World Grain Marketing Systems—Do They Mesh?" Continental Grain Company, May 1975.

Resolution Adopted by the Steering Committee. Cattle Feeders Tax Committee, Phoenix, Arizona, June 5, 1973.

LETTERS.

Brunthauer, Carroll G., Memphis, Tennessee. Letter to the author, October 7, 1975.

Hammer, Marvin P., Continental Grain Company, New York. Letter to the author, October 14, 1975.

CHAPTER 9. OMNIVORE IN ACTION: A CASE STUDY

Several beer industry presidents and executives provided detailed information to me in personal letters such as the following:

Beal, L. J., Spoetzl Brewery, September 16, 1974.

Birdsong, E.L., Pearl Brewing Company, August 20, 1974.

Combs, Edwin S., Rainier Brewing Company, August 27, 1974.

Hoffberger, Jerold, The National Brewing Company, August 23, 1974.

Leinenkugel, William, Leinenkugel Brewery, August 29, 1974.

Matt, F.X., West End Brewing Company, August 26, 1974.

Maytag, Fritz, Steam Beer Brewing Company, September 25, 1974.

Meyer, Gerald, Grain Belt Breweries, August 23, 1974.

Pflugfelder, R.E., Jackson Brewing Company, August 22, 1974.

Russo, Robert, Coors, August 30, 1974.

Schmidt, Robert A., Olympia Brewing Company, March 3, 1975.

Personal letters were also received from:

Bokat, Karen, Federal Trade Commission, September 13, 1974.

Doty, Russell, Minnesota Pollution Control Agency, August 30, 1974.

Karth, Joseph, Congressman, November 5, 1974.

O'Shea, William, Brewers' Association of America, August 30, 1974.

Secondary sources included:

BOOKS.
Berg, Thomas L. *Mismarketing: Case Histories of Marketing Misfires.* Garden City: Doubleday, 1971.
One Hundred Years of Brewing. New York: Arno Press, 1974.

MAGAZINES AND NEWSPAPERS.
Burck, Charles C. "While the Big Brewers Quaff, The Little Ones Thirst," *Fortune,* November 1972.
Business Week: March 24, 1973; January 26, 1974; October 13, 1975; March 8, 1976.
"Brewing Industry," *Valu-Line,* July 19, 1974.
Des Moines Register, January 18, 1976.
Journal of Commerce, January 16, 1976.
Miami Herald, November 6, 1974.
Minneapolis Tribune: February 17, 1974; May 5, 1974.
Modern Brewery Age: April 5, 1975; April 12, 1975; April 19, 1975; May 31, 1975.
Money, February 26, 1976.
O'Malley, Michael. "Leinenkugel's Beer," *Wisconsin,* Winter 1973.
The Times, London, March 29, 1976.
Wall Street Journal: October 26, 1973; June 6, 1974; August 20, 1974; September 24, 1974; December 26, 1974; January 3, 1975; September 16, 1975.

GOVERNMENT PUBLICATIONS.
In The Matter of Adolph Coors Company Docket No. 8845. Federal Trade Commission, July 24, 1973.

CHAPTER 10. YOU CAN DEPEND ON U.S.—OR CAN YOU?

Senators Hubert Humphrey and Herman Talmadge, as well as Representative Keith Sebelius, were helpful in providing much of the information on the foreign policy aspects of our food supplies. Other sources include:

MAGAZINES AND NEWSPAPERS.
Anthan, George. "Political Curb Voted for Food for Peace," *Des Moines Register,* September 6, 1975.
"Ban Retained on Sales to U.S.S.R.," *Milling and Baking News,* August 12, 1975.
"Biting Morality," *Milling and Baking News,* August 12, 1975.
"Butz Stripped of Power on Farm and Food Policy," *NFO Reporter,* October 1975.
"CIA and World Food," *Milling and Baking News,* March 25, 1975.
"Congress Studies Legislation Revising P.L. 480 Programs," *Milling and Baking News,* October 7, 1975.
Cook, Louise. "Grain Sales to Russia Called Problems of Words," *Dallas Times Herald,* September 15, 1975.
"Defends FAS Market Development Role," *Milling and Baking News,* October 22, 1974.
"Food as a Weapon, Will U.S. Ever Use It?" *U.S. News and World Report,* June 2, 1975.

Goldberg, Ray A. "U.S. Agribusiness Breaks Out of Isolation," *Harvard Business Review*, May-June 1975.

"Guidance to Grain Trade on Aftermath of Mississippi Floods," *The Times*, London, November 26, 1975.

House, Karen Elliott. "No Win Issue?" *Wall Street Journal*, August 6, 1975.

———. "Soviet Grain Pact's Benefits Are Disputed As Finishing Touches Put on Accord," *ibid.*, October 3, 1975.

King, Seth R. "Are Grain Sales to the Soviet in U.S. Interest?" *The New York Times*, August 1, 1975.

"Kissinger Announces Reserves System," *Milling and Baking News*, May 20, 1975.

McClung, John. "Bill in Europe to Unveil U.S. Grain Reserves Plan," *Feedstuffs*, September 29, 1975.

Morgan, Dan. "Wheat Marketing Differs Widely in Canada and U.S.," *Winnipeg Free Press*, September 20, 1975.

Natz, Daryl. "Peavey Chief Doubts Usefulness of U.S.–Soviet Grain Agreement," *Feedstuffs*, December 15, 1975.

"No Economic Gains from Export Limit," *Milling and Baking News*, October 14, 1975.

"Offer Views on Export Reporting System," *Milling and Baking News*, October 22, 1974.

"A One-Member Agricultural OPEC," *Minneapolis Tribune*, December 15, 1975.

"President Sets Out Policy on Grain Sales to Soviet Union," *Milling and Baking News*, September 18, 1975.

"Proposal for Grain Reserve System Valued at $4.5 Billion Made by U.S.," *Wall Street Journal*, October 7, 1975.

Schramm, Carl J. "The Perils of Wheat Trading Without a Grains Policy," *Ag World*, May 1975.

"Should U.S. Clamp Down on Grain Sales?" *U.S. News and World Report*, September 15, 1975.

"Soviet Oil for U.S. Grain Talked," *Dallas Times Herald*, September 14, 1975.

Strout, Richard L. "Food Power—A Diplomatic Weapon?" *Ag World*, November 1975.

"U.S. Food Power: Ultimate Weapon in World Politics?" *Business Week*, December 15, 1975.

"U.S. Trade Opinion Split on Soviet Buying Intentions," *Commodities Bulletin*, December 12, 1975.

Ward, Mike. "Revealing Ivan's Nightly Jaunts a Nyet, Nyet at Wheat Board," *Winnipeg Free Press*, July 19, 1975.

"Was The Export Ban Enforceable?" *Pro Farmer*, December 6, 1975.

"Weaver Bill Dropped After Hearings." *Milling and Baking News*, November 11, 1975.

"Wheat vs. Oil Issue," *Milling and Baking News*, October 22, 1974.

Wright, Frank. "New Lawmaker's Aim is U.S. Control of Grain Exports," *Minneapolis Tribune*, June 29, 1975.

GOVERNMENT PUBLICATIONS.
Congressional Record: March 21, 1975. May 6, 1975;

Exemption of Foreign-owned Reserves from Export Controls. U.S. Senate Committee on Agriculture and Forestry, May 22, 1975.

LETTERS AND SPEECHES.

Lebeck, Warren W. "Farm Exports: Will We Bungle America's New Super Strategy?" Speech presented to New York Society of Security Analysts, October 28, 1975.

Weaver, Jim, Congressman, Washington, D.C. Letter to the author, September 10, 1975.

CHAPTER 11. OVER THERE

Although a lot of secondary information on the food situation overseas is available, a great deal of insight was provided by the people in the grain trade. Other sources include:

BOOKS.

Smith, Hedrick. *The Russians.* New York: Quadrangle, 1976.

MAGAZINES AND NEWSPAPERS.

Anderson, Bill. "A Ferment Brews in Poland," *Chicago Tribune,* February 20, 1975.

"Bread Consumption on Upswing in Japan," *Milling and Baking News,* August 19, 1975.

Bryan, Francis E. "Increase Corn Production! But Can They. . . ?" *Ag World,* January 1976.

———. "The New Lands—Key to Soviet Grain Imports," *Pro Farmer,* July 26, 1975.

Chandler, Charles. "More Meat for Russians," *Meat Processing,* November 1975.

Cullison, A. E. "Japanese to Query U.S. on Food Pleas," *Journal of Commerce,* January 10, 1976.

———. "Japan Urged to Stockpile Grain," *ibid.,* June 11, 1975.

"EC Fails to Resolve Ag Problems," *Journal of Commerce,* November 13, 1975.

Garnier, J. F. "Obtain Soybeans Directly from Sources, Eliminating All Intermediaries," *Ag World,* October 1975.

"Italian Farmers Shifting From Wheat to Other Crops," *Journal of Commerce,* December 1, 1975.

"Italy Considers Pasta Law Change," *Journal of Commerce,* December 19, 1975.

"Japan: Growth Stabilization Keystone for the Future," *Journal of Commerce,* June 23, 1975.

Malloy, Michael T. "Soviet Ocean of Grain Isn't Enough," *Ag World,* September 1975.

"Muscovites Urged to Conserve on Bread," *Milling and Baking News,* October 28, 1975.

Palmer, Lane. "Can Siberia Grow More Grain?" *Farm Journal,* October 1975.

———. "Will the Soviets Buy More Grain?" *ibid.,* September 1975.

Schmidt, Kolleen. "Japan's Interest Goes Beyond Grain," *Feedstuffs,* December 17, 1973.

Seigart, Alice. "Europe's Farms Becoming Too Much of a Good Thing," *Chicago Tribune,* September 9, 1975.

"Soviet Citizens Urged to Conserve Bread," *Milling and Baking News*, September 17, 1974.
"Soviets Begin Upgrading of Poultry Industry," *Feedstuffs*, January 6, 1975.
"Speculation Grows About the State of U.S.S.R. Economy, Leader's Future," *Journal of Commerce*, December 10, 1975.
"U.S. Agriculture Secretary Delivers Strong Attacks on CAP," *Agra Europe*, December 5, 1975.
"The U.S.S.R.: New Prospects for Trade," *Journal of Commerce*, December 7, 1973.
"U.S.S.R. Builds New Grain Facilities," *Milling and Baking News*, September 10, 1974.
U.S.S.R. National Affairs: Agricultural Affairs, October 10, 1974 (provided by *Soviet Business & Trade*).
"U.S.S.R. Sees Gains on Wheat in U.S. Pact," *Milling and Baking News*, April 22, 1975.
Yanov, Alexander. "Why Russia Must Purchase Grain," *Minneapolis Tribune*, January 11, 1976.
Yates, Ronald. "The Finest Food Money Can Import," *Chicago Tribune*, December 3, 1975.

GOVERNMENT PUBLICATIONS.
"Most Foreign Food Price Rises Exceed U.S. Increases," USDA Foreign Agriculture Circular, December 8, 1975.
"Report on U.S.S.R. Winter Wheat 1975," USDA Foreign Agriculture Circular, July 1975.
The Soviet Grain Balance, 1960–73, CIA.

CHAPTER 12. ONE IN A MILLION

A great deal of the background for this chapter came from my work in the Peace Corps. In addition, the following published material was used:

BOOKS.
Cranshaw, Edward. *Khrushchev Remembers*. Boston: Little, Brown & Co., 1970.
Lockwood, Lee. *Castro's Cuba, Cuba's Fidel*. New York: Random House, 1969.
Manley, Michael. *The Politics of Change*. London: Andre Deutsch, 1974.
Myrdal, Gunnar. *Asian Drama*. New York: Pantheon, 1968.
Snow, Edgar. *The Long Revolution*. New York: Random House, 1972.
Wharton, Clifton R., Jr. (ed.). *Subsistence Agriculture and Economic Development*. Chicago: Aldine Publishing Co., 1965.

MAGAZINES AND NEWSPAPERS.
Agra Europe, December 12, 1975.
"ASA Promotes Soy for Nutrition," *Soybean Digest*, May 1975.
"ASA Proposes Halt to Aid for Competing Crops," *Milling and Baking News*, September 2, 1975.
Burki, Shahid Javed, and Yusuf, Shahid. "Population: Exploring the Food-Fertility Link," *Finance and Development*, December 1975.

Decker, Truman. "Latin America Population to Surpass Europe's," *Miami Herald,* December 16, 1975.

Lewin, Robert M. "Many Countries Curbing Food Output," *Journal of Commerce,* June 4, 1975.

NFO Reporter, December 1974.

Onis, Juan de. "FAO is Gloomy on Food Outlook," *The New York Times,* June 26, 1975.

The Other Side: September and December 1974; February and May 1975; January 1976.

Richardson, David. "Inside a Nation Where Democracy is Faltering," *U.S. News and World Report,* September 15, 1975.

Tucker, Kernan. "Birth Control Talk Called U.S. Babykill," *Miami Herald,* January 6, 1976.

"U.S.S.R. Says Grain Purchases Sign of a Rich Country," *Milling and Baking News,* January 6, 1976.

Wall Street Journal, November 6, 1975.

Survey of International Development, November-December 1975.

PAMPHLETS.

"Declaration on Population and Food," *The Environmental Fund,* 1976.

"1975 Resolutions," American Soybean Association.

CHAPTER 13. FOOD IN THE FUTURE

A number of food futurists and planners, particularly Dr. Alvan Pyne of International Multifoods, provided valuable information. Other sources include:

BOOKS.

Shepard, Paul. *The Tender Carnivore and the Sacred Game.* New York: Charles Scribner's Sons, 1973.

MAGAZINES AND NEWSPAPERS.

"Acceptance Encourages Bigger Soy Protein Market," *Feedstuffs,* October 20, 1975.

Bateman, Michael. "The Strange New Taste of Tomorrow," *The Sunday Times,* London, January 19, 1975.

Bylinsky, Gene. "A New Scientific Effort to Boost Food Output," *Ag World,* September 1975.

Clark, Lindly H., Jr., "Future Food," *Wall Street Journal,* November 17, 1975.

"Food Protein from Petroleum—It's Here," *Farm Journal,* March 1976.

"Home Grinding of Wheat," *Milling and Baking News,* January 20, 1976.

"Hybrid Wheat Holds Promise for Future," *Milling and Baking News,* June 17, 1975.

Lanier, Verle E. "Soybeans—Feed Today, Food Tomorrow," *Foreign Agriculture,* October 15, 1975.

Lindeman, Bard. "Meat-Heavy American Diet Is Killer, Scientist Warns," *Miami Herald,* January 20, 1976.

Lublin, Joann S. "High Protein Yeast Derived from Petroleum May Someday Help Nourish Hungry Countries," *Wall Street Journal,* September 24, 1975.

"Major Advances in Crops Listed," *Milling and Baking News,* January 20, 1976.

Nagdeman, Julian J. "No Fish Story: Aquaculture May Still be the Wave of the Future," *Barron's,* January 19, 1976.

"NIOC Working to Turn Oil into Food," *Kayhan International,* Tehran, November 22, 1975.

"Non-Plant Protein for U.S.S.R.," *Commodities Bulletin,* January 23, 1976.

Stepp, Carl. "Food May be Hazardous to Your Health," *Miami Herald,* November 13, 1975.

"They've Come a Long Way," *Soybean Digest,* October 1975.

"U.S. Agriculture Faces Upper Limit," *Milling and Baking News,* February 25, 1975.

"U.S. World Food Policy Makes Sense," *Milling and Baking News,* June 24, 1975.

Wagniere, Frederic. "How To Become the World's Bread Basket," *Ag World,* July 1975.

Winski, Joseph M. "Back to Basics Trend in U.S. Eating Habits Appears Entrenched," *Wall Street Journal,* May 29, 1975.

GOVERNMENT PUBLICATIONS.

Alternative Futures for U.S. Agriculture, USDA, September 25, 1975.

LETTERS AND PAPERS.

Bauman, H. E., Vice President, Science and Technology, Pillsbury Company. Letter to the author, April 19, 1976.

Farrell, Kenneth R. "Food and Agriculture in the Next Quarter Century." Paper presented to Planning Executives Institute, San Francisco, May 23, 1975.

Stone, David E., Product Manager, Food Proteins, Ralston Purina Company. Letter to the author, April 10, 1976.

Ullensvang, Dr. Leon P., Executive Director, Planning and Development, Pet Incorporated. Letter to the author, January 8, 1976.

INDEX

Abourezk, James, 114
Afghanistan, 215
Africa, 50, 215
Agnew, Spiro, 105, 108
Agribusiness Accountability Project, 47, 113, 114, 210
Agribusiness Council, 210
Agricultural Communications Council, 113
Agricultural Stabilization and Conservation Service, 114
Agriculture Committee (House), 50-1, 53, 117, 120
Agriculture Committee (Senate), 52, 55-6, 103, 162, 166
Agriculture and Consumer Protection Act of 1973, 51
Agriculture Council of America, 43-5
Agromet, 65
Agway, 123
Alamar Association, 106
Alioto, Joseph, 134, 138
Allende, Salvador, 150
American Agricultural Marketing Association, 115
American Bakeries Co., 129, 162
American Bakers' Ass'n, 52, 129
American Dairy Goat Ass'n, 37
American Farm Bureau, 37-8, 52-4, 165, 183
AFL-CIO, 12, 42, 52
American Management Ass'n, 106
American National Cattlemen's Ass'n, 31
American Society of Farm Managers and Appraisers, 34
American Soybean Ass'n, 37, 118, 210
American Stores, 134
Amoco Foods, 219
Anchor Steam, 149, 151
Anderson-Clayton, 80
Anderson, Jack, 159
Anderson, Wendell, 198
Andreas, Dwayne, 121, 181
Anheuser-Busch, 147-8, 154

A & P, 134, 137
Apple Malt Duck, 150
Archer Daniels Midland, 80-1, 83, 95, 121, 198
Argentina, 120-1, 163, 169, 214
Armour, 131, 133
Ashbrook, John M., 51-2
Associated Milk Producers, 37
Associated Milk Producers, Inc., 42, 123-5
Aswan High Dam, 194, 207-8
Auslam, Dave, 14-15
Australia, 100, 119, 159, 196, 198

Bagley, William, 61
Bahktiari, Mustafa, 14
Baibakov, Nikolai, 190
Baker, Bobby, 105
Ball, John, 12-13, 106
Ballantine Brewery, 142, 145
Baltic Exchange, London, 99
Baltz, Donald, 24
Barker, Bernard, 121
Baruch, Bernard, 37
Bean, Atherton, 10, 127
Beckman, Arnell, 41
Beef, 53
Beeson, Monte, 10, 17, 65
Bell, Richard, 175
Belousov, Nikolai, 119
Bingham, Jonathan, 168, 170
Birdsong, Lee, 149
Blatz Brewery, 154
Blitz-Weinhard beer, 145
Blue Earth County, 19, 20, 119
Boeing, 116
Boerma, Addeke H., 170, 172
Bolivia, 196, 203-4
Borden Food, 126, 129, 137
Borlaug, Norman, 56
Born Brothers, 120
Boumediene, Houari, 182